SO-AIK-941

November, 1995

INSIDE WASHINGTON

Dr. Leslie

Your insights on
the Jamaican Market
are greatly appreciated).

Bill (Capitol)

Inside Washington

Government Resources for International Business

by

William A. Delphos

Venture Publishing, NA
A Division of Venture Marketing

Recipient, Presidential E-Award for Export Service

Copyright © 1995 by

William A. Delphos

Venture Publishing, N.A.
3000 K Street, NW, Suite 690
Washington, DC 20007

All Rights Reserved

Printed in the United States of America

Library of Congress Cataloging-in-Publication Data

Delphos, William A. (William Arthur), 1951-
Inside Washington: Government Resources for International Business / edited by
Alan J. Beard, Steven T. Hofmann, and Joel T. Weber

Entirely new, rev., and updated ed. of Washington's Best Kept Secrets. © 1983 /
Inside Washington. © 1988 / Inside Washington © 1992

1. Corporations, American-Government policy-Information services-United States.
2. International business enterprises-Information services-United States. 3.
Industrial promotion-Information services-United States. 4. United
States-Commerce-Information services. I. Delphos, William A. (William Arthur),
1951-

ISBN 1-883917-08-5

Venture
Publishing

Additional copies of this publication may be
ordered by calling (202) 337-6300.

10, 9, 8, 7, 6, 5, 4,

Table of Contents

CHAPTER SIX

CHAPTER SEVEN

ACKNOWLEDGMENTS

The publication of this book would not have been possible without the dedication and cooperation of a significant number of people, both within our organization as well as in the government. We would like to express our gratitude for their contributions.

Our diligent and dedicated research team spent many hours working with government agencies and multilateral development organizations to provide the most up-to-date, comprehensive information possible. Once the information was obtained, it was synthesized and rewritten for the business audience based on our practical use of many of the programs. The assistance of Alexis Coppedge, Brian Mason, Mark Mondik, and Matt Ziegler throughout was invaluable. Thanks also go to the unfailing eyes of Judy Laufman.

Alan J. Beard

Steven T. Hofmann

Joel T. Weber

May 1995

Washington, DC

PREFACE

Imagine walking into the neighborhood grocery store to buy a jar of chunky peanut butter. As you enter the store, you're stunned to discover that the aisles have been rearranged. Instead of familiar product groups, the displays are organized by manufacturer -- Procter & Gamble, General Foods, Del Monte, Beatrice Foods, and so forth.

What should have been a simple shopping excursion has now become a bizarre hunting expedition, where success rests on a combination of dogged determination and almanac-like knowledge. Who manufactures peanut butter? Which company makes chunky peanut butter? And who makes chunky peanut butter in a reusable plastic tub?

The book is designed to unscramble the scores of government programs available for American firms seeking to do business abroad -- taking them off the shelves now marked Department of Commerce, Export-Import Bank, Small Business Administration, Overseas Private Investment Corporation, International Finance Corporation, and so forth, and putting them onto more logical shelves such as financing, regulations and market information.

Thirteen Washington-based agencies offer most of the key international business assistance. An additional dozen agencies and multilateral development organizations provide services for U.S. businesses seeking to enter the international marketplace. The goal of this guide is to make information about government assistance more accessible to the American business community.

When I first arrived in Washington in 1981 to take an appointment at the Overseas Private Investment Corporation (OPIC), I was amazed at the range and scope of government resources available to help companies expand overseas. I realized that I could have used many of the programs in my previous position as Managing Director of International Operations at a large multinational corporation. Market research also confirmed that the vast majority of business executives were also unaware of these well-kept secrets.

Over the past 14 years, Washington's approach to supporting the overseas expansion of U.S. companies has changed significantly. Through government efforts such as Export Now the Trade Promotion Coordinating Committee (TPCC), agencies are working more closely with each other to assist the business community. Agencies such as Ex-Im Bank, OPIC, and the Trade and Development Agency (TDA) are taking a much more pro-active approach. The Departments of Commerce and State have even begun advocating U.S. business positions abroad.

While the U.S. Government agencies have been "reinventing" themselves, multilateral development banks have recognized the critical role of private industry in developing markets. They have adjusted their lending programs accordingly. Not only are billions of dollars being lent to enterprises on the basis of sound economics, but development banks are actively working with private businesses to create sustainable growth. Technical assistance, training and improved procurement procedures make projects funded by these organizations a multi-billion-dollar opportunity few companies can afford to pass up.

Finally, government in general is working smarter to promote economic development here and abroad. U.S. agencies are more sensitive to overseas competition and are more willing than ever to neutralize the effects of subsidized financing from our competitors. Recognizing the shortage of investment capital in the developing world, the U.S. Government has taken the lead to support a number of private investment funds which can shore-up good overseas projects where existing lending programs are insufficient.

While it would be an exaggeration to suggest that this publication is all-inclusive, every effort has been made to include detailed descriptions of the major government programs available for U.S. businesses considering overseas operations. It is our hope that it will make a significant contribution to strengthening the working partnership between the private sector and the government -- a partnership that is critical if we are to be competitive in the international marketplace.

William A. Delphos

May 1995

Washington, DC

INTRODUCTION

WINNING GLOBALLY

Now that time and distance have been so compressed that a U.S. business executive can fly to Paris for lunch and return the same day, "business as usual" has a decidedly new dimension. New technologies in communication, the free flow of capital, and instant access to an almost limitless supply of information have triggered a revolution posing tremendous challenges and opportunities for the modern business executive.

Only a few years ago, a company limited its search for new markets to exploring opportunities in other cities and other states. Although some of the nation's larger companies looked for growth in other nations, the majority of U.S. businesses were satisfied with the U.S. marketplace. Today, the character of commerce is vastly different. Foreign companies have invested heavily in the United States, bringing global competition to America's doorstep. The U.S. business executive must now look for new avenues of growth, and many are realizing that the best opportunities may lie beyond the water's edge.

The Potential

Multinational corporations have long recognized the value of international expansion, and their investments have made enormous contributions to accelerating trade and economic growth in many areas of the world. But if the United States is to maintain a competitive position in world commerce, we must broaden our effort by encouraging more small- and medium-sized firms to enter international markets, especially those in the developing world, which are the fastest-growing markets for U.S. goods and services.

Winning at Home

The stage is now set for a new era of growth and the U.S. business community has an uncommon opportunity to restore its competitive leadership. It would be difficult to overestimate the importance of this effort. To a great extent, our success will depend on teamwork between the government and the business community, and the effective use of federal services could mean the difference between success and failure.

This book is designed as a ready reference manual, compiling information on the scores of government-supported business assistance programs classified by some as well-kept secrets. This wall of secrecy has not been built by government alone, although government has contributed to the confusion by dividing both programs and information sources among various departments and agencies. At least some of the obscurity can be attributed to the business community's previous lack of interest in international operations. This guide seeks to eliminate the confusion by putting all the pieces in one place so that the array of government programs becomes a solution rather than a puzzle.

About the Book

Most of the trade and investment incentive programs which help U.S. business compete internationally are administered by the federal government and multilateral organizations located in Washington,DC. Organizations which provide such assistance include the Departments of Agriculture and Commerce, the Office of the U.S. Trade Representative, the U.S. Agency for International Development, Export-Import Bank, Overseas Private Investment Corporation, Small Business Administration, the U.S. Environmental Protection Agency, the U.S. Trade and Development Agency, the World Bank, and the International Finance Corporation. Brief descriptions of the functions of these organizations and how they relate to promoting international business development can be found at the end of this chapter.

Until now, businesses seeking the appropriate federal assistance program or individual to help them abroad were forced to wander through the bureaucratic labyrinth of Washington in search of an answer. With this reference guide, however, the maze of agency authority lines has been erased. In its place is a "repackaged" presentation of government programs for business, arranged according to type of assistance available rather than by agency. To further illustrate how these programs can best be used by U.S. businesses, case studies are highlighted in each chapter.

Readers unfamiliar with the international marketplace should notice that the chapters flow logically from "getting started" information to the nuts-and-bolts of putting a business deal together. To help the reader quickly identify and locate information on a specific agency or program, the beginning of each chapter contains a matrix outlining the agencies, programs, and types of financing or services offered.

Chapter 1: Obtaining Information

Chapter 1 outlines the wide array of business information available to U.S. firms considering international operations, including market background reports, statistical profiles, country economic analyses and international demographic data.

Chapter 2: Targeting Opportunities

Chapter 2 contains information on specific programs -- data banks, search services and contract bid notifications -- as well as publications and information resources that are designed to help businesses identify international trade and investment opportunities.

Chapter 3: Regulations and Requirements

Chapter 3 explores the regulations and requirements of doing international business. There also is a valuable overview of taxation issues, including Foreign Shared Corporations and profit repatriation.

Chapter 4: Business Development Assistance

Chapter 4 provides detailed descriptions of the U.S. Government, multilateral, and private programs which provide feasibility study funding and/or assistance. It also profiles programs that offer general training, advice and assistance.

Chapter 5: Export Financing

Chapter 5 describes the loan, loan guarantee and letter of credit programs available to support the exporting efforts of U.S. businesses.

Chapter 6: Investment and Project Financing

Chapter 6 focuses on programs that provide investment or project financing.

Chapter 7: Covering the Deal

Chapter 7 details how to obtain insurance or other forms of protecting an international venture.

In addition to the contact individuals noted throughout the book, the appendices include: U.S. Department of Commerce District Offices; Small Business Administration Field Offices; Small Business Development Centers; State Government International Trade Offices; U.S. Embassies and Consulates Abroad; Country Desk Officers at the Departments of Commerce, State and the Agency for International Development; domestic and foreign offices of Multilateral Donor Agencies; and Foreign Embassies in the United States.

No single volume could fully describe the scope and diversity of the thousands of international enterprises involving U.S. firms or the hundreds of government programs that have been used to help executives undertaking such enterprises. Nevertheless, every effort has been made to present as much information as possible in an easy-to-understand format that can help make business decisions more effective and productive.

FEDERAL TRADE PROMOTION AGENCIES

Within the U.S. Government, foreign governments, and multilateral organizations, many programs exist to help American firms compete and expand internationally. While each government agency has its own mandate and resources for assisting exporters, all U.S. Government agencies operate under the auspices of the Trade Promotion Coordinating Committee (TPCC). Chaired by the Secretary of Commerce, the TPCC is an inter-agency policy working group which coordinates and implements all U.S. export promotion programs. Towards this goal, the TPCC develops strategies for streamlining and improving the myriad U.S. government and private sources of export assistance. In addition, the TPCC is a valuable information resource concerning U.S. export assistance programs.

Department of Commerce (DOC)

The Department of Commerce's International Trade Administration (ITA) coordinates issues relating to trade programs and international export policies, along with assistance and information for U.S. exporters. ITA units include domestic and overseas commercial officers, country experts and industry experts that promote products and offer services and programs for the U.S. exporting community. ITA is staffed by trade specialists in 48 district offices and 19 branch offices in industrial and commercial centers nationwide.

Through commercial sections located in U.S. embassies and consulates, the U.S. & Foreign Commercial Service (US&FCS) operates in 128 cities in 67 countries and is composed of 150 U.S. officers and 480 nationals of the various host countries. The US&FCS is principally charged with assisting U.S. businesses through one-on-one counseling, collecting and disseminating market insight information, representing U.S. commercial interests to host-country governments and an array of international trade shows and missions, as well as supporting other U.S. agencies' international programs.

U.S. Export-Import Bank (Ex-Im Bank)

The Export-Import Bank of the United States (Ex-Im Bank) provides financing support to facilitate exports of U.S. goods and services. Ex-Im Bank provides credit protection for U.S. exporters and their lenders by insuring repayment in the event of default by a foreign buyer. With a long and successful history of funding exports of U.S. equipment and technology, Ex-Im Bank finances a wide variety of American exports, ranging from engineering services to feasibility studies to design and construction services. Ex-Im Bank emphasizes the stimulation of small business transactions and the expansion of project finance capabilities, as well as aggressively promoting exports of U.S. goods and services.

Overseas Private Investment Corporation (OPIC)

The Overseas Private Investment Corporation (OPIC) is a U.S. government agency that promotes private investment in developing countries through financing, political risk insurance and various investor services. These programs are available for development projects that involve U.S. investment; do not have an adverse impact on the U.S. economy or employment; and have strong, positive benefits for the host country. Financing can be obtained for up to 50 percent of the cost of establishing an overseas venture and is available for projects involving U.S. investors with strong "track records" in the same or similar business. OPIC operates its programs in more than 140 developing countries.

Small Business Administration (SBA)

The U.S. Small Business Administration (SBA) offers financial assistance, counseling, export workshops and training to help small- and medium-sized U.S. firms enter international markets. It provides loans and loan guarantees to U.S. companies for equipment, facilities, materials, working capital and business development support for selected export market development activities. Export counseling services and marketing information are available at no cost from the agency's Service Corps of Retired Executives (SCORE) and by university students who participate in the Small Business Institute Program. In addition, Small Business Development Centers (SBDCs) based at universities offer business counseling and assistance. SBA has 79 district offices in the United States.

U.S. Agency for International Development (USAID)

The U.S. Agency for International Development (USAID) supports traditional assistance projects to further economic and social development in industrializing countries. This is done through specific development projects, debt-for-equity swaps, loans and grants given on concessional terms to less developed countries. Areas of assistance include agriculture, health, population control, education, human resources, housing, as well as support for private voluntary organizations. USAID also provides funding for population assistance, economic reform and stabilization and for other poverty alleviation programs. USAID maintains posts at 64 U.S. embassies abroad.

Trade and Development Agency (TDA)

The U.S. Trade and Development Agency (TDA) funds project identification missions, feasibility studies, orientation visits and reverse trade missions, technical symposia, training, information dissemination and procurement promotion for major development projects in developing and middle-income countries. TDA funding is geared toward introducing foreign government officials and multilateral organizations to U.S. companies and technology in the hope that they would be used during project implementation. TDA also seeks to introduce U.S. companies to exporting to developing and middle-income countries.

U.S. Trade Representative (USTR)

The Office of the U.S. Trade Representative (USTR) is a cabinet-level agency that is responsible for the direction of trade negotiations, formulating overall trade policy, and bilateral and multilateral negotiations pertaining to international environmental trade. USTR represents the United States at meetings of the General Agreement on Tariffs and Trade (GATT) and the Organization for Economic Cooperation and Development (OECD) as well as in negotiations with the United Nations Conference on Trade and Development (UNCTAD). USTR is also responsible for administering trade cases that provide relief from unfair trade practices.

Environmental Protection Agency (EPA)

While known domestically as a federal regulatory agency, the Environmental Protection Agency (EPA) is a leading advocate of the U.S. environmental industry's interests in the world market. EPA is also a primary source of manuals, directories, clearinghouses and databases and other information on environmentally sound technologies. EPA sponsors and participates in technology cooperation programs, many of which involve international development projects. Through EPA, companies can obtain information on the implementation of environmental regulations in developing countries, learn about EPA's technology transfer and technical assistance programs, and access computerized information on environmental technologies and regional environmental development projects.

Department of Energy (DOE)

The U.S. Department of Energy is a valuable source of technical, market, and financial assistance for U.S. firms specializing in energy-related industries, especially those with a positive environmental impact. DOE chairs the Committee on Renewable Energy Commerce and Trade (CORECT), an inter-agency working group of 14 federal agencies formed in 1984 to advance commerce and trade in renewable energy technologies by bringing together potential users, funding sources and U.S. industry members to ensure that U.S. renewable energy applications are considered for viable applications throughout the world.

Department of Agriculture (USDA)

Through its Commodity Credit Corporation, the Department of Agriculture (USDA) administers export sales and donations for foreign use through other agencies and provides export guarantees to foreign buyers. Its Foreign Agricultural Service gathers worldwide information through representatives stationed in 70 U.S. embassies, develops data to support trade, and works to reduce trade barriers. Its Office of International Cooperation and Development is responsible for international and technical cooperation for development assistance programs.

Department of State

Several offices of the U.S. Department of State offer both assistance for exporters valuable information resources. The Office of Business and Export Affairs provides export assistance to U.S. businesses on market conditions and export regulations for other countries. The Office of Trade and Commercial Affairs assists U.S. companies with protecting patents, trademarks and copyrights against infringement while working in a foreign marketplace. Country Desk officers can provide information on the current state of political, economic, and social affairs in a specific country, as well as provide contact information and advice for people visiting a foreign country for the first time.

National Association of State Development Agencies (NASDA)

State programs can often fill financing gaps not addressed by federal and private entities. U.S. firms can access these state programs to complement federal funding options. Some state programs provide export counseling or technical assistance, while others offer financial support for international activities. Many state trade programs work with Ex-Im Bank to help exporters arrange financing, including Florida, Maryland, Michigan, Minnesota, Oklahoma, Texas, Virginia and Washington. Maine, New Hampshire and Vermont have similar cooperative arrangements with Ex-Im Bank to support exports.

MULTILATERAL ORGANIZATIONS & DEVELOPMENT BANKS

The World Bank

The International Bank for Reconstruction and Development (IBRD or World Bank), headquartered in Washington, DC, is responsible for providing both financial and technical assistance to developing countries to stimulate economic development. Owned by more than 140 member governments, the Bank makes structural adjustment loans to help developing countries effect policy changes and lends funds to credit-worthy countries or their agencies, generally for specific development projects. Through its procurement program, contract opportunities for suppliers of goods and services are available through international competitive bidding. The Bank maintains representative offices in 57 foreign countries.

International Finance Corporation

The International Finance Corporation (IFC), a member of the World Bank Group, is a multilateral development institution that promotes productive private investment that will contribute to the economic growth of its developing member countries. Its principal objective is to provide the financing, technical assistance and management needed to develop productive investment opportunities. The IFC seeks to encourage the flow of private capital, both domestically and internationally, through the establishment or expansion of local capital markets and financial institutions.

United Nations Development Programme (UNDP)

The United Nations Development Programme (UNDP) is the central planning, funding and coordinating organization for technical cooperation in the United Nations system. As an inter-governmental agency of the United Nations, UNDP provides grants, technical assistance and policy advice for assistance projects in most developing countries. For the past four decades, UNDP has helped developing countries build their human resources and institutions, productive use of natural resources and planning and managerial capabilities. This is achieved by co-designing and co-financing technical cooperation and also through pre-investment projects with developing countries. UNDP receives funding from donor countries which is then used to provide expertise (technical assistance and advice) for development projects.

Asian Development Bank (ADB)

The Asian Development Bank (ADB), headquartered in Manila, Philippines, has become a major catalyst in promoting the development of the most populous and fast-growing region in the world. ADB is owned by the governments of 36 countries from the Asia/Pacific region and 16 countries from Europe and North America. The Bank has mobilized international resources for both its ordinary and concessional lending operations to accelerate economic and social growth in the Asia/Pacific region through financial and technical assistance.

African Development Bank (AfDB)

Since it began operations in 1966, the African Development Bank (AfDB) has committed more than $22.3 billion for over 1,600 loans and grants to 51 African countries. Headquartered in Abidjan, Côte d'Ivoire, the AfDB is the major source of external public financing on the continent. The AfDB assists financially viable projects which have significant economic merit by catalyzing the flow of domestic and external resources. Bank Assistance is provided directly to private enterprises and financial institutions and is also available indirectly through private financial institutions such as development, commercial and merchant banks.

European Bank for Reconstruction and Development (EBRD)

The European Bank for Reconstruction and Development (EBRD) lends and invests exclusively for projects and investment programs in the countries of Central and Eastern Europe, including the former-Soviet republics. The EBRD plays a catalytic role in stimulating capital and investment from both public and private sources. With limited resources relative to the scale of need in the region, EBRD emphasizes the quality of its projects and the added value it brings to them. The EBRD requires that its projects have a "multiplier effect," such as demonstration value, mobilization of co-financing, or relief of infrastructural bottlenecks that constrain private sector development. The EBRD assists projects that encounter difficulty in securing financing. It shares and minimizes investor risk; promotes foreign direct investment; encourages co-financing by reducing risk through its preferred creditor status; enables mobilization of domestic capital; and complements the efforts of other lenders.

Inter-American Development Bank (IDB)

The Inter-American Development Bank (IDB), headquartered in Washington, DC, has been a major lender to its Latin American and Caribbean members since its inception. Its cumulative lending and technical cooperation amounted to $56.8 billion by the end of 1992. IDB is currently the principal source of external finance for most Latin American countries. The Inter-American Investment Corporation (IIC), an affiliate of the Inter-American Development Bank (IDB), provides financing for private-sector investment projects in Latin America and the Caribbean. IIC was capitalized in 1986 with $200 million with the primary objective of promoting the development of private enterprise in IDB's regional member countries.

Japanese Ministry of International Trade and Industry (MITI)

As the primary government authority for trade, the Ministry of International Trade and Industry (MITI) formulates and implements Japan's trade and industrial policy. MITI delegates a part of its trade policy and program to the Japan External Trade Organization and supervises the export-import financing programs of the Export-Import Bank of Japan. MITI also operates an export insurance program with the U.S. Export-Import Bank (Ex-Im Bank) which helps U.S. companies participate in international activities.

Export-Import Bank of Japan (JEXIM)

The Export-Import Bank of Japan (JEXIM) was founded in 1950 as an independent governmental financial institution. JEXIM's objective is to encourage and supplement financing by commercial banks and other Japanese financial institutions to facilitate economic interchange between Japan and foreign countries. While most assistance is intended for Japanese firms purchasing imports, JEXIM has begun a new program to assist non-Japanese firms exporting manufactured goods to Japan.

Japan International Cooperation Agency (JICA) / Overseas Economic Cooperation Fund (OECF)

Both the Japan International Cooperation Agency (JICA) and the Overseas Economic Cooperation Fund (OECF) distribute Japan's Official Development Assistance (ODA), Japan's foreign aid for developing countries. The OECF provides loans to both foreign governments, corporations registered in Japan and corporations registered in developing countries for development projects. JICA's primary function is to provide technical assistance and development grants for feasibility studies to recipient countries and private businesses. Both organizations offer opportunities for foreign corporations.

Global Environment Facility (GEF)

The Global Environment Facility (GEF) provides grants and concessional funds to developing countries for investment projects, technical assistance and research for the activities with global environment benefits. GEF resources are intended to facilitate projects with global environmental benefits for which official development funds are not normally available to complement, not substitute for, regular aid programs. GEF activities are implemented as follows: UNDP provides technical assistance, the U.N. Environmental Programme provides scientific and environmental advice, the World Bank supports GEF investment operations and administers project funding, and regional development banks collaborate in investment operations. GEF finances projects targeted solely at global environmental problems and allows middle-income countries that have significant environmental problems (e.g., Hong Kong) to borrow money from GEF at low-interest rates.

GOVERNMENT-BACKED EQUITY FUNDS

The Government-Backed Equity Funds are privately managed equity pools designed to foster development of small- and medium-sized enterprises in specific markets or regions of the world. Enterprise Funds have been established by the U.S. Agency for International Development (USAID) to provide capital to commercially viable projects in the form of equity capital and/or extended credit for start-up or expansion in Central and Eastern Europe (CEE) and the Newly Independent States (NIS) of the former-Soviet Union. The Enterprise Funds are expected to raise additional capital from private and public sources.

Loans and equity contributions range from $500,000 to several million dollars and are offered directly or in conjunction with commercial banks acting as intermediaries. These funds offer equity investment support, technical assistance and training related to actual or potential investments and loans.

The Enterprise Funds for Eastern Europe and the NIS include:

- Czech-American Enterprise Fund
- Slovak-American Enterprise Fund
- Hungarian-American Enterprise Fund
- Polish-American Enterprise Fund/Polish Equity Fund
- The Russian-American Enterprise Fund
- Environmental Enterprises Assistance Fund
- Western NIS Enterprise Fund
- Central Asian-American Enterprise Fund
- Defense Enterprise Fund

The Government-Backed Equity Funds (both existing and planned) include:

- Bancroft Eastern Europe Fund
- Poland Partners Fund
- New Europe East Investment Fund
- Central European Telecom Investment Fund
- Central Environmental Protection Fund (CEPF)
- Ecofund
- First Hungary Fund
- Global Environment Emerging Markets Fund
- East Europe Development Fund
- Pioneer Poland Fund
- Renaissance Partners Fund
- Czech National Environmental Fund
- National Fund for Environmental Protection & Water Management
- Slovak National Fund
- Alliance ScanEast Fund
- Fund for Large Enterprises in Russia
- Russia Partners Fund

- Agribusiness Partners International Fund
- South America Private Equity Growth Fund
- Central and Eastern European-NIS Property Fund
- First NIS Regional Fund
- Framlington Investment Fund for Russia
- EBRD Regional Venture Funds (Russia)
- Urals Regional Venture Fund
- EBRD-Small Business Fund
- Africa Growth Fund, L.P.
- Asia Pacific Growth Fund
- Global Environment Fund (GEF)

REGIONAL DEVELOPMENT FUNDS

Andean Development Corporation

The Andean Development Corporation (Corporacion Andina de Formento-CAF), headquartered in Venezuela, began operations in 1970. CAF provides technical and financial support for a variety of industry sectors in the Andean countries of Bolivia, Colombia, Ecuador, Peru and Venezuela. CAF's authorized capital of $2.1 billion consists of $900 million of subscribed capital, $453 million of paid-in capital, and $448 million of guarantee capital. In addition to its capital resources, CAF conducts fund-raising activities with international public and private financial institutions, including the Inter-American Development Bank, the U.S. Agency for International Development, and international private banks.

Bahamas Development Bank (BDB)

The Bahamas Development Bank (BDB) provides medium- and long-term financing for public and private development projects. Financing includes loans, guarantees, and equity participation. Technical assistance is also available for project development.

Caribbean Development Program

Established in 1986, Puerto Rico's Caribbean Development Program (CDP) provides financial assistance for projects in Puerto Rico and beneficiary states of the Caribbean Basin Initiative (CBI) by taking advantage of Section 936 of the U.S. Internal Revenue Code. Under Section 936, U.S. corporations receive partial tax exemption on income earned in Puerto Rico provided that the corporation reinvests profits in projects in Puerto Rico. In 1986, the U.S. Congress extended this tax exemption to beneficiary states of the CBI. The Caribbean Basin Projects Financing Authority (CARIFA) is an additional source of CDP financing for medium- and large-scale projects in eligible CBI states.

Caribbean Development Bank (CDB)

Working in association with the Caribbean Common Market (CARICOM), the Caribbean Development Bank (CDB) provides long-term financing for development projects in the Caribbean. With $210 million in capital resources, the CDB, headquartered in Barbados, provides loans and letters of credit for private-sector projects in manufacturing, forestry, fishing, tourism, and mining. Since 1970, the CDB has provided over $350 million in loans and $78 million in letters of credit for these sectors. Financing for pre-feasibility and feasibility studies is also available.

Caribbean Financial Services Corporation (CFSC)

Established in 1984, the Caribbean Financial Services Corporation (CFSC) works in cooperation with the U.S. Agency for International Development (USAID) and the European Investment Bank (EIB) to provide financing and assistance for development projects in the English-speaking Caribbean. With capital resources of $21 million, the CFSC provides medium- and long-term financing and equity for projects and institutions that enhance the region's foreign-exchange earning capability.

Central American Bank for Economic Integration (CABEI)

The Central American Bank for Economic Integration (CABEI) is a source of financial assistance for member governments of the Central American Common Market (CACM) (Costa Rica, El Salvador, Guatemala, Honduras, and Nicaragua) to support regional development projects.

Colombian Private Investment Fund

The Colombian Private Investment Fund provides medium- and long-term financing with working capital and fixed investments for industrial development projects.

Costa Rica Private Investment Corporation (PIC)

Working in cooperation with the U.S. Agency for International Development, the German Finance Corporation, and the United Kingdom's Commonwealth Development Corporation, the Costa Rica Private Investment Corporation (PIC) provides financing and equity for projects which improve regional exports. With $45 million in resources, the PIC provides medium- and long-term financing and equity participation for eligible projects throughout Central America, although primarily in Costa Rica.

North American Development Bank (NADBank)

The North American Development Bank (NADBank) was created following the ratification of the North American Free Trade Agreement (NAFTA) to finance border development and environmental improvement projects as well as provide support for community adjustment and investment for the United States and Mexico. Established with a capital base of $450 million, the NADBank will be further capitalized by $2.55 billion of callable capital from the United States and Mexico. The NADBank has not yet fully defined its mandate in Mexico beyond border environmental-remediation projects.

Japan Development Bank (JDB)

Established in 1951, the Japan Development Bank (JDB) is wholly owned by the Japanese government. JDB was established to promote Japan's industrial development and socio-economic growth by offering long-term and low-interest loans for various projects originating in the private sector. JDB has provided financing to foreign-affiliated companies in Japan, using the same standards as those used for domestic firms. Loans to foreign affiliated companies have increased rapidly since FY 1984 when JDB created two loan programs entitled "Facilities for Imported Products" and "Promotion of Foreign Direct Investment in Japan."

Private Investment Fund for the Americas (PIFA)

Established by the Strategic Resources Corporation with a a capital base of $500 million, the Private Investment Fund for the Americas (PIFA) is designed to support infrastructure development in Latin America and the Caribbean.

CHAPTER ONE

Obtaining Information

Before expanding into the international market, business executives should learn as much as possible about the opportunities and obstacles they are most likely to encounter. Foreign markets are poorly understood by many Americans. To successfully penetrate those lucrative markets, research on the targeted countries is essential.

Many executives are unaware of the publications and services that the government offers to assist in collecting market information. By using these resources properly, not only can costly mistakes be avoided but unforeseen opportunities can be discovered as well. Most services are available either free-of-charge or at a minimal cost. This chapter details some of the programs that can provide critical information with which to make decisions to expand into lucrative foreign markets.

The following is a brief list of the key topics described in Chapter One:

- Country and Trade Information
- Current Affairs
- Industry Information
- Export Information
- Fax-Back Services
- Contact Information
- Geographic and Regional Information
- Export Assistance.

Published Information

A variety of government, multilateral and private sector publications comprise an excellent base of resources for international market research. This section describes relevant publications for executives attempting to conduct market research. Computerized information and "people resources" are also included in this chapter.

The *Atlas of United States Foreign Relations* is a compilation of documents addressing international organizations, elements of the world economy, trade and investments, development assistance and national security. This atlas presents background information on international markets such as special agreements or initiatives between the U.S. and a foreign country. Cost: $5.00 per copy. (Payment is accepted by credit card or pre-payment by personal check.)

Contact:
Superintendent of Documents
U.S. Government Printing Office
Washington, DC 20402
Tel: (202) 512-1800

The *1994 World Factbook* provides accurate, up-to-date information on countries and geographic areas of the world, including maps for each entry and fold-out color maps of major regions. Entries for each country cover geography, demography, government, economy, communications and defense forces. Published annually by the Central Intelligence Agency, this volume includes charts on the United Nations system, international organizations and their members, and regional maps.

(Publication No. 041-015-00174-4) Cost: $29.00 per copy; outside the U.S., Canada, and Mexico, $64. (Payment is accepted by credit card or pre-payment by personal check.)

Contact:
Superintendent of Documents
U.S. Government Printing Office
Washington, DC 20402
Tel: (202) 512-1800

International Business Practices, a Commerce Department publication, describes the legal aspects of doing business in 117 countries. The book is organized by region; each country section describes business organizations, export-import laws, commercial policies, foreign investment, intellectual property rights, taxation, regulatory agencies, and useful contacts. The book also includes chapters on export finance, export management and trading companies, foreign sales corporations, the Foreign Corrupt Practices Act, and international sales and agents. Publication No. 003-009-00622-8.

Contact:
Superintendent of Documents
U.S. Government Printing Office
Washington, DC 20402
Tel: (202) 512-1800

The *Foreign Broadcast Information Service (FBIS)* monitors foreign broadcasts, news agency transmissions, newspapers, periodicals, and government statements. FBIS publishes translations of these materials in hard copy daily and in microfiche weekly. FBIS publications are available for most countries in Asia, Africa, Latin America, and Eastern Europe. Cost: $625.00 per year (add $100.00 for each additional category).

Contact:
National Technical Information Service
5285 Port Royal Road
Springfield, VA 22161
Tel: (703) 487-4650
Fax: (703) 321-8547
E-Mail: ORDERS@NTIS.FEDWORLD.GOV

Business America is a monthly magazine from the Department of Commerce (DOC) that helps U.S. exporters penetrate international markets by providing current and newsworthy information on opportunities for international trade and methods of business. A typical issue includes: an analysis of U.S. trade policy; a "how-to" article for new exporters; a review of international economic trends; and news of federal actions affecting trade. *Business America* also includes trade news from DOC, other U.S. Government agencies, and foreign governments; and provides information on trade and investment opportunities abroad. Each issue features a calendar of upcoming catalogue shows, exhibitions, seminars and international trade fairs. Cost: Annual subscription, 12 issues, $32.00 in the U.S.; $40.00 foreign. Single copies: $3.00 in the U.S.

Contact:
Superintendent of Documents
U.S. Government Printing Office
Washington, DC 20402
Tel: (202) 512-1800

Editorial Office:
Business America
Department of Commerce
Room 3414
14th Street and Constitution Avenue, NW
Washington, DC 20230
Tel: (202) 482-3251
Fax: (202) 482-5819

A Department of Commerce publication, *A Basic Guide to Exporting,* outlines the steps involved in exporting and provides practical information and sources of government assistance to exporters. It is available for $9.50. (Publication Number 003-009-00487-0)

Contact:
Superintendent of Documents
U.S. Government Printing Office
Washington, DC 20402
Tel: (202) 512-1800

The Small Business Administration's *Exporters' Guide to Federal Resources for Small Businesses* identifies major federal programs designed to assist small business owners in exporting. The cost is $4.75. (Publication Number 045-000-00263-2)

Contact:
Superintendent of Documents
U.S. Government Printing Office
Washington, DC 20402
Tel: (202) 512-1800

The *International Trade Statistics Yearbook* presents statistical analysis of overall foreign trade by regions and countries, as well as world exports by origin, destination, and product category. The publication costs $125.00.

Contact:
United Nations Publications
Room DC 2-0853
New York, NY 10017
Tel: (212) 963-8302
Fax: (212) 963-3489

The **World Bank** produces many publications and information services about international activities and programs of the World Bank Group. A complete Index of Publications and Guide to Information Products and Services is available from the World Bank Bookstore, located in Washington, DC, at the corner of 18th Street and Pennsylvania Avenue, NW.

Contact:
World Bank Bookstore
701 18th Street, NW
Washington, DC 20433
Tel: (202) 473-1155
Fax: (202) 676-0581

The **National Technical Information Service (NTIS)** disseminates the results of U.S. and foreign government-sponsored research, development and engineering activities. As a source for U.S. government scientific and technical information, NTIS manages software, data files and databases produced by federal agencies and allows U.S. firms to access the results of over 15,000 U.S. government-sponsored research and engineering programs. NTIS presents its findings in the form of newsletters, computer searches and data files. Selected publications and services of NTIS include:

- Newsletter Abstracts
- NTIS Published Searches
- Federal Research in Progress (FEDRIP) Database
- NTIS Bibliographic Database
- Foreign Technology Newsletter Abstracts.

Contact:
National Technical Information Service
5285 Port Royal Road
Springfield, VA 22161
Tel: (703) 487-4650
Fax: (703) 321-8547
E-Mail: ORDERS@NTIS.FEDWORLD.GOV

Overseas Business Reports (OBR), a series prepared by the Department of Commerce International Economic Policy Division's country specialists, provide helpful background data for evaluating export markets. The series discusses marketing factors in individual countries; presents economic and commercial profiles of countries and regions; issues semi-annual outlooks for U.S. trade with countries and geographical regions; and publishes selected statistical reports on the direction, volume, and nature of U.S. foreign trade. Cost: Annual subscription $16.00 in the U.S.; $20.00 abroad.

Contact:
U.S. Department of Commerce
International Economic Policy Division
1441 L Street, NW
Washington, DC 20230
Tel: (202) 482-3022

Automated Trade Locator Assistance System (ATLAS) of the U.S. Small Business Administration provides access to international market and trade information. For a particular product, ATLAS reports indicate the top importing countries, import quantities, dollar volumes, and five-year market trends. Data is presented in user-friendly formats that are easily analyzed. This service is available free of charge through SBA district offices.

Contact:
Nearest SBA District Office. See Appendix C.

Country Trade Statistics from the Department of Commerce (DOC) can provide data on all U.S. exports over the most recent five-year period. These reports indicate which U.S. industries currently present the best opportunity for exports to a particular country. Each report contains four key statistical tables showing the leading U.S. exports to target regions with which the U.S. maintains commercial relations.

Contact:
Nearest DOC District Office. See Appendix B.

Trends is a weekly publication produced by the National Technical Information Service (NTIS) that offers expert analysis of foreign and domestic political developments in the former Soviet Union, Eastern Europe, China and other selected countries in Asia, as well as selected countries of Latin America. *Trends* articles, which are based on in-depth examinations of media reports, examine major political and environmental developments which place the country's current activities into context and identify policy directions. *Trends* is released to the public six months after the date of publication. Cost: $250.00 per year in the U.S., Canada and Mexico; $500.00 foreign.

Contact:
National Technical Information Service
5285 Port Royal Road
Springfield, VA 22161
Tel: (703) 487-4630
Fax: (703) 321-8547
E-Mail: ORDERS@NTIS.FEDWORLD.GOV

Country Market Profiles are produced by the U.S. Department of Agriculture (USDA) and present country-specific descriptions of 40 overseas markets for high-value agricultural products. These 2-to-4-page descriptions include market overviews, economic trends, and information on U.S. market positions, foreign competition, and general export-labeling and licensing requirements.

Contact:
Foreign Agricultural Service Information Division, Publications Branch
USDA
14th Street & Independence Avenue, SW
Washington, DC 20250
Tel: (202) 720-7937
Fax: (202) 720-3229

Handbook of Economic Statistics is an annual publication prepared by the Central Intelligence Agency that contains basic statistics for comparing economic performance of countries around the world. New data and statistics are included for commodities, high technology and manufactured goods. Cost: $32.00; outside the United States, Canada and Mexico, $64.00. Order no.: PB92-928024/CAU.

Contact:
National Technical Information Service
5285 Port Royal Road
Springfield, VA 22161
Tel: (703) 487-4650
Fax: (703) 321-8547
E-Mail: ORDERS@NTIS.FEDWORLD.GOV

Industry Studies from the Department of Commerce (DOC) examine the present and future international competitiveness of various industries. Topics include industry performance, recent foreign competition, U.S. and foreign government assistance, and trends and assessments of future global competitiveness. DOC has over 20 industry studies in its series. Cost: $4.00 - $6.00 each.

Contact:
Office of Trade Information and Analysis
U.S. Department of Commerce
HCHB 2219
14th Street & Constitution Avenue, NW
Washington, DC 20230
Tel: (202) 482-4944
Fax: (202) 482-3968

The *Economist Intelligence Unit* publishes extensive country reports quarterly with up-to-date analysis and market information. Regional statistics are provided, including social and political analysis. Specific reports are published on various regions. This information is useful to any business executive who needs to forecast future trends in banking, investments and corporate finance.

Contact:
The Economist Intelligence Unit, Limited
Subscriptions Department
P.O. Box 200
Harold Hill
Ramford, Essex RN3 8UX, U.K.
Tel: 011-(44) 1-322-289194
Fax: 011-(44) 1-708-371850

The *International Herald Tribune* is published daily in the U.S. and worldwide, and covers international news. Special sections are included on a weekly basis, including an environment, health and science section and a money report. Delivered six days a week (no Sunday paper), the *Tribune* is delivered daily in major cities in the U.S. and Canada, including: Washington, Chicago, Philadelphia, Boston, Atlanta, Miami, Houston, Phoenix, Tucson, Denver, San Francisco, Los Angeles, Montreal and Toronto.

Because the newspaper is co-owned by *The New York Times* and *The Washington Post*, each issue contains stories that have been published in both papers as well as articles written specifically for the *Tribune*. Worldwide circulation is nearly 200,000. Cost: One-year subscription, $377.00; six months, $205.00; three months, $115.00.

Contact:
International Herald Tribune
850 3rd Avenue, Eighth Floor
New York, NY 10022
Tel: (800) 882-2884
Fax: (212) 755-8785

The *Journal of Commerce*, a daily newspaper published by the Knight-Ridder Business Information Service, covers all business subjects, including international and domestic trade. It includes current market information, industry news and trade forecasts, specifically by industry sector. Foreign exchange information and dollar exchange rates are published daily, along with information on trade relations and major trade pacts. The *Journal of Commerce* presents information on imports and exports and lists a schedule of upcoming trade missions by their sponsoring agencies, including federal and state development agencies. Information on export opportunities is supplied by the Department of Commerce. Cost: One-year subscription rate, $310.00; 6-month subscription, $180.00; 3-month subscription, $99.00. Single copy: $1.25. One-year subscription in Canada: $410.00; International one-year subscription: $465.00.

Contact:
For subscription inquiries and address changes:
The Journal of Commerce
445 Marshall Street
Philipsburg, NJ 08865
Tel: (800) 221-3777
Tel: (908) 859-1300

Electronic Sources of Information

A number of market information services are available electronically, or by telephone/facsimile connection. Some of the advantages of these "high-tech" information solutions are the speed with which business executives can obtain relevant and useful information on international business trends.

FAX-BACK SERVICES

In 1992, the U.S. Department of Commerce (DOC) began installing a network of instant fax-transmission servers. DOC estimated that over 85 percent of the inquiries which the country desk officers in the Trade Development Division receive each year can be answered by the information contained on the instant fax servers. The documents on the fax servers are updated regularly, and next-step contact information is often included on the fax sheets.

For companies exploring the international marketplace, these free fax services can be invaluable sources of information. The instant fax servers are organized by region, so each will contain documents specific to those markets. The information offered by each regional fax server should answer many basic questions about international business. The Commerce Department fax servers are as follows:

The Office of Africa, Near East and South Asia (ANESA) at the Department of Commerce operates **ANESA Flash Facts**, which provides key market information for these regions. Documents available through this service include: foreign investment climate statements, international market insight reports, and general and specific guides for American exporters interested in doing business overseas. The ANESA Flash Fax service is available 24 hours a day, seven days a week. To receive a main menu of document options, dial the ANESA Flash Fax number from a touch-tone phone, follow the instructions and the information will be faxed automatically upon request. Each document includes a telephone number through which firms can request next-step information.

Contact:
U.S. Department of Commerce
International Trade Administration
Africa/Near East/South Asia Division
To connect with a fax hotline: (202) 482-1064
To speak with a country desk officer: (202) 482-1860

EEBICFLASH, operated by the Eastern Europe Business Information Center (EEBIC), provides quick access to information on countries in Central and Eastern Europe. This resource offers access to hundreds of documents which cover: exporting and financing, current trade and business opportunities, upcoming trade events, and country information. To receive a main menu of document options, dial the hotline number from a touch-tone phone, follow the instructions, and the information will be faxed automatically upon request. An information number is provided at the end of each document to allow the recipient to discuss the information with a country specialist.

Contact:
U.S. Department of Commerce
International Trade Administration
Eastern Europe Division
To connect with the fax hotline: (202) 482-5745
To speak with an EEBIC staff member: (202) 482-2645

The **Flashfax BISNIS Bank** is a 24-hour fax line containing information on opportunities in the Newly Independent States of the former Soviet Union. The fax line maintains three document menus. Menu 1, document #0001, contains trade and investment opportunities and trade promotion information. Menu 2, document #0002, has industry- and country-specific information as well as financing alternatives. Menu 3, document #0003, contains information on BISNIS publications.

Contact:
U.S. Department of Commerce
International Trade Administration
BISNIS Office
To connect with the Flashfax BISNIS hotline: (202) 482-3145
To speak with a BISNIS staff member: (202) 482-4655

The **PacRim Hotline** at the Department of Commerce is a telephone information service that provides convenient access to current trade-related documents from East Asia and the Pacific Region. The hotline provides a wide variety of facts and data. To receive a main menu that lists the available documents, follow the instructions given from the hotline. The requested documents will then be faxed within 30 minutes. After the faxes have been sent and reviewed, country desk officers are available to discuss them. The countries featured include: Australia, Cambodia, Indonesia, South Korea (U.S. embargo status is provided for North Korea), Laos, Malaysia, New Zealand, the Philippines, Singapore, Taiwan, Thailand and Vietnam.

Contact:
U.S. Department of Commerce
International Trade Administration
Asia and the Pacific Rim Division

To connect with the fax hotline: (202) 482-3875, 482-4957, or 482-3646
To speak with a Pacific Rim country desk officer: (202) 482-4958

The **Amerifax** information service offers a variety of information on the North American Free Trade Agreement (NAFTA) and its signatory countries as well as information on Latin America and Caribbean. Option #1 of Amerifax provides information on Canada and Mexico as well as NAFTA. Document #5000 contains information on the making of NAFTA Rules of Origin Determination. Information on the Mexican tariff schedule is provided on document #6000, and the Canadian tariff schedule is document #7000. Option #2 of Amerifax provides information on Latin America and the Caribbean. Document #0100 is a listing of documents on this region. The main menu is Document #0101.

Contact:
U.S. Department of Commerce
International Trade Administration
Office of NAFTA, Office of Latin America and the Caribbean
Tel: (202) 482-0305

COMPUTERIZED DATABANKS

The U.S. Environmental Protection Agency (EPA) has resources to assist business executives with environmental market development. **INFOTERRA** is an informational liaison service that connects business executives to EPA environmental experts. This program can be used to locate environment-related technology information services, including the EPA library and information network. In addition to referring international clients to U.S. experts, INFOTERRA/U.S.A. has the capacity to search over 500 EPA international and commercial databases and access EPA and other government agency reports on environmental activities. INFOTERRA is linked to EPA program offices nationwide to provide details on international environmental activities.

With over 600 sources listed in the directory, this service is part of the INFOTERRA network, the environmental research and referral arm of the United Nations Environment Programme (UNEP). The network consists of 138 member countries, each of which maintains a register of environmental experts. This registry is part of the INFOTERRA International Directory of Sources, which disseminates environmental expertise on over 1,000 environmental topics.

Contact:
INFOTERRA/U.S.A. National Focal Point
INFOTERRA-3404
Environmental Protection Agency
401 M Street, SW
Washington, DC 20460
Tel: (202) 260-5917
Fax: (202) 260-3923

The **National Technical Information Service (NTIS) World Data Bank
II** is a computer-generated mapping system of the world. Maps of four geographic areas
(North America, South America, Europe/Africa and Asia) are contained on magnetic
tapes and can be displayed at various scales by coastlines, rivers or international
boundaries. This digital format is useful for visual displays of geographic information.
To update the information, a large-capacity hard drive is necessary. World Data Bank
II is available in individual volumes or as a complete set. Cartographic Automatic
Mapping (CAM) can be used for output of World Data Bank II files. Cost: $560.00.

Contact:
National Technical Information Service
5285 Port Royal Road
Springfield, VA 22161
Tel: (703) 487-4650
Fax: (703) 321-8547
E-Mail: ORDERS@NTIS.FEDWORLD.GOV

The **Export and Import Trade Data Base**, provided by the U.S. Department
of Commerce Trade Data Services Branch, provides worldwide export and import
statistics tracked by mode of transportation and port of entry or exit. Available
classification levels include the Harmonized System on Commodity Classification,
Standard International Trade Classification, Standard Industrial Classification-based
codes, and End-Use Classification. Customized tabulations and reports can be prepared
to user specifications. Prices begin at $25 and vary according to user requirements and
job size.

Contact:
U.S. Bureau of the Census
Foreign Trade Division, Rm 2279
Trade Data Services Branch
FOB #3
Washington, DC 20233
Tel: (301) 457-2311
Fax: (301) 457-4615

People Resources and Services

The government supports a number of counseling services, training seminars and research services which assist U.S. companies in designing an approach to the international marketplace. Most of these services are offered free-of-charge: however, for some training seminars or information searches a nominal charge may apply.

The **Trade Information Center (TIC)** is often the first point of contact for U.S. exporters. This hotline, staffed by U.S. Department of Commerce personnel, directs business executives to the appropriate offices within the U.S. Government agencies which assist exporters. Information is provided free-of-charge, and companies may use a special "800" number to access the center.

Contact:
U.S. Department of Commerce
Trade Information Center (TIC)
Tel: (800) USA-TRAD(E)

The **Eastern Europe Business Information Center (EEBIC)** at the Department of Commerce is designed to provide information on doing business in Eastern Europe. To increase the involvement of small- and medium-sized companies in Eastern Europe, the Center issues a series entitled *Eastern Europe Looks for Partners*, alerting companies to specific East European opportunities in energy, environment and telecommunications.

Contact:
U.S. Department of Commerce
Eastern Europe Business Information Center (EEBIC), Rm 7414
14th Street and Constitution Avenue, NW
Washington, DC 20230
Tel: (202) 482-2645
Fax: (202) 482-4473

Business Information Service for the Newly Independent States (BISNIS)
provides information on commercial opportunities in the Newly Independent States (NIS), sources of financing, current lists of trade contacts, and U.S. Government programs supporting trade and investment in the region. BISNIS publishes a monthly bulletin containing information on upcoming trade promotion events, updates on U.S. Government programs in the region, and practical advice on doing business in the NIS.

Contact:
U.S. Department of Commerce
ITA/BISNIS
14th Street and Constitution Avenue, NW
Washington, DC 20230
Tel: (202) 482-4655
Fax: (202) 482-2293

The **Japan Export Information Center (JEIC)** assists U.S. companies interested in developing export business to Japan by providing business counseling services and current information on exporting to Japan, Japanese business customs and practices, market entry alternatives, economic conditions, available market information and research, standards and product-testing procedures, tariffs and non-tariff barriers. The export marketing guide, *Destination Japan: A Business Guide for the 90s*, is published by JEIC, which also maintains a commercial library and counsels on various aspects of doing business in Japan. The JEIC also works with the Japanese Government to adapt Japanese import promotion programs to the needs of U.S. exporters.

Contact:
U.S. Department of Commerce
Office of Japan, Rm H-2320
14th Street and Constitution Avenue, NW
Washington, DC 20230
Tel: (202) 482-2425
Fax: (202) 482-0469

Single Internal Market Information Service (SIMIS) serves as the major contact point within the U.S. Government for U.S. business questions on commercial and trade implications of the European Union's (EU) Single Market program. Maintaining a comprehensive database of EU directives and regulations, SIMIS also supports specialized documentation published by the EU, the U.S. Government, and the private sector. SIMIS provides a basic information packet on EU 1992, sectorial guides to EU legislation, informational seminars, and business counseling.

Contact:
U.S. Department of Commerce
Single Internal Market Information Service
14th Street and Constitution Avenue, NW
Washington, DC 20230
Tel: (202) 482-5276
Fax: (202) 482-2155

For small companies who are new to the export market, the **Service Corps of Retired Executives (SCORE)** provides one-on-one counseling and training seminars by individuals who have had years of practical experience in international trade. SCORE volunteers assist small firms in evaluating export potential and in strengthening domestic operations by identifying financial, managerial, or technical problems. Each SCORE office also offers a series of presentations on international business for the local business community.

Contact:
Small Business Administration
National SCORE Office
409 3rd Street, SW
Washington, DC 20416
Tel: 1-800-634-0245
Fax: (202) 205-7636

The Kutztown University Small Business Development Center's Export Development Program (EDP) is one of the most innovative, cost-effective export promotion programs for small- and medium-sized manufacturers. One of the services that the EDP has developed is a trade leads matching system, the Automated Export Identifier System (AEIS). In addition, the EDP has established an office in Brussels, Belgium to provide assistance to South Central Pennsylvania companies. The Central Pennsylvania Export Representative for Trade (CPERT) has helped over 27 Pennsylvania companies to penetrate the European market.

The **Small Business Development Centers (SBDC)** targets small business owners who are new to export, and offer counseling, training, managerial and trade finance assistance. While counseling services are provided at no cost to the small business exporter, nominal fees are generally charged for export training seminars and other SBDC-sponsored export events.

Contact:
Office of Small Business Development
U.S. Small Business Administration
409 3rd Street SW
Washington, DC 20416
Tel: (202) 205-6766
Fax: (202) 205-7727
or
See Appendix H for the nearest Small Business Development Center

The **Economic Research Service (ERS)** of the U.S. Department of Agriculture (USDA) provides economic data, models, and research information about the agricultural economies and policies of foreign countries. The ERS also provides information concerning agricultural trade and aid relationships between foreign countries and the United States. The ERS has the following divisions to assist U.S. companies:

- The International Economics Division collects and analyzes extensive information on foreign country and commodity markets for U.S. agricultural products; forecasts changes in these markets; and conducts research on longer-term agricultural supply, demand and trade issues. Regional branches evaluate individual country markets, as well as such regional groupings as the European Union (EU). Analysts also collect and interpret current information on developments in commodity markets and foreign government policies that can influence internationally traded commodities.

- The Trade Policy Branch furnishes current information on the trade strategies of other countries and on activities of international organizations such as the Food and Agriculture Organization (FAO), the Organization for Economic Cooperation and Development (OECD), the General Agreement on Tariffs and Trade (GATT) and the United Nations Conference on Trade and Development (UNCTAD). This branch also analyzes alternative trade policies and their implications for U.S. agricultural trade.

- The Global Analysis Branch regularly generates and distributes a wide variety of world price and quantity data for commodities of major interest to U.S. exporters, such as grains and livestock products. This branch maintains a large database of agricultural export and import statistics for a variety of countries.

Contact:

Information Division
ERS-USDA
Room 228
1301 New York Avenue, NW
Washington, DC 20005-4788
Tel: (202) 219-0494
Fax: (202) 219-0308

Buying Info: 1(800) 999-6779
Electronic Info: (202) 720-5505
Bulletin Board Info: (202) 219-0012

The **World Traders Data Reports (WTDR)**, a service of the Department of Commerce, provides U.S. companies with information on foreign businesses. Reports contain information on foreign companies such as the type of organization, year established, relative size, number of employees, general reputation, territory covered, language preferred, product lines handled, principal owners, and financial and trade references. Each report also contains a general comment on the firm's reliability as assessed by the U.S. Commercial Officer who conducted the investigation. Reports on firms located in the United States, Puerto Rico, U.S. Trust Territories, or in the republics of the former Soviet Union are not available. Cost: $100.00 per search.

Contact:
Nearest Commerce Department District Office. See Appendix B.

The **Office of Multilateral Affairs (OMA)** serves as a contact point for U.S. multilateral trade policy issues related to the General Agreement on Tariffs and Trade (GATT), the Organization for Economic Cooperation and Development (OECD), the United Nations, and other international organizations. The following trade policy areas are serviced by OMA: Generalized System Preferences (GSP), Section 301 and special 301 issues, intellectual property rights, Multilateral Trade Negotiations (MTN) including Uruguay Round, trade and the environment, and related trade policy initiatives.

Contact:
U.S. Department of Commerce
Office of Multilateral Affairs
14th Street and Constitution Avenue, NW
Washington, DC 20230
Tel: (202) 482-0603
Fax: (202) 482-5939

The **Office of the U.S. Trade Representative (USTR)** provides publications to exporters challenged by foreign barriers to trade and unfair trade practices. Offices are organized according to sectorial responsibilities.

Contact

Agricultural Affairs
Tel: (202) 395-6127

Office of Industry
Tel: (202) 395-5656

Science and Technology
Tel: (202) 395-3324

Investment
Tel: (202) 395-7271

Intellectual Property Services
Tel: (202) 395-4510

Environmental & Natural Services
Tel: (202) 395-7320

Office of Textiles
Tel: (202) 395-3026

CHAPTER TWO

Targeting Opportunities

Numerous government programs and publications can help business executives market their products and services abroad. Publications and database services identify everything from projects to potential partners, and government experts can provide insight into the best methods of penetrating a given market. Most of these sources of information are provided for free or at a nominal cost; therefore, they can make an important difference for small businesses or companies just beginning to commit to the international marketplace.

Since, in most countries, relationships must be well-developed before business transactions take place, laying the groundwork and establishing a network are important first steps. This chapter outlines published, computerized and "people" resources that help U.S. firms target international opportunities.

The following is a list of information resources and services for targeting market opportunities located in Chapter Two:

- Foreign Trade Leads
- Contact Information
- Published Information
- Export Rules and Regulations
- Market-Specific Counseling
- Project Procurement Information
- Market, Country, and Trade Information
- U.S. Development Project Information
- Project Procurement Announcements
- Feasibility Study Announcements
- Multilateral Development Bank Information.

- Consultant Registries
- Consultant Services
- Trade Missions
- Export Counseling
- Market Information
- Export Information
- Advertising Abroad

PUBLISHED INFORMATION

Commerce Business Daily (CBD), a publication of the Department of Commerce, contains international trade leads and commodity requirements of foreign governments. Published five times weekly, this publication lists U.S. Government procurement invitations, subcontracting leads, contract awards, sales of surplus property and foreign business opportunities, with contact names and phone numbers. The CBD office at DOC will provide a complete listing of companies that distribute CBD in electronic form. Cost: Annual subscription, $324.00 (first-class postage); $275.00 (second-class postage) in the U.S. Six-month subscription $162.00 (first-class postage); $137.50 (second-class postage). Single copies are not sold. (Publication No. 703-013-00000-7)

Contact:
Superintendent of Documents
U.S. Government Printing Office
Washington, DC 20402
Tel: (202) 512-1800

For a sample copy or to receive CBD through electronic services

Department of Commerce
14th Street and Constitution Avenue, NW
Room 2852
Washington, DC 20230
Tel: (202) 482-0632
Fax: (202) 482-5467

U.S. Agency for International Development (USAID) ***Financial Export Opportunities and Procurement Information Bulletins*** are available to any U.S. company on the USAID mailing list. Foreign government requirements for U.S. products are advertised in these two bulletins published by USAID's Office of Small and Disadvantaged Business Utilization (OSDBU). Contact OSDBU to receive an application for the mailing list to receive these publications free-of-charge.

Contact:
Office of Business Relations
U.S. Agency for International Development
OSDBU/MRC, Room 1200A, SA-14
Washington, DC 20523
Tel: (703) 875-1551
Fax: (703) 875-1862

The *U.S. Trade and Development Agency (TDA) Biweekly Report* alerts manufacturers and suppliers of upcoming projects and encourages them to contact consulting engineers and construction engineers about international project procurement. The report gives U.S. firms an opportunity to participate in the preliminary stages of large, international projects. By publishing this guide, TDA also increases the likelihood that U.S. goods and services will be used in executing the project.

The *Historical Project Activities Report* includes information on TDA development activities in the following regions: Asia/Pacific, Africa/Middle East, Latin America/Caribbean and the Newly Independent States. Information in these monthly reports includes: announcements of upcoming orientation visits or other activities sponsored by TDA; announcements of definitional missions; feasibility study bidding; announcements of firms chosen to perform feasibility studies; and information about World Bank and other multilateral projects to which TDA has provided assistance.

Contact:
Congressional Information Bureau, Inc.
U.S. Trade and Development Biweekly Report
3030 Clarendon Blvd., Suite 202
Rosslyn, VA 22201
Tel: (703) 516-4801
Fax: (703) 516-4804

ADB Business Opportunities, a monthly publication from the Manila-headquartered Asian Development Bank (ADB), lists all proposed projects, advance action on procurement, technical assistance projects, consultants recruiting and retroactive financing projects within ADB. It also lists procurement notices and final contract awards. New projects are listed in *Business Opportunities* as early as possible after ADB is satisfied that such projects have satisfied preliminary criteria for ADB funding.

The rate for an international subscription by airmail is $30.00 for one year (12 issues), which must be paid in advance by check, draft, or international money order drawn on a U.S. bank in U.S. dollars and payable to the Asian Development Bank. Any questions regarding subscriptions should be addressed to the Information Office.

Contact:
Subscription Information Office
Asian Development Bank
P.O. Box 789
1099 Manila, Philippines
Tel: 011 (63-2) 711-3851
Fax: 011 (63-2) 741-7961

Development Business is a biweekly publication of the United Nations that provides procurement information on development projects financed by the World Bank, regional development banks and other international organizations. The publication contains information about new project proposals, approvals and contract awards. Included with a subscription to *Development Business* is a subscription to the World Bank, Asian Development Bank, Inter-American Development Bank, and African Development Bank Monthly Operational Summaries. Beginning mid-1995, subscriptions will also include the International Business Opportunities Service (IBOS), a biweekly report on contracting opportunities. Cost: $350.00 per year.

Contact:
United Nations Publications
Development Business
P.O. Box 5850 GCPO
New York, NY 10163
Tel: (212) 963-1515
Fax: (212) 963-1381

IDB Projects is a listing of project proposals, the status of projects underway, procurement notices, and business opportunities offered by the Inter-American Development Bank. The publication includes contact information for the IDB as well as an overview of IDB's operations. The subscription cost for 10 issues is $150.00 per year.

Contact:
Office of External Relations
Intern-American Development Bank
1300 New York Avenue, NW
Washington, DC 20577
Tel: (202) 623-1397
Fax: (202) 623-1403

The *United Nations Inter-Agency Procurement Services Office (IAPSO)* collects and distributes procurement data for UNPD-sponsored or affiliated projects. Advance information furnished to IAPSO from UNDP's network of 113 resident representatives is transmitted regularly for publication and circulated by IAPSO to national trade missions. The office is a critical point of contact for equipment and service suppliers interested in becoming involved with the United Nations procurement system. IAPSO can act as a procurement agent on specific requests from the international aid community. To share information on suppliers efficiently, IAPSO has a computerized data bank of potential suppliers, which is accessed by appropriate U.N. agencies.

Contact:
United Nations Development Programme
Inter-Agency Procurement Services Office
Norre Voldgade 94
DK - 1358 Copenhagen K
Denmark
Tel: 011 (45) 33 15 40 88
Fax: 011 (45) 33 15 32 51

The monthly newsletter *Procurement Opportunities*, published by the European Bank for Reconstruction and Development (EBRD), provides information on procurement opportunities at all stages of a project's development. Procurement, co-financing notices and contract award information are included in the publication. A subscription to the newsletter can be obtained from the EBRD's headquarters in London for an annual fee of £85.00. EBRD also offers a facsimile service detailing procurement opportunities.

Contact:
Procurement Opportunities
Subscriptions Department
European Bank for Reconstruction and Development
82-84 Peckham Rye
London SE15 4HB U.K.
Tel: 011 (44) 171-639-0333
Fax: 011 (44) 171-358-9568

The **Overseas Economic Cooperation Fund (OECF)** is the main financial institution for Japan's Official Development Assistance (ODA) program. OECF provides loans to foreign governments and corporations for development-related projects. U.S. environmental firms can become involved with OECF projects through subcontracting opportunities from financed projects. Contractors should contact the OECF office in Washington, DC to be placed on a *Press Release* list that will announce signed agreements and give contact information for the main contractors receiving financing.

Please note: Countries applying for OECF assistance will submit a short list of subcontractors to OECF with project development plans. OECF will then access the World Bank DACON Database to check the subcontractor's qualifications and experience. As a general rule, if the subcontractor is not listed on DACON, OECF will not contact the subcontractor for consulting or contracting services.

The releases that are sent out through the Washington, DC office are received several days late, as the main OECF office in Tokyo announces all project signings. If contractors have representatives in Tokyo, they should contact the Tokyo office to receive the press releases the same day they are issued.

Contact:
Washington, DC Representative
Overseas Economic Cooperation Fund
2100 Pennsylvania Avenue, NW
Suite 535
Washington, DC 20037
Tel: (202) 463-7492
Fax: (202) 463-7496

Tokyo Headquarters
Overseas Economic Cooperation Fund
Takebashi Godo Building
1-4-1, Otemachi
Chiyoda-ku, Tokyo 100
Japan
Tel: 011 (81-3) 3215-1311
Fax: 011 (81-3) 3215-2897 or 3215-2896

U.S. Department of Agriculture Foreign Buyer Lists are maintained on a database of more than 17,000 foreign firms classified by their demand for certain kinds of agricultural products. Business executives can use Foreign Buyer Lists to match their products to potential customers worldwide. The lists include company name, contact name, address, telephone, telex and facsimile numbers. The lists are updated annually and can be ordered by commodity for the entire world or by country for all commodities. Cost: $15.00 for each list which can be done according to product or country.

Contact:
AgExport Connections
FAS/USDA
Room 4939-S
14th Street and Independence Avenue, SW
Washington, DC 20250-1000
Tel: (202) 720-7103
Fax: (202) 690-4374

The *1992 Industry & Product Classification Manual*, prepared by the Department of Commerce and Bureau of the Census, divides the Standard Industrial Classification (SIC) four-digit codes into greater detail. The industries covered are transportation; communications; electric, gas and sanitary services; wholesale trade; retail trade; and services divisions.

The manual describes industrial coverage of economic and agriculture censuses within the context of each SIC division, explains the Census Bureau's interpretation in applying the establishment concept, and includes an alphabetical index to industries for various activities and products in each SIC division. Cost: $25.00 in the United States, Canada and Mexico; $50.00 foreign.

Contact:
National Technical Information Service
5285 Port Royal Road
Springfield, VA 22161
Tel: (703) 487-4650
Fax: (703) 321-8547
E-Mail: ORDERS@NTIS.FEDWORLD.GOV

The *AgExport Action Kit* of the U.S. Department of Agriculture provides U.S. exporters with information on potential foreign buyers of food and agricultural products. The AgExport Action Kit is available from the Foreign Agricultural Service free of charge.

Contact:
AgExport Connections
USDA
14th Street and Independence Avenue, SW
Washington, DC 20250
Tel: (202) 720-7103
Fax: (202) 690-4374

The *Export Yellow Pages/Technology Pages/Green Pages* are annual export directories of exporters and export-service providers that are produced and distributed in cooperation with the U.S. Department of Commerce. *The Green Pages,* an export directory of environmental goods and services, is bound into The Export Yellow Pages and reprinted separately as a stand-alone directory. In 1995, 20,000 stand-alone copies of *The Green Pages* and 25,000 copies of the *Technology Pages* were distributed throughout the world. In addition to overseas distribution, *The Green Pages, The Technology Pages*, and *The Export Yellow Pages* are featured publications for *World Trade Week* and are distributed at trade shows in the U.S. and abroad.

A business card-sized advertisement in The Export Yellow Pages has helped North American Beauty Services of Glen Burnie, Maryland, to identify an additional 15 international distributors for the company's beauty and hair care products and led to substantial growth in export business.

Although North American Beauty Services advertises in a number of international trade magazines, the company president, Mr. Harry Schwartz, believes that The Export Yellow Pages is one of the most cost-effective methods of reaching international distributors. "The response to our ad in The Export Yellow Pages has been overwhelmingly positive. We are so excited about the opportunities continued advertising can bring, that we have decided to upgrade to a half-page advertisement this year."

The *NAFTA Export Pages* will connect buyers and sellers throughout the United States, Canada, and Mexico. The publication is slated to debut in September 1995, with a distribution of 175,000 copies and a CD-ROM version which will include all company listings and advertisements.

The inaugural edition of the *NAFTA Export Pages* will feature more than 50,000 suppliers from all three NAFTA countries and will be produced in English, Spanish, and French. U.S. companies will be listed alongside their Mexican and Canadian counterparts. All companies listed in the book will receive a copy of the publication free-of-charge. Buyer groups will also be targeted for distribution through the NAFTA markets and worldwide, including industry purchasing managers, government procurement officials, distributors, agents and other intermediaries.

Contact:
For advertising information: Tel: (800) 288-2582
To obtain a copy of the directory and/or to be listed in future editions:
Local Department of Commerce District Office (See Appendix B)

Commercial News U.S.A. (CNUSA), a Department of Commerce (DOC) publication, provides worldwide publicity for U.S. products available for immediate export. Published 10 times yearly and distributed outside the U.S., this service enables foreign firms to identify and contact U.S. exporters of specific products, giving the U.S. company a direct indication of market interest and generating sales leads, agent contacts and other benefits. Specific regions may be targeted in advertising.

Each edition of CNUSA contains short descriptions of 150 to 200 new products, together with the names and addresses of the exporters and product photographs. It is distributed to 137,000 agents, distributors, government officials and end-users in 155 countries, as well as 1.3 million electronic bulletin-board users. *CNUSA* is sent to Chambers of

Commerce abroad and DOC district offices. Product data in this publication ultimately reaches 500,000 business and government leaders worldwide. U.S. services that are eligible must have been in business in the U.S. for a minimum of three years.

Contact:
Nearest DOC District Office (See Appendix B) or

Commercial News U.S.A.
U.S. Department of Commerce
Room 1310
14th Street and Constitution Avenue, NW
Washington, DC 20230
Tel: (202) 482-4918
Fax: (202) 482-5362

The **Energy Sector Management Assistance Project (ESMAP),** sponsored by the United Nations Development Programme (UNDP) and the World Bank, assists developing countries in managing their energy sectors to promote efficient, equitable and environmentally sound development. ESMAP publishes a quarterly newsletter, *The ESMAP Connection,* which is available free of charge. The newsletter highlights recent ESMAP publications, technical notes and briefs of projects being sponsored through the program.

Contact:
Energy Sector Management Assistance Project
Power Development/Efficiency & Household Fuels Division
The World Bank
1818 H Street, NW
Washington, DC 20433
Tel: (202) 473-3412
Fax: (202) 477-0545

Electronic Sources of Information

The **USAID Consultant Registry Information System (ACRIS)** is a computerized database that assists small, medium and disadvantaged U.S. businesses and individual consultants competing for USAID technical service contracts. Maintained by the Office of Small and Disadvantaged Business Utilization (OSDBU), ACRIS brings U.S. technical service businesses and individual consultants to the attention of USAID personnel.

ACRIS lists U.S. firms, individuals and their technical service capabilities and matches services needed in USAID-financed projects with private-sector capabilities. ACRIS contains data on areas of expertise, corporate experience, and other items of interest to USAID.

A firm may register in ACRIS by submitting its corporate capability statement to OSDBU for review. Once OSDBU has determined that a firm has the expertise and capabilities needed by USAID, the firm will be provided with forms.

While registration in ACRIS is not required to be considered for USAID contracting opportunities, this database is used by OSDBU to help identify potential contractors.

Contact:
Office of Small & Disadvantaged Business Utilization
U.S. Agency for International Development
Room 1200A, SA-14
Washington, DC 20523
Tel: (703) 875-1551
Fax: (703) 875-1862

The World Bank's **DACON (Data on Consultants) Information Center** maintains a computerized data bank that lists information on qualifications of consulting firms which have participated in multilateral bank-financed projects. Cost: Free. To register, firms should obtain an information packet and set of diskettes from the World Bank.

Contact:
DACON Information Center
The World Bank
1818 H Street, NW
Washington, DC 20433
Tel: (202) 458-4095
Fax: (202) 334-0003

Direct From the U.S.A. is a video catalog show that the U.S. and Foreign Commercial Service (US&FCS) office in Manila has designed as a cost-effective way for U.S. firms to test the Philippines market for specific products and services. Designed for small- and medium-sized American companies that are not located in the Philippines, this program provides exposure to potential Philippine agents, distributors and business partners at a two-week exhibition in the U.S. Commercial Center in Manila, and at similar displays in the country's fastest-growing provincial capitals. American firms are encouraged to contact the office below as soon as possible, since space is limited. The participation fee covers all pre-show publicity, event staging costs and customized lists of interested Philippine companies. Cost: $150.

Contact:
Commercial Librarian
U.S. Embassy Manila
Commercial Section
APO AP 96440
Tel: 011 (63 2) 818-6476
Fax: 011 (63 2) 818-2684

The **Economic Bulletin Board (EBB)** is a personal computer-based electronic bulletin board within the Department of Commerce that provides trade leads and current statistical releases from federal agencies. Users can also access files by downloading them to a personal computer. As an on-line source, EBB provides information from the Bureau of Economic Analysis, the Bureau of the Census, the Bureau of Labor Statistics, the Federal Reserve Board, and the Department of the Treasury, among others. Government reports and statistics are updated daily on EBB, which can be accessed 24 hours a day via computer modem.

General topics addressed in the EBB include energy data, daily trade opportunities, major economic indicators, U.S. Trade Representative Press Releases, regional economic statistics and foreign trade data. Subscription rates vary for computer type. Connect time is billed quarterly, calculated by hourly rates. To become familiar with EBB, a free, limited-access service is available by calling EBB and using "GUEST" as the User ID password. Guest users may not download data files.

Contact:
Economic Bulletin Board
U.S. Department of Commerce
Office of Statistics/USA
HCHB Room 4885
Washington, DC 20230
Tel: (202) 482-1986
Fax: (202) 482-2164
E-Mail: STAT-USA@DOC.GOV

The **Environmental Technology Network for Asia (ETNA)** is a computer database that disseminates free-of-charge, environmental opportunity notices received from the Asia-based Technology Cooperation offices. Managed by the U.S. Agency for International Development (USAID) Center for Trade and Investment Services, ETNA matches opportunity notices to appropriate U.S. environmental companies registered with its database. Companies whose services match a particular project's requirements in Asia are alerted by fax to facilitate a quick response. To register, U.S. firms complete the ETNA registration mailer available from United States-Asia Environmental Partnership (US-AEP). Opportunity notices are also sent to a network of 48 state development agencies, 14 trade associations and other organizations.

Contact:
Environmental Technology Network for Asia
U.S. Agency for International Development
Center for Trade and Investment Services
515 22nd Street, NW
Room 100, SA-2
Washington, DC 20523-0229
Tel: (202) 663-2674 or (800) 872-4348
Fax: (202) 663-2760

U.S.-Asia Environmental Partnership (US-AEP) Trade Leads provides detailed information on environmentally related business opportunities in Asia that have been gathered by its Technology Representatives. Offices of Technology Cooperation, managed by the U.S. and Foreign Commercial Service (US&FCS) of the Department of Commerce, are located in Hong Kong, India, Indonesia, Malaysia, the Philippines, Singapore, Taiwan and Thailand. Information on these leads is available through the Environmental Technology Network for Asia (ETNA), which is detailed on the previous page.

Contact:
Environmental Technology Network for Asia
Center for Trade and Investment Services
515 22nd Street, NW
Room 100, SA-2
Washington, DC 20523-0229
Tel: (202) 663-2674 or (800) 872-4348
Fax: (202) 663-2760

The **Export Contact List Service** is a database retrieval service that provides exporters with names of prospective international customers by country or industry. Administered by the Department of Commerce, the U.S. exporter specifies the SIC code, geographic area and the type of contacts desired (distributor, retailer, etc.). The service provides the names and contact information, along with company background and product or service specialty. Names are collected and maintained by Commerce Department district offices and commercial officers at foreign posts. Contact list prices vary according to the format selected. The minimum fee is $10.00. The cost varies based on the number of countries, the product lines chosen and the number of names received ($0.25 per name on label).

Contact:
Nearest Commerce Department District Office (See Appendix B)

The **Global Export Manager (GEM)**, produced by the National Association of State Development Agencies (NASDA), is an automated international business opportunity management package designed to notify local companies of international business opportunities. GEM allows business executives to match companies with foreign buyers and procurement opportunities through the database, saving both time and money. US-AEP's ETNA (see above) is run on the GEM system.

GEM has three main components: an ExPro Trade Opportunity Matching System (the main component), the NASDA State Export Program Database (SEPD), and the Market Research Information Retrieval System. GEM allows business executives to produce standard and customized reports tracking project progress and to access updated information on-line from SEPD. Interested businesses can schedule demonstrations of GEM and NASDA services either on-site or at the NASDA office in Washington, DC.

The U.S. Trade and Development Agency (TDA) is using GEM to disseminate information on potential international procurement opportunities to states. The states then match the opportunities with client companies. TDA is also developing a series of training programs in the field for both export service providers and private businesses on how to use development business opportunities to make an export sale.

A new program, the Foreign Office Trade Opportunity Generator (FOTOGen), is a satellite trade-opportunity entry system that can be loaded onto either a laptop or a desktop computer. FOTOGen is ideal for use by overseas offices, or for U.S.-based employees traveling overseas, to gather trade opportunities to match with the ExPro system of GEM at the home office.

Contact:
National Association of State Development Agencies
750 First Street, NE
Suite 710
Washington, DC 20002
Tel: (202) 898-1302
Fax: (202) 898-1312

The **National Trade Data Bank (NTDB)** from the National Technical Information Service maintains trade and export promotion data collected from 14 federal agencies, including the Central Intelligence Agency, Environmental Protection Agency, U.S. Department of Commerce, Export-Import Bank of the United States, Overseas Private Investment Corporation, Small Business Administration, and Office of the U.S. Trade Representative. The information on NTDB assists companies to identify trends, write proposals and create business plans. Provided on two 4.72-inch plastic discs using Compact Disk-Read Only Memory (CD-ROM), the NTDB includes over 90,000 documents with up-to-date information on international economies, basic export information and foreign trade.

The **Foreign Traders Index**, also included in NTDB, identifies foreign firms seeking to import U.S. products. Cost: $360.00 for annual subscription of 12 issues; $35.00 for a single issue from the most recent month. The NTDB CD-ROMs are also available at federal depository libraries across the country. Selected reports and publications that are available include: World Factbook, Handbook of Economic Statistics, U.S. International Transactions, U.S. Direct Investment Abroad, U.S. Industrial Outlook, and *International Market Research*.

Contact:
National Technical Information Service
5285 Port Royal Road
Springfield, VA 22161
Tel: (703) 487-4650 (to order single issues)
Fax: (703) 321-8547
E-Mail: ORDERS@NTIS.FEDWORLD.GOV

Trade Opportunities Program (TOPS) is a Commerce Department service that provides sales leads from international firms seeking to buy or represent U.S. products and services. U.S. commercial officers worldwide gather leads through local channels and forward them to Washington, DC, where they are distributed, in print and electronically, through the Department of Commerce's Economic Bulletin Board (EBB).

These leads include details of specifications, quantities, end-use, delivery and bid deadlines. Cost: There is a nominal annual fee and connect-time charge. Most district offices charge $0.25 per name, although not all offices provide this service. Contact a local office to confirm what services are provided, or access TOPS through the EBB.

Contact:
Nearest Commerce Department District Office (See Appendix B)

For general information on TOPS:
Trade Information Center
Tel: (202) 482-0003
Tel: (800) U.S.A.-TRAD(E) (872-8723)

To access the Economic Bulletin Board:
Tel: (202) 482-1986
Fax: (202) 482-2164

The **U.S. Small Business Administration** offers exporters access to application information, SBA services, and other export assistance information via **SBA Online** service. This service is available 23 hours a day, all year around.

For a fee, the Online service allows greater access to SBA's programs and data resources, including research data banks, news groups, office mail, and other program information.

Contact:
For access to the basic SBA Online, (800) 697-4636.
For access to fee-based Online service, (900) 463-4636, or (202) 401-9600.

The **Research Strategic Venture Partners (RSVP)** is available via SBA's Online service. This computerized database provides profiles of foreign companies seeking small- and medium-sized U.S. companies for joint-venture opportunities. Profiles can be sorted by country, product of interest, or both. The RSVP also permits profiled companies to follow up with companies that have accessed their profiles.

Contact:
SBA Office of International Trade
409 Third Street, SW, Suite 6100
Washington, DC 20416
Tel: (202) 205-6720
Fax: (202) 205-7272

Trade Leads enables U.S. business executives to reach out directly to foreign buyers. The USDA's 80 overseas offices send inquiries from foreign buyers interested in purchasing U.S. food products to USDA's headquarters in Washington, DC each day. More than 2,500 trade leads are passed on to interested U.S. suppliers each year. Specifically, trade leads cover products such as grocery products; dairy, livestock, poultry and seafood products; horticultural and tropical products; grains, feeds and pulses; cotton, tobacco and seeds; forest products; and oilseeds and oilseed products. Each trade lead gives details on how to locate the foreign buyer; specific products in demand, the desired quantity, packaging requirements, timing of deliveries, and type of quotation required; and the foreign buyer's bank reference.

Contact:
AgExport Connections
FAS/USDA
Room 4939-S
14th Street & Independence Avenue, SW
Washington, DC 20250-1000
Tel: (202) 720-7103
Fax: (202) 690-4374

U.S. Supplier Lists, maintained by the U.S. Department of Agriculture's Foreign Agricultural Service, are designed to meet the needs of prospective exporters and foreign purchasers of U.S. products seeking sources of U.S. food and agricultural products. The lists are categorized by Harmonized System (HS) codes and include name, address, telephone/telex/fax, Standard Industrial Classification (SIC) codes, sales information, and year the firm was established. Cost: $15.00 per list by HS code.

Contact:
AgExport Connections
FAS/USDA
Room 4939-S
14th Street and Independence Avenue, SW
Washington, DC 20250-1000
Tel: (202) 720-7103
Fax: (202) 690-4374

The **Computerized Information Delivery Service (CIDS)** provides instant access to USDA reports, news releases, and other agricultural information to any location immediately after release. The CIDS provides information on trade leads, market reports, economic outlooks, and crop and livestock statistics for a fee.

Contact:
U.S. Department of Agriculture
Computerized Information Delivery Service (CIDS)
Tel: (202) 720-2791
Fax: (202) 690-1131

Sent by satellite to over one hundred countries, *"Doing Business,"* a privately managed, monthly half-hour televised business program, highlights innovation and excellence in U.S. businesses. Segments on new products, services, and processes of interest to overseas buyers as well as promising research are featured in the program.

Contact:
Worldnet Television
601 D Street, NW
Washington, DC 20547
Tel: (202) 501-8450
Fax: (202) 501-6076

A component of the National Agricultural Library, **Agriculture Trade and Marketing Information Center** assists in locating relevant material from the large collection of trade and marketing information. The center also provides copies of research and data from its AGRICOLA database. User assistance for accessing the National Agricultural Library's online systems is also provided. These systems include: ISIS (Integrated System for Information Services), AGRICOLA (Agricultural OnLine Access database), ALF (Agricultural Libraries Forum), and the library's electronic bulletin board.

Contact:
Agriculture Trade & Marketing Information Center
National Agriculture Library
Tel: (301) 504-5509
Fax: (301) 504-5472

People Resources/Services

Both **Country and Industry Desk Officers** of the U.S. Department of Commerce can provide expert market research assistance to U.S. companies. The International Trade Administration is divided into two divisions: Trade Development and International Economic Policy. Professional staff at Trade Development focus on an industry-specific approach to the international market, while Country Desk Officers focus on an individual country or region. Industry and Country Desk Officers can offer key insights into the international marketplace. To obtain contact information for individual country desk officers, contact the Trade Information Center at the Department of Commerce (or see Appendix A); to contact Industry Desk Officers, contact the Trade Information Center.

Contact:
Trade Information Center
Tel: (800) USA-TRAD(E) (872-8723)
Fax: (202) 482-4473

Mailing address for all desk officers:
Country/Industry Desk Officer
U.S. Department of Commerce
14th Street and Constitution Avenue, NW
Washington, DC 20230
See Appendix A for country-specific telephone numbers.

The **Infrastructure Finance Advisory Service (IFAS)** offers information about infrastructure projects and markets, advice on identifying sources of finance from the U.S. Government and the private sector, and assistance in mobilizing technical and financial resources to strengthen bids. IFAS is a cooperative effort of the U.S. Agency for International Development (USAID), the U.S. Export-Import Bank (Ex-Im Bank), the Overseas Private Investment Corporation (OPIC), the Small Business Administration (SBA), and the U.S. Trade and Development Agency (TDA).

IFAS serves U.S. equipment manufacturers, contractors and project developers with bidding on public tenders, developing Build-Own-Operate or Build-Operate-Transfer projects, and establishing joint ventures. Companies can receive current information on opportunities, including fact sheets, country-specific data and regional trade activities for building business relationships. All IFAS services are currently free-of-charge and clients are not required to have prior international experience.

Contact:
Infrastructure Finance Advisory Service
K & M Engineering & Consulting Corp.
2001 L Street, NW, Suite 906
Washington, DC 20036
Tel: (202) 466-6485
Fax: (202) 466-4772

United States-Asia Environmental Partnership
1133 20th Street, NW, Suite 300
Washington, DC 20036
Tel: (202) 835-0333
Fax: (202) 835-0366

Office of Multilateral Development Bank Operations (MDBO) is the
liaison office within the Department of Commerce that facilitates access to
representatives from multilateral banks, including the World Bank. MDBO offers
information and assistance to U.S. companies that are interested in supplying goods and
services to overseas construction, engineering, manufacturing and investment projects.
This office can counsel U.S. companies on the project procurement process.

In addition, the MDBO maintains a library of information on current and planned MDB
projects. The MDBO information center is open Monday through Friday, from 9:00
a.m.- 5:00 p.m.

Contact:
Office of Multilateral Development Bank Operations
U.S. Department of Commerce
14th Street and Constitution Avenue, NW
Washington, DC 20230
Tel: (202) 482-4332
Fax: (202) 273-0927

Multilateral Development Bank (MDB) Representatives can assist U.S.
exporters with business leads and provide counseling on MDB projects. The U.S.
Department of Commerce has assigned members of the U.S. & Foreign Commercial
Service (US&FCS) to each of the major MDBs. The major MDBs (African
Development Bank (AfDB), Asian Development Bank (ADB), the European Bank for
Reconstruction and Development (EBRD), and Inter-American Development Bank
(IDB)) maintain in-country representative offices. These offices can supplement
published MDB project information and may be able to identify trade opportunities
stemming from potential MDB projects.

Contact:
Office of Multilateral Development Bank Operations
U.S. Department of Commerce
14th Street and Constitution Avenue, NW
Washington, DC 20230
Tel: (202) 482-4332
Fax: (202) 273-0927
or
See Appendix F for a complete listing of MDB in-country offices.

The **Office of Small and Disadvantaged Business Utilization (OSDBU)** at USAID assists U.S. firms interested in contracting with USAID-sponsored projects. OSDBU administers the procurement set-aside programs and keeps businesses informed of procurement opportunities. The office is an initial point of contact at USAID for U.S. businesses, particularly small and minority- and women-owned firms. The primary concern of the office is to help these firms participate fully in USAID-financed contracts and procurements. OSDBU offers in-depth information and counseling on USAID programs, contracting and sub-contracting opportunities, and marketing and operational strategies for conducting business with USAID.

Contact:
Office of Small and Disadvantaged Business Utilization
U.S. Agency for International Development
Room 1200A, SA-14
Washington, DC 20523
Tel: (703) 875-1551
Fax: (703) 875-1862

Foreign Embassies in the United States can provide key market research information. This directory of foreign embassies lists key attaches and consular officers who could provide U.S. firms with contact information for government officials and local companies, as well as insights into local business regulations and climate.

Contact:
See Appendix E.

The World Bank's **Public Information Center** makes many World Bank documents available through the Internet, including Project Information Documents, Environmental Data Sheets, the publications catalogue and an overview of the World Bank's public information system. Internet users accessing the Bank's information system through NCSA Mosaic or other World Wide Web navigation tools should use the following universal resource locator: **http://www.worldbank.org**. The server address to access the system via "gopher" is: **gopher.worldbank.org**. In the event of a problem accessing the World Bank's system through the Internet, send electronic mail to: **pic@worldbank.org.** Visitors to Washington can also visit the center and obtain documents in person. Most publications are provided free-of-charge; however, Staff Appraisal Reports and some other technical data are priced at $15.00.

Contact:
Public Information Center
The World Bank
1776 G Street, NW
Washington, DC 20433
Tel: (202) 458-5454
Fax: (202) 522-1500
E-Mail: PIC@WORLDBANK.ORG

The **Center for Trade and Investment Services (CTIS)** serves as a single source of information on USAID programs and procurement opportunities. CTIS manages the US-AEP Environmental Technology Network for Asia (ETNA), which receives notice of environmental opportunities in Asia/Pacific and electronically matches them to U.S. environmental companies that are registered on the database.

CTIS facilitates business opportunities for U.S. firms in USAID-supported countries, but it is *not* a U.S. export promotion office. Rather, it provides value-added counseling (timely and targeted information) and research services by identifying and analyzing critical market intelligence and business opportunities for its clients. Through a nationwide network of federal and private-sector associations, CTIS provides information domestically and throughout the developing world.

Contact:
Center for Trade and Investment Services
U.S. Agency for International Development
320 21st Street, NW
Washington, DC 20523
Tel: (202) 663-2660
Fax: (202) 663-2670

The **International Partnerships for the Commercialization of Technology (INPACT),** sponsored by the U.S. Department of Commerce, provides information and counseling for countries that show interest in linking their smaller firms with U.S. counterparts. The INPACT program includes development and execution of bilateral agreements, training and project screening, and aid in identifying networks of potential partners and resources in the United States.

INPACT companies are traditionally smaller, non-defense firms which are making use of novel applications of existing technology. Joint ventures formed through INPACT must adhere to existing laws and regulations in the participating countries, including U.S. trade regulations and export controls.

Contact:
International Operations
Technical Policy Analysis and Studies
U.S. Department of Commerce
Room 4816
14th Street and Constitution Avenue, NW
Washington, DC 20230
Tel: (202) 482-2123
Fax: (202) 482-4498

The **Foreign Agricultural Service (FAS)** maintains 20 overseas Agricultural Trade Offices (ATOs) to help exporters of U.S. farm and forest products in overseas markets. These offices supply U.S. exporters with up-to-the-minute information on the market, potential customers, and promotional opportunities. Each ATO has library facilities, conference rooms, and office space. Some ATOs have kitchen and food demonstration areas that can be used to hold food tastings for potential clients. Offices are located in the following cities

China:	Beijing, Guanzhou
Germany:	Hamburg
Japan:	Osaka, Tokyo
Korea:	Seoul
Mexico:	Mexico City
Saudi Arabia:	Riyadh, Jeddah
Taiwan:	Taipei
United Kingdom:	London
Hong Kong	
Singapore	
United Arab Emirates.	

Contact:
Coordinator
Foreign Ag-Affairs Office
USDA
14th Street and Independence Avenue, SW
Washington, DC 20250
Tel: (202) 720-6138
Fax: (202) 720-8316
or see Appendix J

For agricultural exporters seeking foreign market information, **U.S. Trade Assistance and Promotion Office (TAPO)** is the initial contact point within the Foreign Agricultural Service (FAS). TAPO maintains a wide range of information, including market overviews and other research generated by the FAS Agricultural Trade Offices (ATOs).

Contact:
TAPO
U.S. Department of Agriculture
14th Street & Independence Avenue, SW
Washington, DC 20250
Tel: (202) 720-7420
Fax: (202) 690-4374

Trade Missions can help to promote the sale of U.S. goods and services throughout the world. These missions also help U.S. exporters to establish relationships with sales agents and other foreign representatives.

Seminar missions are multi-country business trips designed to facilitate the sale of sophisticated products and technology. During a mission, a team of U.S. industry representatives presents brochures and product literature to potential foreign buyers, agents and distributors.

Specialized trade missions are planned, organized and led by the U.S. Department of Commerce (DOC). Generally, missions are limited to representatives of eight U.S. firms. Participants pay their own travel expenses and reimburse the Department of Commerce for its mission support costs.

A number of government-approved trade missions are organized by trade associations, chambers of commerce, state development agencies and similar groups with the advice and support of the U.S. Department of Commerce. DOC assists in planning these missions through its Export Development Offices, the Foreign Commercial Service, and Foreign Service Posts.

Contact:
Nearest Commerce Department District Office. See Appendix B.

The Commerce Department's Agent/Distributor Service has helped Neuro Scan, a Herndon, Virginia, manufacturer of software and medical equipment for brain research, to penetrate markets in the Middle East and Taiwan. Through the assistance of the Richmond, Virginia, office of the U.S. Department of Commerce, Neuro Scan was able to identify credible foreign agents and distributors. The company now has over 22 distributors, primarily in Europe and the Far East, and maintains support offices in the Netherlands.

The **Agent/Distributor Service,** administered by the Department of Commerce, helps U.S. companies find interested and qualified foreign agents or distributors for their products or services. On request, U.S. foreign commercial specialists will seek a foreign representative for a U.S. company's product line. A report will be developed and sent to the requesting company providing information on up to six qualified representatives interested in representing the U.S. company. The reports includes the name and address of the foreign firm, name and title of contact person, telephone number, cable address and telex number, and brief comments about the firm or its stated interest in the proposal. A search usually requires 30 days. Cost: $125.00 per report.

POM Incorporated started exporting nine years ago with little expectation of success. The Russellville, AR, manufacturer of parking meter systems needed to establish a foreign distribution system yet had no experience or international contacts to utilize. After consulting with the Department of Commerce's Little Rock district office, POM began utilizing the Agent/Distributor Service to develop contacts with foreign distributors and various offices of the Foreign Commercial Service. With continuing advice from the Agent/Distributor Service, POM has built a widespread network of agents and distributors covering 50 countries. All are closely linked via communication networks, regular office newsletters and other means of support to ensure that they maintain close links with POM's home office.

Contact:
Nearest Commerce Department District Office. See Appendix B.

The **Gold Key Service (GKS)** is a customized contact information service developed for U.S. companies visiting foreign markets. This business facilitation service is provided by the U.S. Government through a private-sector contractor and can arrange in-country appointments with potential partners. Local US&FCS offices can provide market information, export counseling, export assistance and programs to U.S. exporters. Many of the offices can provide information on customized services and facilitate contacts through US&FCS international offices. A comprehensive briefing by US&FCS personnel is included in the GKS basic package.

The service requires a minimum of three weeks' lead time to ensure meaningful appointments and to prepare a briefing for the user. The request for this service should be accompanied by 10-15 packages of the company's product literature (translated into necessary languages) including a price list. In addition, providing the following information can assist GKS:

- Your company's goals and objectives
- A brief outline of your competitors in the U.S. and abroad
- The exact dates for which your firm requires appointments
- The names and titles of all individuals on the trip and any foreign language abilities
- A copy of the traveler's itinerary, including telephone and fax numbers where your party can be reached.

The estimated price of the basic service is $250.00 per day with a minimum of four appointments and a maximum of six appointments scheduled per day. GKS can also provide interpreter/translation services as well as clerical assistance and meeting location services.

Using assistance and services provided by the Department of Commerce, Pollution Controls Exports (PCE) of Somers, Connecticut, is now selling its products to over 20 countries throughout the world. By contacting their local Department of Commerce and Small Business Administration District Office, PCE was able to tap into government information sources at an early date.

The Company has also used Commerce Department services such as the Agent/Distributor Service and the Gold Key Service, a custom-tailored service for U.S. firms planning to visit a foreign market.

Contact:
See your local Commerce Department District Office. See Appendix B.

The **U.S. & Foreign Commercial Service (US&FCS)** of the Department of Commerce operates 68 District Offices that assist U.S. exporters. Local US&FCS offices can provide market information, export counseling, export assistance and programs to U.S. exporters. Many of the offices can provide information on customized services and facilitate contacts through US&FCS international offices. US&FCS market-research services are listed below. A recent interagency effort established a number of **U.S. Export Assistance Centers (USEACs)** throughout the United States which can help U.S. firms take advantage of other government services as well. The four existing USEACs are included in the listing of US&FCS district offices.

The **Customized Sales Services (CSS)** is a customized service which provides firms with key marketing and foreign representation information for specific products. U.S. & Foreign Commercial Service staff conduct interviews to obtain marketing background on the product, such as sales potential in the market, comparable products, distribution channels, going price, competitive factors and qualified purchasers. CSS is currently available through most countries in the Asia/Pacific. The cost varies from $500.00 to $2,000.00 depending on the country.

Contact:

To Identify Local Department of Commerce District Office call:

Trade Information Center
Tel: (800) USA-TRAD(E) (872-8723)
Fax: (202) 482-4473
or
See Appendix B for Export Assistance Centers

Small Business Administration District Offices offer U.S. exporters export counseling and assistance, market research and referrals to other government programs that assist in international market studies.

Contact:
Local Small Business Administration District Office (See Appendix C)

Market Development Cooperators, which are agricultural nonprofit associations, work with the Foreign Agricultural Service to promote and expand international markets for U.S. products. More than 50 foreign agricultural associations, 7,000 processors and handlers, and 1,500 farm cooperatives representing several million farmers participate in this program. U.S. companies can receive assistance in expanding international markets for their food products by contacting the Market Development Cooperator for their respective industry.

Contact:
Foreign Agricultural Service
USDA
Room 5089-S
Washington, DC 20250
Tel: (202) 720-4761
Fax: (202) 690-3606

State International Trade Offices offer trade information, market research, business leads, export seminars and a variety of other services to assist U.S. firms. Most state international trade offices have representatives abroad who are liaisons to the region for the state and its businesses. State offices can help identify business opportunities and contact potential partners for interested companies. For more information on the services available from the state offices, contact the office directly.

Contact:
Local State International Trade Offices (See Appendix G)

US-AEP Environmental Technology Representatives are commercial officers who serve in nine Asian cities. These representatives, sponsored in conjunction with the United States-Asia Environmental Partnership (US-AEP) and the U.S. & Foreign Commercial Service, identify preliminary market opportunities and assist U.S. firms in making key contacts. They also provide local businesses with information about U.S. environmental technologies, among others.

The technology representatives assist U.S. businesses by actively promoting appropriate energy products and services. They can also facilitate business relationships between companies, organize local events and seminars locally to showcase U.S. technology and products, and can assist in locating potential partners. The representatives will research trade and investment laws, policies and regulations and identify trade leads when necessary for U.S. businesses.

Representatives are located in: Bangkok, Thailand; Bombay, India; Hong Kong; Jakarta, Indonesia; Kuala Lumpur, Malaysia; Manila, Philippines; Seoul, Korea; Singapore; and Taipei, Taiwan. In addition, US-AEP has a regional representative at the Asian Development Bank in Manila who focuses on energy and environmental infrastructure projects.

Contact:
Headquarters
United States-Asia Environmental Partnership (US-AEP)
1133 20th Street, NW, Suite 300
Washington, DC 20036
Tel: (202) 835-0033
Fax: (202) 835-0366

Additional Addresses:

Technology Representatives in Asia/Pacific

Asian Development Bank
US-AEP Commercial FCS/ADB
Thomas Jefferson Cultural Center,
3rd Floor
395 Sen. Gil J. Puyat Avenue
Makati, Metro Manila, Philippines
Tel: 011 (63-2) 813-3248
Fax: 011 (63-2) 816-7684

US-AEP Hong Kong
HKPC Building - Suite 4E, 4/F
78 Tat Chee Avenue
Kowloon, Hong Kong
Tel: 011 (852) 776-0015
Fax: 011 (852) 779-2963

US-AEP India
American Center
4 New Marine Lines
Bombay, 400 020-09 India
Tel: 011 (91-22) 262-4590
Fax: 011 (91-22) 262-4595

US-AEP Indonesia
9th Floor ATD Plaza
Jalan M.H. Thamrin Kav. 3
Jakarta 10340, Indonesia
Tel: 011 (62-21) 601-8483
Fax: 011 (62-21) 601-8487

US-AEP Korea
Leema Building, Suite 424
146-1, Susong-dong, Chongro-ku
Seoul, Korea 110-140
Tel: 011 (822) 734-6558
Fax: 011 (822) 734-6559

US-AEP Malaysia
Suite 2002, Menara Tan and Tan
207 Jalan Tan Razak
Kuala Lumpur, Malaysia 50400
Tel: 011 (60-3) 264-0018
Fax: 011 (60-3) 264-0026

US-AEP Philippines
Thomas Jefferson Cultural Center,
2nd Floor
395 Sen. Gil J. Puyat Avenue
Makati, Metro Manila, Philippines
Tel: 011 (63-2) 852-877
Fax: 011 (63-2) 818-2676

US-AEP Singapore
One Colombo Court, #04-07A
Singapore, 0617
Tel: 011 (65) 334-3141
Fax: 011 (65) 334-1757

US-AEP Taiwan
Commercial Section,
American Trade Center
Taipei World Trade Center
International Trade Building
Room 3207, 32/F
333 Keelung Road, Section 1
Taipei, Taiwan 10548
Tel: 011 (886-2) 757-7043
Fax: 011 (886-2) 757-7086

US-AEP Thailand
Diethelm Towers, Tower A
93/1 Wireless Road, Suite 302
Bangkok 10330 Thailand
Tel: 011 (66-2) 252-5040
Fax: 011 (66-2) 255-2915

The purpose of **American Business Centers (ABCs)** in the former Soviet Union is to provide American companies with a positive working environment and services essential to doing business in the region. Plans are underway to place five ABCs within Foreign Service posts in Vladivostok, St. Petersburg, Tashkent, Almaty, and Kiev. Seven solo ABCs will be established and operated by non-federal entities through cooperative agreements with the Department of Commerce. The centers will seek to provide business development services including short-term office and exhibit space, market research and counseling, interpretation and translation services, telecommunications and computer equipment, and assistance in making NIS contacts.

Contact:
Business Information Service for the Newly Independent States
Tel: (202) 482-4655
Fax: (202) 482-2293

JETRO's Business Support Centres, located in Tokyo and four other major cities, provide assistance to foreign businesses in the initial stages of business activities in Japan. Facilities include:

- Office space, complete with fax and copy machines;
- The Help Desk, manned by five JETRO advisors that provide consulting on utilizing the Japanese market;
- A business library containing reference books, statistics, directories, reports and educational videos;
- Meeting rooms; and
- A JETRO Database terminal.

The JETRO Business Support Centre is open weekdays from 9:30 a.m. to 5:00 p.m.

Contact
JETRO Business Support Center
Akasaka Twin Tower
2-17-22 Akasaka
Minato-ku, Tokyo 107, Japan
Tel: 011 (81) 3-5562-3131

CHAPTER THREE

Regulations and Requirements

Before undertaking an international venture, American firms should be aware of foreign country agreements that must first be obtained, host-country regulations regarding certain types of business, tax incentives and requirements and general regulations affecting trade between the United States and foreign countries. This chapter reviews these subjects, under five major sub-groupings:

International Agreements and Treaties: How to locate information on investment treaties, trade barriers and foreign government approvals.

Rules, Regulations and Standards: Where to find information and programs to assist U.S. firms with trade disputes, product standards, customs and export restrictions.

Export License Assistance: Where to obtain information about applying for export licenses and submitting license applications.

Accounting/Tax Information: Tax rules governing U.S. individuals and companies abroad and U.S. Government incentives for operating abroad.

Host-Country Incentives: Investment incentives available in foreign countries for U.S. businesses investing in those countries including import duty exemptions, tax holidays and training grants.

The following is a list of key topics discussed in Chapter Three:

- Investment and Taxation Treaties
- Export Assistance Services
- Industry- and Commodity-Specific Export Information
- Taxation Assistance Services
- Tax Requirements for Exports and Foreign-Based Corporations
- Foreign Tax Incentives.

International Agreements and Treaties

Treaties in Force: A List of Treaties and Other International Agreements of the United States in Force on January 1, 1994, published annually by the U.S. Department of State, includes bilateral and multilateral agreements in effect as of January 1, 1994, and an appendix listing documents affecting international copyright regulations of the United States. Cost: $28.00 in the U.S.

Contact:
Superintendent of Documents
U.S. Government Printing Office
Washington, DC 20402
Tel: (202) 512-1800

Treaties and Other International Acts Series contains the texts of agreements entered into by the United States with other nations. Annual subscription: $220.00 in U.S.

Contact:
Superintendent of Documents
U.S. Government Printing Office
Washington, DC 20402
Tel: (202) 512-1800

The **Office of the U.S. Trade Representative (USTR)** was created by the Trade Expansion Act of 1962 to negotiate and administer all trade agreements on behalf of the United States. In addition, the USTR serves as representative for the United States in the major international trade organizations. The USTR has two major responsibilities:

- **Act as the President's chief advisor on international trade policy.** Primary responsibility within the U.S. Government for developing international trade policy and for coordinating its implementation. This includes negotiating with the United Nations, OECD and other multilateral organizations on trade and commodity issues.

- **Serve as the country's chief negotiator for international trade agreements**. The USTR is also responsible for policy guidance on issues relating to international trade, including: 1) expansion of U.S. exports; 2) matters concerning the General Agreement on Tariffs and Trade (GATT); 3) bilateral trade and commodity issues; 4) international trade issues involving energy and the environment; and 5) orchestrate investment matters that are related to trade.

Contact:
Office of the U.S. Trade Representative
International Programs
600 17th Street, NW
Washington, DC 20506
Tel: (202) 395-3606
Fax: (202) 395-3911

A *Bilateral Investment Treaty (BIT)* is a reciprocal agreement between the U.S. Government and a foreign government which outlines the treatment of investors in the two countries. These treaties are ratified by the Senate thereby creating an international obligation for the U.S. and the treaty partner and thus superseding domestic law.

The U.S. Government seeks to negotiate BITs that contain the following major elements:

- Most-favored-nation or national treatment (with limited exceptions), whichever is better, for the U.S. investor abroad.

- Guarantees of prompt, adequate and effective compensation for expropriation, as well as the right to transfer such compensation at the prevailing exchange rate on the date of expropriation.

- The right of investors to make free transfers of currency in connection with the investment at the prevailing exchange rate.

- A legal framework for the settlement of disputes between a firm and host country and between governments, based on prevailing standards of international law including the possibility of third-party arbitration.

- A treaty of at least ten years' duration.

The U.S. currently has BITs with Bangladesh, Cameroon, Grenada, Morocco, Panama, Senegal, Turkey and Zaire.

The USTR can provide copies of BITs, which are pending Senate ratification, and a list of countries that have entered into BIT negotiations with the United States.

Contact:
Office of Industry and Services
Office of the U.S. Trade Representative
600 17th Street, NW, Room 422
Washington, DC 20506
Tel: (202) 395-7271
Fax: (202) 395-3911

The **Service Industries and Finance Division** at the Commerce Department provides counseling and advice on U.S. and foreign country laws, regulations and practices affecting international trade and investment. Staff members offer information and help U.S. firms research laws on taxation; antitrust, patent and trademark rights; licensing patents; foreign agents, distributors, and joint ventures; product liability; and other issues related to exporting and international investment.

Contact:
Service Industries and Finance Division
U.S. Department of Commerce
Room 1104
14th Street & Constitution Avenue, NW
Washington, DC 20230
Tel: (202) 482-5131
Fax: (202) 482-4775

The **Office of Business and Export Affairs** is a point of contact in the State Department for U.S. companies requiring assistance with international business.

Contact:
Trade and Commercial Affairs
U.S. Department of State
Room 3831A
Washington, DC 20520
Tel: (202) 647-2532
Fax: (202) 647-1537

National Trade Estimate Report on Foreign Trade Barriers, published in October 1987, examines the most significant barriers of United States trading partners. Each deterrent is examined in depth by country, with additional information on their effects and best counter measures. The information is provided by the Executive Office of the President, Office of the United States Trade Representative, Department of Agriculture and Department of Commerce. Cost: $17.00 per copy in the U.S.; $21.25 foreign. Order no.: S/N 041-001-00326-6.

Contact:
Superintendent of Documents
U.S. Government Printing Office
Washington, DC 20402
Tel: (202) 512-1800

Within the National Oceanographic and Atmospheric Administration (NOAA), the National Marine Fisheries Service's (NMFS) **Office of Trade Analysis and Operations** addresses trade problems affecting U.S. fishery exports. The Trade Analysis and Operations office works in coordination with the United States Trade Representative, the International Trade Administration and the International Trade Commission. These activities support bilateral and multilateral trade negotiations and actions by U.S. industry under United States trade law.

Contact:
Office of Trade and Industry Services
National Marine Fisheries Services
1315 East-West Highway
Silver Spring, MD 20910
Tel: (301) 713-2272
Fax: (301) 713-2258

The **Foreign Agricultural Service (FAS)** of the U. S. Agriculture Department (USDA) identifies and works to mitigate foreign trade barriers and practices that impede exports of U.S. farm products. Agricultural representatives play a major role in trying to remove tariff or non-tariff barriers affecting market access. FAS has offices at the headquarters of the European Union (EU) in Brussels, and at the international negotiations center in Geneva. FAS also maintains contact with the United Nations Food and Agricultural Organization in Rome.

A company that has identified a barrier to exporting its products to a foreign country should contact a Market Development Cooperator group (i.e., trade association). The Cooperator and the Department of Agriculture will work together to resolve the barrier. A company that believes it has been treated unfairly by a foreign government in a trade issue, such as losing a tender to a higher bidder, should also contact the Cooperator. Exporters without cooperator representation can contact USDA directly.

Contact:
FAS/USDA
Room 5057, South Building
Washington, DC 20250
Tel: (202) 720-6343
Fax: (202) 690-3606

Rules, Regulations & Standards

The **U.S. Patent and Trademark Office (PTO)** administers the patent and trademark laws of the United States. After examining patent and trademark applications, PTO grants protection to qualified inventions and federal registration to qualified trademarks. The PTO also provides information concerning international patents and trademarks.

Contact:
U.S. Patent and Trademark Office
Center for Patent and Trademark Information
2231 Crystal Drive
Arlington, VA 22202
Tel: (703) 308-5557
Fax: (703) 308-5247

The **Service Industries and Finance Division** of the Commerce Department can help U.S. firms with countertrade issues. In dealings with Eastern Europe, U.S. firms may find it necessary to utilize barter and countertrade practices. As the economies of Eastern Europe move toward the free market, requests for barter and countertrade should decrease.

Contact:
Service Industries and Finance Division
U.S. Department of Commerce
Room 1104
Washington, DC 20230
Tel: (202) 482-5131
Fax: (202) 482-4775

The **Animal and Plant Health Inspection Service (APHIS)** within the U.S. Department of Agriculture provides U.S. agricultural exporters with information concerning foreign import requirements for livestock and fresh vegetables. APHIS also inspects live animals, plants and agricultural products.

Contact:
Animal and Plant Health Inspection Service
Federal Building, Room 764
6505 Belcrest Road
Hyattsville, MD 20782
Tel: (301) 436-8892
Fax: (301) 436-8318

The **Office of Trade and Commercial Affairs** within the U.S. State Department is responsible for policies relating to the foreign protection of U.S. patents, trademarks and copyrights. It follows developments that might result in erosion of this protection, especially in developing nations. It also works with the U.S. Patent and Trademark Office and the Copyright Office. The Office provides consultation to U.S. companies faced with possible patent, trademark- or copyright-infringement problems.

Contact:
Office of Trade and Commercial Affairs
U.S. Department of State
Room 2835
Washington, DC 20520
Tel: (202) 647-0304
Fax: (202) 647-1537

The problems started when Minnesota Mining & Manufacturing Company (3M) failed to pay a fee that is required to keep patents in force in the United Kingdom. The patent in question covered plastic scouring pads used to clean pots and pans. Assuming that 3M's patent was now null and void, a British firm, Bondina Ltd., began to manufacture the same kind of scouring pads. In response, 3M brought an infringement suit against Bondina. A major issue was whether the product was the result of a "real invention" or whether it was merely an "obvious development" in technology undeserving of patent protection. Eventually, 3M won the restoration of its patent, but not before risking loss of its patent along with a major share of the scouring-pad market.

The **Office of Food Safety and Technical Services** **(FSTS)** responds to issues related to food safety regulations and barriers which affect international trade of U.S. agricultural products. Issues include: commodity complaints, foreign product labeling and food standards, sanitary regulations, pesticide residues, and other technical requirements for importing U.S. products into foreign markets.

Contact:
Food Safety and Technical Services
FAS/USDA
Room 5545-S
14th Street and Independence Avenue, SW
Washington, DC 20250-1000
Tel: (202) 720-1301
Fax: (202) 690-0677

The **Food Safety and Inspection Service** **(FSIS)** of the U.S. Department of Agriculture supplies information regarding foreign import regulations for meat and poultry. FSIS also inspects meat and poultry products to ensure that they meet both U.S. and foreign standards.

Contact:

For information on import regulations:
Food and Safety Inspection Service
USDA
Room 327-E, Administration Bldg.
Washington, DC 20250
Tel: (202) 720-2952
Fax: (202) 690-1588

For meat and poultry inspections:
Export Coordination Division
Food Safety and Inspection Service
USDA
Room 0019, South Building
Washington, DC 20250
Tel: (202) 720-9051
Fax: (202) 690-3856

The **Federal Grain Inspection Service (FGIS)** inspects the grain produced in the United States to ensure that it meets all U.S. standards. U.S. grain for export must be officially inspected and weighed, except for land shipments to Canada and Mexico.

The Federal Grain Inspection Service (FGIS) also maintains an international monitoring staff to handle foreign buyer complaints about U.S. grain. Exporter complaints are ordinarily filed with the agricultural representative in the U.S. embassy of the foreign country (see Appendix D).

Registration is required of each firm that buys, handles, weighs or transports 15,000 or more metric tons of grain annually for sale in foreign commerce. Annual registration costs $135.00 for firms engaged in exporting grain; $270.00 for firms engaged in exporting grain and that own 10 percent or more of another firm that is engaged in interstate commerce.

Contact:

Federal Grain Inspection Service
USDA
Room 1641, South Building
P.O. Box 96454
Washington, DC 20090-6454
Tel: (202) 720-0252
Fax: (202) 720-1015

The **National Marine Fisheries Service (NMFS)** conducts inspections and analyses of fishery commodities for export and issues official U.S. Government certificates attesting to the findings. The U.S. Department of Commerce can provide bilingual certificates for shipments to France and tri-lingual certificates for shipments to Belgium.

The NMFS inspection, certification and/or analytical services are available on a fee-for-service basis for the following:

- Origin and species of fish
- Sanitary condition of processing facilities
- Product inspection for wholesomeness, safety and suitability for human consumption
- Chemical, biological and physical tests for adulterants, contaminants and micro-constituents
- Quantity of contents -- net and drained weight
- Appropriateness of labeling and packaging integrity
- Other (as requested by applicant, including factors related to quality and condition).

Contact:
National Marine Fisheries Service
1335 East-West Highway
Silver Spring, MD 20910
Tel: (301) 713-2355
Fax: (301) 713-4114

The *Export Administration Regulations* is a comprehensive list of the rules controlling exports of U.S. products and requirements for export licensing. An annual subscription includes *Export Administration Bulletins,* which explain recent policy changes and include updated regulations. Cost: $87.00 in the U.S.; $108.75 foreign. Order no.: S/N 903-014-00000-8.

Contact:
Superintendent of Documents
U.S. Government Printing Office
Washington, DC 20402
Tel: (202) 512-1800

The **Agricultural Marketing Service (AMS)** of the U.S. Department of Agriculture provides a voluntary food-quality certification service to help U.S. exporters meet importers' specifications. The service is operated on a user-fee basis; to apply, a copy of the contract specifications must be submitted in advance. AMS reviews the contracts and then works with the companies to develop written specifications that can be certified.

Contact:
Agricultural Marketing Service
USDA
P.O. Box 96456
Washington, DC 20090-6456
Tel: (202) 720-4638
Fax: (202) 720-8477

Dairy Grading Section
Dairy Division
Tel: (202) 690-0531
Fax: (202) 720-4844

Fresh Products Branch
Fruit and Vegetable Division
Tel: (202) 720-5870
Fax: (202) 720-0016

Processed Products Branch
Fruit and Vegetable Division
Tel: (202) 720-4693
Fax: (202) 720-0016

Livestock and Meat Standardization
Livestock and Seed Division
Tel: (202) 720-4486
Fax: (202) 720-3499

Poultry Grading Branch
Poultry Division
Tel: (202) 720-4411
Fax: (202) 690-3165

or the following inspection offices:

Southeast Inspection Office
Duval Building
9450 Koger Boulevard
St. Petersburg, FL 33702
Tel: (813) 893-3271
Fax: (813) 893-3111

Western Inspection Office
5600 Rickenbacker Road
Building No. 7
Bell, CA 90201
Tel: (213) 894-5369
Fax: (213) 894-5398

The **National Center for Standards and Certification Information (NCSCI)** is the central depository and inquiry point for standards information in the United States. NCSCI responds to over 5,000 individual inquiries annually on identification and source availability of standards. NCSCI also prepares directories for specialized standards information.

Contact:
National Bureau of Standards
National Center for Standards and Certification Information
A-629 Administration Building
Gaithersburg, MD 20899
Tel: (301) 975-4040
Fax: (301) 975-2128

Operation of Trade Agreements Program is the International Trade Commission's annual report which includes information on the General Agreement on Tariffs and Trade (GATT), the Export-Import Bank, United States' actions on imports, revisions of trade laws and other information. Cost: Free.

Contact:
Office of Publications
International Trade Commission
500 E Street, SW
Washington, DC 20436
Tel: (202) 205-1807
Fax: (202) 205-2186

The **Trade Remedy Assistance Office** was established as a separate division of the International Trade Commission (ITC) in 1988 to assist eligible small businesses in preparing petitions to the ITC to halt unfair trade practices such as dumping of foreign goods at below-market prices and foreign import restrictions and export subsidies. This office works closely with the Department of Commerce, the U.S. Customs Service, the U.S. Trade Representative and the Department of Labor to provide technical assistance to firms seeking relief under U.S. trade laws.

A small company can file a petition by using the legal services of the office. Successful petitions lead to the imposition of a countervailing or anti-dumping duty.

In a countervailing and anti-dumping duty investigation, the ITC makes its preliminary determination within 45 days after a petition has been filed. Within 120 days of the filing the Commerce Department makes its preliminary determination, followed by an ITC-convened hearing and vote on the matter. If the final determination of the ITC is affirmative, the Commerce Department issues a countervailing duty or anti-dumping order requiring imposition of duties.

Contact:
Director
Trade Remedy Assistance Office
500 E Street, SW, Room 601
Washington, DC 20436
Tel: (202) 205-2200
Tel: (800) 343-9822
Fax: (202) 205-1798

The **U.S. Customs Service** must clear all goods imported into the United States. The Customs Service, with headquarters in Washington, DC, has seven geographical regions that are further divided into districts with ports of entry. The Service is also responsible for administering the import laws of the U.S. Virgin Islands and Puerto Rico.

The following free publications provide information on customs requirements for Imports:

- *U.S. Import Requirements*: General information on U.S. Customs requirements for imported merchandise.
- *Tariff Classifications on U.S. Imports*: How to obtain a binding U.S. Customs duty ruling on items before they are imported.
- *Import Quota*: Summary of import quotas administered by the Customs Service.
- *Notice to Masters of Vessels*: Precautions that masters or owners of vessels should take to avoid penalties and forfeitures.
- *Notice to Carriers of Bonded Merchandise*: Precautions that carriers and customhouse brokers should take to safeguard merchandise moving in-bond and the penalties incurred for violations.
- *Drawback:* How to obtain a duty refund on certain exports.
- *Foreign Trade Zones*: Advantages, use and customs requirements of foreign trade zones.
- *Foreign Assembly of U.S. Components*: Details use of Item 807.00 in the U.S. Tariff Schedule, which permits a reduction in duty to reflect the value of components manufactured in the United States and assembled abroad.

Contact:

U.S. Customs Service
1301 Constitution Avenue, NW
Washington, DC 20229
Tel: (202) 566-8195

U.S. Customs Service
6 World Trade Center
New York, NY 10048
Tel: (212) 466-4444

North Central Region
55 East Monroe Street
Chicago, IL 60603-5790
Tel: (312) 353-4731

Northeast Region
#10 Causeway Street
Boston, MA 02222-1059
Tel: (617) 565-6147

Pacific Region
1 World Trade Center, Suite 705
Long Beach, CA 90831-0700
Tel: (213) 491-7341

South Central Region
423 Canal Street
New Orleans, LA 70130
Tel: (504) 589-6324

Southeast Region
909 Southeast 1st Avenue
Miami, FL 33131
Tel: (305) 536-5952

Southwest Region
5850 San Felipe Street
Houston, TX 77057
Tel: (713) 953-6843

The following publications are available from the **U.S. Customs Service:**

Importing into the United States: Customs and other requirements for importing merchandise into the United States. Cost: $6.50.

Tariff Schedules of the United States Annotated: For use in classification of imported merchandise, for rates of duty and for statistical purposes. Cost: $66.00.

Customs Regulations of the U.S.: Looseleaf volume of regulations interpreting many of the customs, navigation and other laws administered by the U.S. Customs Service. Cost: $68.00.

Customs Bulletin: Weekly pamphlet containing proposed and final amendments to Customs Regulations, notices and administrative decisions of interest to the international trading community, and pertinent decisions of the U.S. Court of International Trade and the U.S. Court of Appeals for the Federal Circuit. Cost: $114.00 in the U.S.; $142.50 foreign. Single copy $2.50 in the U.S.; $3.13 foreign.

Contact:

Superintendent of Documents
U.S. Government Printing Office
Washington, DC 20402
Tel: (202) 512-1800

The **U.S. Customs Service** can provide U.S. companies with decisions on the tariff classification and rate of duty of specific merchandise before it is shipped to the United States. To obtain a decision, the following information must be provided:

- Complete description of the goods, including samples, sketches, diagrams and other illustrative material if the goods cannot be described adequately in writing;
- Method of manufacture or fabrication;
- Specifications and analyses;
- Quantities and costs of the component materials; and
- Commercial designation and chief use in the United States.

Contact:
U.S. Customs Service
Area Director of Customs
New York Seaport
6 World Trade Center, Room 423
New York, NY 10048
Tel: (212) 466-5817
Fax: (212) 466-5099

The ***International Mail Manual*** provides information on correct international postal rates, prohibitions, restrictions, availability of insurance and other special services, as well as information on mailing to individual countries. Subscription service consists of three complete cumulative manuals per year. Cost: $14.00 for annual subscription in the U.S.; $17.50 foreign.

Contact:
Superintendent of Documents
U.S. Government Printing Office
Washington, DC 20402
Tel: (202) 512-1800

The **Office of Food Policy** provides information on export restrictions, involving exports such as coffee, tea, cocoa, sugar, jute, cotton, bananas or hard fibers. These food exports could be affected by restrictions in international commodities agreements.

Contact:
Office of Food Policy
Bureau of Economic and Business Affairs
U.S. Department of State
Room 3526
Washington, DC 20520
Tel: (202) 647-3059
Fax: (202) 647-1894

The **Export Services Branch (ESB)** of the U.S. Department of Agriculture provides technical services, information and research on transportation and packaging problems encountered by exporters and shippers of agricultural products.

Contact:
International Transportation
U.S. Department of Agriculture
Auditors Building, Room 1217S
Washington, DC 20250
Tel: (202) 690-1304
Fax: (202) 690-0338

The **European Marketing Research Center** in Rotterdam, the Netherlands, provides technical assistance to U.S. exporters, including help with lost and damaged exports shipped to the European market. The Center also provides information on foreign requirements for packaging and labeling and spoilage tolerances.

Contact:
European Marketing Research Center
USDA/Agricultural Research Service
c/o American Embassy (The Netherlands)
APO New York 09159
Tel: 011 (31-10) 476-5233

When shipping product or providing quotes for most foreign customers, products must be denominated in metric standards. The **Office of Metric Programs** provides exporters with guidance and assistance on foreign metric import regulations.

Contact:
Office of Metric Programs
National Institute of Standards and Technology
Building 411, Rm A146
Gaithersburg, MD 20899
Tel: (301) 975-3690
Fax: (301) 948-1416

Used for temporary imports/exports that are out of the country for less than a year, the **ATA Carnet** is a special international customs document that is used for professional equipment and commercial sample imports/exports. The carnet is issued in lieu of the usual customs documents required and eliminates value-added taxes, duties, and temporary bonds. The carnet is accepted as a guarantee in forty-six participating countries against the payment of customs duties which sometimes come due on goods that are temporarily imported under a carnet and not re-exported.

Contact:
U.S. Customs Service
1301 Constitution Avenue, NW.
Washington, DC 20229
Tel: (202) 927-0440
Fax: (202) 927-6892

or

U.S. Council for International Business
1212 Avenue of the Americas
18th Floor
New York, NY 10036
Tel: (212) 354-4480
Fax: (212) 944-0012

The **Export Legal Assistance Network (ELAN)** provides free, initial consultations to small companies on the legal aspects of exporting through an arrangement of the Federal Bar Association (FBA). Advice is provided by qualified attorneys from the International Law Council of the FBA.

Contact:
Small Business Administration
409 3rd Street, SW
Washington, DC 20416
Tel: (202) 778-3080
Fax: (202) 778-3063

or

Nearest SBA District Office (see Appendix C)

Export License Assistance

The **Export License Voice Information System (ELVIS)** within the Department of Commerce's Bureau of Export Administration (BXA) is the central resource for information on export licenses and regulations. With a touch-tone telephone **ELVIS** lets you request information through voice-mail and connects you to an export counselor.

ELVIS gives you access to the following services:

- Information on how to obtain commodity classifications;
- Information on the different licenses available: emergency, distribution, project, service supply;
- Ordering export application forms, BXA regulations and publications, getting on the mailing list of the free bi-monthly publication, the *OEL Insider*;
- Obtaining an update on the latest regulations;
- Ordering the most recent additions to the Table of Denial Orders;
- Obtaining helpful export enforcement tips; and
- Receiving a schedule of Export Licensing seminars.

Contact:

Washington, DC
Tel: (202) 482-4811

Southern California
Tel: (714) 660-0144

Northern California
Tel: (408) 748-7450

New England
Tel: (603) 598-4300

The **Export License Application and Information Network (ELAIN)** is an electronic submission service that allows firms to submit export license applications to the Department of Commerce electronically through the Compuserve network. Officials then review, process and issue the license electronically. **ELAIN** can shorten the license approval process from two weeks to three days.

Contact:

Washington, DC
Tel: (202) 482-4811

Southern California
Tel: (714) 660-0144

Northern California
Tel: (408) 748-7450

New England
Tel: (603) 598-4300

The **System for Tracking Export License Applications (STELA)** enables the exporter to access the **Export Control Automated Support System (ECASS)** database by using a touch-tone telephone. The **STELA** system provides exporters with the current application status.

Contact:
Automated Information Staff
U.S. Department of Commerce
Room 3898
14th Street and Constitution Avenue, NW
Washington, DC 20230
Tel: (202) 482-2752 (touch-tone)
Fax: (202) 482-2753 (Exporter Assistance staff)

Accounting/Tax Information

The **Internal Revenue Service (IRS)** assists international taxpayers with the following six publications:

- No. 54: *Tax Guide for U.S. Citizens and Resident Aliens Abroad*
- No. 90: *U.S. Tax Treaties*
- No. 514: *Foreign Tax Credits for U.S. Citizens and Resident Aliens*
- No. 570: *Tax Guide for U.S. Citizens Employed in U.S. Possessions*
- No. 593: *Income Tax Benefits for U.S. Citizens Who Go Overseas*
- No. 686: *Certification for Reduced Rates in Tax Treaty Countries*.

The IRS provides service to U.S. citizens through representatives based in U.S. embassies and consulates in Bonn, Caracas, Riyadh, London, Manila, Mexico City, Nassau, Ottawa, Paris, Rome, Sao Paolo, Singapore, Sydney and Tokyo. The IRS also maintains offices in San Juan, Guam and the U.S. Virgin Islands.

Internal accountants should be fully aware of the regulations passed by the Financial Accounting Standards Board (FASB): Accountants with international interests should review FASB 52, a publication that describes the regulations affecting financial reporting of most companies operating abroad. Cost: $5.50.

Contact:
Order Department
Financial Accounting Standards Board
P.O. Box 3821
Stamford, CT 06150
Tel: (203) 847-0700
Fax: (203) 849-9714

The **International Tax Counsel** within the U.S. Department of the Treasury negotiates tax treaties, reviews and works on proposed regulations and reviews IRS revenue rulings. The International Tax Counsel office also provides up-to-date information on international tax legislation.

Contact:
International Tax Counsel
U.S. Department of the Treasury
Room 3064
15th Street and Pennsylvania Avenue, NW
Washington, DC 20220
Tel: (202) 622-0130
Fax: (202) 622-1772

The **Tax Administration Advisory Service**, a service of the Treasury Department, provides consultation on a wide range of tax issues that affect international business operations.

Contact:
Tax Administration Advisory Service
U.S. Department of the Treasury
950 L'Enfant Plaza South, SW
Washington, DC 20024
Tel: (202) 447-0635
Fax: (202) 287-4332

Taxation of U.S. Citizens Abroad

U.S. citizens and resident aliens who work or live abroad or receive certain types of foreign income or income from U.S. possessions fall under special categories for tax purposes and are granted special exclusions or deductions under certain circumstances. Individuals are advised to consult a tax attorney or accountant to determine whether modifications to the rules have been enacted and their effect, if any, on taxes. See the publications previously listed.

Operating Abroad: U.S. Income Tax Incentives

Major U.S. accounting firms offer comprehensive tax information for U.S. corporations, small businesses and individuals engaged in international commercial transactions. They can provide detailed information on taxation of foreign operations, controlled foreign corporations, sale or liquidation of controlled foreign corporations, foreign tax credits, tax treaties and special U.S. trade incentives as well as tax incentives offered by host countries. (The following summary was provided by the international accounting and consulting firm of Deloitte and Touche.) All case studies in this section are hypothetical. This is a basic introduction to some of the more important tax aspects of foreign trade and investment. Because the tax subjects are complex and rules are modified frequently, business executives are advised to consult a knowledgeable tax advisor.

Tax-Favored Export Entities

U.S. law allows for the establishment of certain entities which receive special tax benefits from the income earned through the export of qualifying goods and services. These are the FSC (Foreign Sales Corporation) and the Interest-Charge DISC (Domestic International Sales Corporation). The qualification requirements and associated benefits of the export incentives are as follows:

Foreign Sales Corporation

To qualify as a FSC, the corporation must be incorporated in a foreign country. It must maintain a "permanent establishment" outside the United States and have at least one director who also resides outside the United States. Additionally, the FSC must meet specified foreign management requirements and perform certain economic processes outside the United States. If the corporation meets these and other technical requirements, up to 15/23 of its income (16/23 for non-corporate shareholders) may be exempt from U.S. tax, while the remainder will be taxed currently. The FSC rules also provide special pricing and income-allocation techniques that help exporters get the maximum tax benefit from the use of this export vehicle.

Small FSC. Small exporters may elect to treat their FSCs as "small FSCs." The amount of export receipts receiving tax-favored treatment is limited to $5 million for this class of FSC. In return, the administrative and operating costs are reduced as the "small FSC" is exempt from the offshore management and economic process requirements of "large FSCs" noted above.

Interest-Charge DISC

Rather than forming a FSC, exporters may establish an "interest-charge" DISC. In contrast to the FSC, this is a domestic entity. To qualify, a domestic corporation must derive at least 95 percent of its gross receipts from exporting activities and 95 percent of its assets must be export-related. If the corporation meets these and other requirements, the DISC provisions of the tax code will allow the deferral (versus the FSC's exemption) of U.S. income taxes on up to 16/17 of export profits derived from a maximum of $10 million of gross receipts annually. Unlike the FSC, the "interest-charge" DISC is not subject to U.S. tax. Its shareholders however, are taxed currently on: the 1/17 of export profits not eligible for deferral (whether distributed or not); any dividends the DISC actually remits from export profits previously deferred from U.S. income tax; and any profits derived from gross receipts in excess of the $10-million limit. In addition, the shareholders must also pay an interest charge on the deferred tax of the DISC. As with the FSC, the DISC rules also provide special pricing and income-allocation techniques to maximize available tax benefits.

Richard W. Adams, president of AWT World Trade Corporation, says he has found an almost hassle-free way to save taxes on export sales of his U.S. products. The Connecticut distributor of industrial castings and brake linings joined forces with other distributors in a new tax-saving vehicle called Shared Foreign Sales Corporation (FSC). AWT's tax savings after participating in a FSC were $6,000, or roughly twice the annual costs involved. "This is an opportunity to be just a little more profitable -- it's icing on the cake," says Mr. Adams.

Licensing Technology to a Foreign User

If a U.S. business decides not to operate abroad but to make its technology available to a foreign user, royalties or other fees received for the use of the technology may be subject to withholding by the foreign country on the gross amount of the fee. Generally, when such a withholding is made, it is creditable against the U.S. income tax payable upon the fee. An income tax treaty between the U.S. and the foreign country may reduce or eliminate this withholding.

For some U.S. businesses that have neither the desire nor the capacity to set up operations overseas, licensing technology may provide a useful alternative. However, it may be best from a business standpoint to establish operations abroad. In that case, significantly different tax considerations come into play (See Transfers of Property to a Foreign Corporation).

With no plans to enter foreign markets on its own, a U.S. manufacturer quickly granted a British firm a license to manufacture and sell the U.S. firm's products in the United Kingdom. In addition, the British firm was granted the exclusive right to sublicense the U.S. company's know-how to the rest of the world. The manufacturer viewed the worldwide sublicensing right as a potential source of royalty income requiring no additional effort on its part. Within a few years, opportunities for the manufacturer's products appeared in several country markets throughout the world. But the licensing agreement barred the manufacturer from any direct participation in those markets. Restricted to modest sublicensing royalties, the U.S. manufacturer could only watch its products generating a much greater income for the British licensee and the sublicensees.

Operating within a Foreign Country

If a U.S. corporation or individual establishes a foreign corporation to carry on activities abroad, its income is generally not subject to U.S. tax until the corporation pays a dividend to the U.S. shareholder. Therefore, U.S. tax on such foreign income may be deferred, although the foreign corporation is wholly owned by a U.S. corporation or individual.

When a dividend is paid, the U.S. Government will allow a credit for withholding tax imposed by the foreign country on the dividend. In the case of a U.S. corporate shareholder owning at least 10 percent of the foreign corporation, a credit is also allowed for all or a portion of any foreign corporate income tax imposed on the foreign corporation.

Operating Abroad Through a Branch of a U.S. Corporation, Partnership or Joint Venture

A U.S. Corporation that has foreign source income through the operation of a branch incurs U.S. corporate taxes on that income as it is earned. If there are foreign losses, those amounts may be used to reduce its U.S. taxable income. If foreign income taxes are paid on the foreign source income, the foreign taxes may be credited against its U.S. taxes (subject to certain limitations if foreign losses have been used to offset U.S. income). U.S. partners or joint ventures must include a share of foreign source income in their U.S. tax returns. U.S. tax is payable on this income, but a credit is allowed for a share of foreign income taxes incurred.

"S Corporations"

Certain provisions of the Internal Revenue Code allow a U.S. corporation that is owned by a small group of U.S. shareholders to elect to pay no U.S. corporate taxes. Instead, each shareholder is taxed on a share of the corporation's income as it is earned and may deduct a share of any losses. Since the corporation is not taxed, the usual double tax burden of operating in the corporate form (i.e., the corporation taxed and the shareholders taxed when dividends are remitted to them) is avoided. Foreign corporate income taxes paid by such a corporation that operates abroad are allowed as credits on the shareholders' U.S. individual tax returns.

Possessions Corporations

Some U.S. possessions, like Puerto Rico, may provide tax incentives for a U.S. corporation that organizes a business there including various tax holidays. If the U.S. corporation also elects to be taxed as a possessions corporation and complies with certain other requirements, the corporation will receive a special tax credit against its U.S. corporate income tax. The credit will equal the U.S. income tax that would have been levied on profits earned by that corporation in the possession. Thus, the corporation may pay no U.S. income tax on those profits. Also, if more than 80 percent of that corporation is owned by a U.S. parent company, any dividends received by that parent company from the possessions corporation will be exempt from U.S. income tax. A U.S. corporation can elect to be taxed as a possessions corporation if at least 80 percent of its gross income is from sources in a possession and 75 percent of that gross income is from the active conduct of business in the possession.

Exemption from Gross Income for Employees Based Abroad

Self-employed U.S. individuals or U.S. employees residing in a foreign country can exempt from U.S. income tax up to $70,000 of foreign earned income (income from the performance of personal services in the foreign country) after 1986. To qualify for this exemption, the employee or self-employed individual must be resident abroad for an entire tax year or be physically present abroad for at least 330 days during a 12-month period. An employee may also be exempt from U.S. income tax on amounts received from his or her employer to cover certain excess housing costs incurred in the foreign country.

Many employers take advantage of these exemptions by reducing the compensation of their overseas employees by an amount equal to the U.S. income tax that the employees would have paid had they remained in the United States.

Foreign Tax Credit Limitation

All U.S. taxpayers are permitted to credit against their U.S. income tax liability foreign income taxes paid or accrued during the taxable year on foreign-source income. In most instances, U.S. corporate taxpayers that receive dividends from a foreign subsidiary in which they own at least 10 percent of the voting stock are allowed to credit the corporate income taxes paid by that subsidiary on the earnings distributed. However, there are limitations on the credit designed to ensure that the foreign tax credit claimed will not exceed the U.S. income tax payable by the U.S. taxpayers on the foreign source income. To the extent the limitation prevents a U.S. taxpayer from crediting all of the foreign income tax paid or accrued, double taxation (U.S. plus foreign) or excessive taxation of the same income may result. Because of a variety of factors, including differences in U.S. and foreign concepts of income, it is not unusual for the amount of creditable foreign tax to be limited in a taxable year. A 2-year carryback and 5-year carryforward period is permitted for those credits so limited, subject to certain requirements.

Transfers of Property to a Foreign Corporation

When a U.S. business organizes a foreign corporation to do business abroad, it often transfers to that foreign corporation tangible property that has appreciated in value (such as equipment or foreign currency), or intangible property that will give rise to future income (such as patents or technical know-how, customer lists, etc.) necessary to the conduct of that business. Any such transfer must be reported to the IRS. The gain realized on a transfer to a subsidiary company would ordinarily not be taxed by the U.S. at the time of transfer. However, since the foreign corporation's income may not be currently subject to U.S. income tax, it would be possible for that corporation to subsequently sell or use that property and avoid any U.S. income tax. To prevent such avoidance, when applied to transfers of property to a foreign corporation, the general rule is that the amount of gain or income to be earned will be recognized and subject to tax. Certain exceptions to this rule exist, including nonrecognition of gain if tangible assets transferred will be used in the active conduct of a trade or business outside the U.S.

Passive Foreign Investment Company (PFIC)

A PFIC is any foreign corporation in which, for any taxable year, 75 percent or more of the gross income consists of passive income, or if at least 50 percent of the average value of the assets produce (or are held to produce) passive income. Ownership percentage by U.S. persons is not a determinant of PFIC status. A PFIC can elect to be treated as a Qualified Electing Fund (QEF) or a Non-Qualified Electing Fund (Non-QEF). A U.S. shareholder in a PFIC electing QEF status must currently include in income his pro rata share of the QEF's net capital gain and other earnings and profits (subject to the taxpayer's election to defer payment of tax and incur an interest charge). A U.S. shareholder in a PFIC which does not elect QEF status must pay tax and an interest charge on the deferred portion of any gain on disposition of PFIC stock and on certain distributions from the PFIC.

The Closely Held Foreign Corporation--Passive Income

As discussed previously, if a U.S. individual organizes a foreign corporation to conduct activities abroad, the income earned by that corporation will normally not be subject to U.S. income tax until the U.S. corporation pays dividends to that individual. However, if more than 50 percent of the corporation's gross income is passive income, e.g., interest, dividends, etc., and more than 50 percent in value or voting power of the corporation's stock is owned by five or fewer U.S. citizens or residents, the corporation will be a "Foreign Personal Holding Company." As such, the corporation's net income will be taxed directly to its U.S. shareholders although not actually distributed to those shareholders as dividends.

Controlled Foreign Corporations

Because the income of a foreign corporation is generally not taxed by the United States until distributed as dividends to its U.S. shareholders, some taxpayers seek to shift income currently taxable by the U.S. to a foreign subsidiary to defer U.S. income tax. The Internal Revenue Code attempts to prevent this by requiring shareholders of so-called controlled foreign corporations (CFC) to pay tax currently on the following types of income earned by the CFC even though such income has not been distributed to the shareholders:

- **Foreign Personal Holding Company Income.** Passive income realized by the CFC such as dividends, interest, rentals, royalties, foreign currency gains, and gains from the sale of property that does not generate active income and certain commodity gains.

- **Foreign Base Company Sales Income.** Income realized by the CFC from the purchase of personal property from a related person and its sale to any person, or the purchase from any person and sale to a related person, if the property is both manufactured and sold for use outside the country in which the CFC is organized.

- **Foreign Base Company Services Income.** Income realized by the CFC from performing services outside its country of incorporation "on behalf of" its U.S. parent or for a related person.

- **Insurance Income.** Income realized by the CFC from insuring or reinsuring property, people, or products situated outside the country in which the CFC is organized.

- **Investment of Earnings in U.S. Property.** To avoid paying taxable dividends to its U.S. parent, the CFC invests its earnings in bonds, stock, or other property of its U.S. parent.

- **Foreign Base Company Shipping Income.** Income derived from the use of any aircraft or vessel in foreign commerce, whether or not the income is earned from a related party.

- **Foreign Base Company Oil-Related Income.** Income realized from "down-stream activities" (transportation, refining, etc.) of petroleum products by major oil producers unless extracted in the CFC's country of incorporation or if the products are sold for use in such country.

Non-Arm's-Length Dealing With a Foreign Corporation

If a U.S. corporation deals with its foreign subsidiary in other than an "arms-length" fashion, the IRS may adjust the U.S. taxpayer's income as if the parties were unrelated. Thus the arm's-length standard requires a related taxpayer to report its income and expenses from transactions with its parent as if it were not related to its parent. (It is, therefore, extremely important that the basis for any intercompany pricing be carefully documented.)

Gain on Disposition of Foreign Subsidiary by U.S. Parent Taxed as Ordinary Income

If a U.S. corporation sells or exchanges (including liquidation) stock of a foreign subsidiary that is a controlled foreign corporation (CFC), any gain recognized by the U.S. corporation on the stock sale will be taxable as dividend income to the extent the gain does not exceed the foreign corporation's earnings and profits attributable to the stock which have not been previously taxed by the United States.

Bribe- and Boycott-Related Income

U.S. taxpayers who use foreign corporations to make illegal bribes or other payments to foreign officials or who participate in economic boycotts against Israel (or other designated countries) may be denied credits for foreign income taxes, deferral from U.S. tax on the foreign subsidiary's income and FSC benefits.

Denial of the Foreign Tax Credit with Respect to Certain Foreign Countries

In general, the foreign tax credit is denied when income is attributable to activities conducted:

- In a country that the Secretary of State has designated as one repeatedly supporting terrorism, or
- In a country with which the U.S. does not have diplomatic relations, or
- In a country the government of which the U.S. does not recognize.

In addition, U.S. shareholders of such a CFC will be taxed currently on the corporation's income attributable to activities conducted in one of the above-described countries.

Miscellaneous U.S. Tax Disincentives to Operating Abroad

Special accelerated cost-recovery tables are applicable to property used primarily outside the United States, so that the depreciation deductions are smaller on this property than on comparable property used in the United States. With limited exceptions, a foreign corporation cannot file a consolidated U.S. income tax return with its U.S. parent. There are also extensive and complicated tax-reporting requirements for foreign operations.

Contact:
Internal Revenue Service
950 L'Enfant Plaza South, SW
Washington, DC 20024
Tel: (202) 447-0635
Fax: (202) 287-4332

Host-Country Incentives

The following is a checklist of some incentives offered by countries to attract investment. The "package" of incentives listed below varies with the country and may vary significantly within a country, depending on how attractive a particular investment is to the country's economy. The most attractive investment would have some of the following attributes:

- Be a large employer of local labor
- Earn hard currencies from exports
- Use local raw materials
- Train local managers and technicians
- Help develop locally owned suppliers
- Make a maximum reinvestment of profits in the local company
- Provide goods that are a substitute for imports.

Tax and Tariff Incentives

Income Tax Incentives

- Corporate income tax holidays (exemptions from income tax) that may be limited or unlimited in time and amount
- Accelerated depreciation
- Investment tax credit in addition to depreciation
- Tax exemption or rebate of taxes to the extent funds are used to acquire public bonds
- Increased deduction allowed for business entertainment in connection with export sales
- "Double deduction" of export promotion expenses
- Royalty or fee income of a foreign transferor of technology may be free of withholding of income tax
- Foreign contractor's taxable income may be determined by a favorable formula
- Reduced personal taxation of foreign managers and technicians
- Reduced withholding of income tax on dividends to foreign shareholders from approved investment

Other Tax Incentives

- Exemption from excise taxes on imported machinery and equipment
- Exemption from registration duties, stamp taxes, or capital taxes upon incorporation
- Exemption from property taxes
- Exemption from sales, value added and excise taxes with respect to export sales

- Tariff Incentives
- Waivers on import of machinery, equipment and raw materials
- Access to regional common markets
- Tariff-free foreign trade zones

Non-Tax Incentives

Financial Assistance

- Grants for purchase of land, buildings and machinery
- Grants for expenditure of export market development
- Grants to aid research and feasibility studies
- Government land provided for factory sites
- Low-cost rentals in government-owned industrial parks
- Low-cost financing

Other

- Assistance in locating plant sites, employees, suppliers and markets
- Preference in purchases by government agencies
- Protection of market from competition
- Purchase of government-owned raw materials (e.g., oil and gas) at less than market price
- Guarantee of availability of foreign exchange to purchase equipment and raw materials and to pay interest, fees for technology and dividends
- Work permits granted to imported technicians and managers

The foregoing checklist is intended only to illustrate the variety of incentives that are offered by host countries, many of which are negotiable during the preinvestment stage. A prospective investor's market and investment feasibility study should include a thorough investigation of the tax and non-tax incentives, as well as the disincentives to doing business in a particular country. Further information can be obtained from major accounting firms, foreign ministries, U.S. embassies and financial institutions abroad, as well as U.S. Government agencies.

CHAPTER FOUR

Business Development Assistance: Study Funding, Technical Advisory Services and Training

Once companies have decided on an approach to a foreign market, business executives should then evaluate the commercial feasibility of expanding overseas. Often, the costs associated with evaluating the foreign market -- overseas travel, hiring consultants and formulating a business plan -- can be prohibitive. These expenses may eliminate all but the strongest prospects from being pursued.

U.S. Government agencies and multilateral organizations administer a variety of programs aimed at sharing the cost of developing international projects. Resources range from travel reimbursement to hiring consultants to conducting feasibility studies. Many of these institutions also offer diverse technical assistance services. These programs and services are described in this chapter.

The following is a list of key topics found in Chapter Four:

- Feasibility Study Funding
- Technical Assistance Funding
- Agricultural Business Development Assistance
- Multilateral and Regional Sources of Funding Assistance
- Research and Development Funding
- Export Training Services.

Study Funding

U.S. Trade and Development Agency

The **U.S. Trade and Development Agency (TDA)** can help U.S. companies in the initial stages of project development. TDA provides grants for feasibility studies, orientation visits, and conferences that present U.S. technology and equipment capabilities for the subject sector. TDA's early support improves the likelihood that U.S. technology, equipment, and services will be used in project implementation. TDA priority sectors include infrastructure, telecommunications, and natural resource development. Feasibility studies may include calculations of cost-benefit, market and cash-flow assessments; plans for processing raw materials; plant operations analysis; and market and financial analysis to formulate the optimal approach to the project. In addition,TDA selectively funds orientation visits to the U.S. for high-level officials who are responsible for major upcoming capital infrastructure projects. TDA also funds a variety of conferences and symposia intended to familiarize officials of foreign governments with U.S. goods and services, as well as to encourage U.S. companies to export to industrializing countries.

TDA supports feasibility studies for public-sector projects in developing countries which offer significant trade opportunities for U.S. suppliers. TDA support enables the host government to determine the technical and economic viability of a project with the application of U.S. technology. Feasibility study contracts are awarded to U.S. companies which submit bids in response to these solicitations; the host government selects the winning firm. TDA will fund 100 percent of a feasibility study for a public-sector project supported by a host government. Grants range in size from $30,000 to $2 million.

Private-sector projects developed by a U.S. company that will be a significant investor in the project may be eligible for cost-shared funding assistance. The investor is required to finance the cost of the feasibility study, but TDA will reimburse the investor for up to 50 percent of those costs once the study is complete. Subsequent financing for project implementation must be identified before TDA will commit to provide assistance. Host-government approval is required to conduct feasibility studies.

Any U.S. company can submit a feasibility study proposal for a private sector project to TDA. Proposals will be evaluated on the basis of host-government approval, priority attached to the project by the host government, and an evaluation of technical and financial factors. TDA also reviews the level and nature of competition for the project, level of expertise of the proposing firm, budgetary constraints, level of equity proposed by the U.S. company and other related factors.

There is no application form to solicit TDA assistance. International competitive bidding announcements for feasibility study funding appear in the *Commerce Business Daily*, which specifies project work and country studies, along with target budgets.

In 1992, the Romanian Railways (CFR) initiated the development and execution of a long-term plan to improve the overall quality of its existing railway system. In this regard, Hewlett Packard (HP) participated in a pilot project to restructure CFR's Passenger Ticketing and Reservation systems. The Passenger Ticketing and Reservations pilot project was installed at the Bucharest North Station and has been operating successfully for the past three years. With the success of the pilot program, CFR proposed similar Information Technology (IT) applications to the main rail stations throughout Romania.

Before making an investment of this magnitude, CFR proposed to conduct a comprehensive feasibility study and roll-out plan to build upon the results of the pilot program at the Bucharest North Station. While HP has been a leading IT system provider in Romania, it faced significant competition on this project from ICL (a UK-based Fujitsu group), Groupe Bull, and Siemens. In 1995, TDA agreed to provide a grant of $258,000 to HP to conduct the feasibility study with HP assuming some share of the study's cost. This assured HP continued participation in the project with the possibility of future contracts to supply equipment and services.

Contact:
U.S. Trade and Development Agency
1621 North Kent Street
Rosslyn, VA 22209
Tel: (703) 875-4357
Fax: (703) 875-4009

Export-Import Bank of the United States (Ex-Im Bank)

Feasibility and Design Assistance

The **Export-Import Bank of the United States (Ex-Im Bank)** finances feasibility studies for projects through its Direct Loan and Guarantee programs. In the area of direct credits and guarantees for foreign buyers, Ex-Im Bank offers fixed-rate, medium-term loans to help finance project-related feasibility studies and pre-construction design and engineering services up to $10 million through its Engineering Multiplier Program. Ex-Im Bank's Working Capital Loan Program also can be used to support pre-export costs, such as marketing, assuming the exporter has sufficient collateral.

Terms and Conditions:

Loans to successful applicants will cover up to 85 percent of the U.S. costs. Feasibility studies that cost over $10 million can be financed through a combination of the Engineering Multiplier Program and the regular lending program. If Ex-Im Bank undertakes final project financing, loan payments can refinanced in the long-term financing package.

Contact:
Export-Import Bank of the United States
Engineering Department
811 Vermont Avenue, NW
Washington, DC 20571
Tel: (202) 565-3570
Fax: (202) 565-3584

Market Promotion Project (MPP)

The **Market Promotion Project (MPP)** is administered by the U.S. Department of Agriculture's (USDA) Foreign Agricultural Service (FAS) through the Food, Agriculture, Conservation and Trade Act of 1990. The program directs funds or commodities from USDA's Commodity Credit Corporation (CCC) to provide U.S. producers with financing to promote U.S. agricultural products. For fiscal 1991, MPP allocated $200 million to 47 projects to promote U.S. agricultural commodities.

Activities financed by the MPP vary from commodity to commodity and include activities such as market research and product promotion activities. Among the commodities included are: nectarines, pears, plums, canned peaches and fruit cocktail, table and concord grapes, apples, wood products, poultry and eggs, soybeans, dried prunes, almonds, walnuts, raisins, fresh and processed citrus, rice, frozen potatoes, confectionery and other processed food products, red meat, salmon, avocados, kiwi, pistachios, sweet and tart cherries, processed corn, wine, cotton, strawberries, hops, bourbon, dry beans, honey, peanuts, mink pelts, ginseng, dates, processed tomato products and sunflower seeds.

Terms and Conditions:

The MPP uses surplus stocks or funds from the CCC to partially reimburse agricultural organizations conducting specific foreign market development projects for eligible products in certain countries.

Application Procedures:

Deadlines for proposals for MPP programs are published in the *Federal Register*. Once a proposal has been approved by the USDA, participating companies sign a program agreement with the CCC. The companies must then submit activity plans to FAS outlining specific activities and budgets.

Contact:
Market Promotion Program
USDA
Room 4932
14th Street and Independence Avenue, SW
Washington, DC 20250-1000
Tel: (202) 720-4327
Fax: (202) 720-8461

Dairy Export Incentive Program (DEIP)

The **Dairy Export Incentive Program (DEIP)**, a program administered by the CCC, operates on a bid bonus system and issues generic certificates which can be exchanged for CCC-owned commodities. CCC will make payments to entities selling U.S. dairy products for export.

Terms and Conditions:

CCC will make payments to entities selling U.S. dairy products for export. Such sales must be additional and may not displace commercial export sales.

Contact:
Commodity Credit Corporation
Operations Division, Room 4503
USDA
14th Street and Independence Avenue, SW
Washington, DC 20250-1000
Tel: (202) 382-9150
Fax: (202) 382-8235

Private-Sector Energy Development (PSED)

The PSED program of the Center for International Electric Power Development is operated under the auspices of USAID's Office of Energy. It is designed to assist the private sector in participating in resolving electric power shortages faced by developing countries. To accomplish this, the Center sponsors the Private-Sector Energy Development Feasibility Study Fund which provides financial support to the private sector for the development of private-sector energy/power projects, such as private-power generation or cogeneration plants.

This will cover up to 50 percent of the cost of prefeasibility and feasibility studies. If the feasibility study leads to the implementation of the project, the PSED share of the feasibility study cost shall be refunded to the U.S. Treasury by the applicant, with zero-percent interest. If the proposed project does not achieve financial closure within three years, the applicant will be forgiven from refunding the PSED share of the feasibility study cost.

Generally an applicant to the PSED Fund must propose an environmentally sound, privately owned and operated energy/power project in USAID-assisted country. Applicants must be companies under U.S. management, have 51 percent of the stock owned by U.S. citizens or be owned by citizens of USAID-assisted countries, and be able to demonstrate sufficient financial capability to share the expenses. At a minimum, proposed projects must meet the environmental standards of the World Bank and/or of the host country.

The applicant should have prior and current experience with developing, implementing, operating and/or owning the type of project it proposes to develop with USAID's support. Prior international experience is preferred. The proposed project should provide an opportunity for the export of U.S. goods and services over the course of the project's development, implementation and operation.

Applicants must demonstrate private ownership of, or participation in, the proposed project either through direct or third-party investments. Small and minority-owned businesses are especially encouraged to apply to this fund.

Examples of types of projects submitted to the PSED include, but are not limited to: hydroelectric, waste-to-energy, geothermal power stations and combined-cycle plants. The capacity of most proposed projects is in the 1 MW to 300 MW range.

The PSED supports the following activities:

- Private Energy/Power Project Development Assistance
- Private-Power Database of Project Opportunities
- Technical Assistance to Project Sponsors and Utilities
- Assistance with Project Financing Programs
- Cost-Sharing Feasibility Study Fund for Private Companies.

Contact:

By Mail:
Center for International Electric Power Development
Office of Energy
U.S. Agency for International Development
SA-18, Room 508
Washington, DC 20523

By Courier:
Private Sector Energy Development Program
U.S. Agency for International Development
1611 N. Kent Street, Suite 200
Rosslyn, VA 22209
Tel: (703) 524-4400
Fax: (703) 524-3164

Institutional Grant Facility

The World Bank has a $25-million grant fund called the **Institutional Grant Facility (IGF)** which provides grants for technical assistance projects. IGF provides grants up to $500,000 to cover the cost of upstream institutional development and capacity building. All World Bank borrowers may apply for IGF grants. Grants are awarded for technical assistance, not for project preparation or for planned or on-going Bank-financed activities.

The Bank committee responsible for grant approval gives special consideration to innovative business plans. As a major source of technical assistance, the Bank has a close working relationship with the United Nations Development Programme (UNDP), the Development Assistance Committee of the OECD, and many of the specialized agencies of the U.N. system.

Contact:
Procurement Service, Asia Technical Department
The World Bank
1818 H Street, NW
Washington, DC 20433
Tel: (202) 458-2912
Fax: (202) 477-3129

United Nations Development Programme

The **United Nations Development Programme (UNDP)** is an intergovernmental agency of the United Nations that is instrumental in providing technical assistance and policy advice for projects in developing countries. UNDP receives funding from donor countries which is then used to provide expertise (technical assistance and advice) for development projects. UNDP partners with the World Bank and the United Nations Environment Programme (UNEP) to target projects for environmental development, specifically through joint management of the Global Environment Facility (GEF). UNDP assists with country environmental reports, which eventually shape environmental policy and can target priority areas in a country's development plans. UNDP has several grant programs that provide financial support to develop international projects.

Contact:
United Nations Development Programme
Executive Coordinator, Global Environment Facility
Environment and Natural Resources Group/BPPE
1 United Nations Plaza
New York, NY 10017
Tel: (212) 906-5044
Fax: (212) 906-6947

Washington, DC Office
1889 F Street, NW
Washington, DC 20006
Tel: (202) 289-8674
Fax: (202) 842-2998

Investment Feasibility Study Facility

The **Investment Feasibility Study Facility (IFSF)** is a $1-million revolving fund which finances feasibility studies to support investment decisions in developing countries. IFSF assists potentially viable investment projects in developing countries to attract domestic and/or foreign capital from private and other sources, including development finance institutions (DFIs). IFSF provides short-term, low-cost financing for feasibility studies. Should a feasibility study result in a capital investment, the cost of the study is reimbursed to IFSF from the investment flow. Amounts recovered will then be available to finance other studies.

This fund is designed to ensure that appropriate investment procedures are followed and that investment follow-up is carried out. Studies must be sponsored by a DFI or a private financing institution. The host government must endorse the proposal and/or make an official request to UNDP. While the cost of the feasibility analysis depends upon the type of study under consideration, costs for studies performed to date have averaged $45,000 apiece.

All parties involved, including the government, the entrepreneur and the sponsoring financial institution must agree that the actual cost of the study will be reimbursed to UNDP from the first disbursement of funds to the investment project by the Sponsoring Financial Institution (SFI). If the study does not lead to any investment on the part of the SFI, the costs are absorbed by IFSF.

A brief proposal including all data available on the project (a description of the proposed feasibility study, capital structure, marketing strategies, sales plans, and project financing proposals) should be prepared. Sponsor background is useful for an initial assessment.

Contact:
Private Sector Development Programme
United Nations Development Programme
One United Nations Plaza
TM - Ninth Floor
New York, NY 10017
Tel: (212) 697-4595 or 697-9692
Fax: (212) 697-5058

Regional Assistance Programs

African Development Bank (AfDB)

The **African Development Bank (AfDB)**, headquartered in Abidjan, Côte d'Ivoire, has committed over $22.3 billion to more than 1,600 loans and grants to 51 African countries since it began operations in 1966. The AfDB is the major source of external public financing on the continent, committing several billion in new loans and grants each year.

AfDB participates in technical cooperation, facilitating investment and lending operations through feasibility studies, project preparation and implementation activities.

Interested firms must submit bids for evaluation under an international competitive-award process which is coordinated between the host government and AfDB. Many bids for technical assistance projects are announced in international publications such as the United Nations' *Development Business*.

Firms may pre-qualify by filing their experience and capabilities with AfDB in advance. AfDB uses its Data on Consultants (DACON) roster to maintain up-to-date information on consulting firms eligible to assist in operations it funds. Firms should ensure that their DACON forms on file with AfDB are less than two years old, and are encouraged to update their DACON forms to reflect significant new activities that enhance their capabilities.

AfDB maintains field offices in several African member countries. (See Appendix F for a listing of these AfDB contacts.) AfDB field offices may assist U.S. companies with business advisory services and project identification.

Contact:
Headquarters
African Development Bank
P.O. Box 1387, Abidjan 01
Côte d'Ivoire

US&FCS -- AfDB
AfDB Liaison Officer
U.S. Embassy Abidjan
5 Rue Jesse Owens
01 B.P. 1712
Abidjan 01, Cote d'Ivoire
Tel: 011 (225) 21-09-79, ext. 350
Fax: 011 (225) 22-24-37 (Direct)
Fax: 011 (225) 22-32-59 (Embassy)

Asian Development Bank (ADB)

The **Asian Development Bank (ADB)** has been a major lender for infrastructural and environmental development to its Asian members since its inception in 1966. Historically, ADB's lending has been at the government level. With the recent wave of privatization of industry throughout the Asia/Pacific region, ADB's relatively small private sector investment arm has been absorbed within the rest of bank operations.

ADB maintains field offices in Bangladesh, Indonesia, India, Nepal and the South Pacific. (See Appendix F for a listing of these ADB contacts.) The U.S.-Asia Environmental Partnership (US-AEP) has a technology representative at ADB headquarters in Manila to assist U.S. companies with business advisory services and project identification.

ADB has funded numerous technical assistance projects in the region, generally for industrial development or major infrastructure planning. Such funding would be channeled to the host government and the scope of work would be developed between ADB and the recipient. Technical assistance projects are announced in international publications such as the United Nations' *Development Business*. Firms may pre-qualify by filing their experience and capabilities with ADB in advance.

Interested firms must submit bids for evaluation under an international competitive-award process. There is no program whereby a private firm can initiate a funding request on behalf of itself.

Contact:
Headquarters
Asian Development Bank
P.O. Box 789
1099 Manila, Philippines
Tel: 011 (63-2) 711-3851
Fax: 011 (63-2) 741-7961, 632-6816

European Bank for Reconstruction and Development

The **European Bank for Reconstruction and Development (EBRD)**, since it began operations in April 1991, has lent and invested exclusively for projects and investment programs in the countries of Central and Eastern Europe, including the former Soviet Union. The EBRD has become one of the primary sources of equity capital in the region.

EBRD provides technical cooperation and assistance to facilitate investment. Many of EBRD's technical cooperation projects assist lending operations by providing feasibility studies, project preparation, and implementation activities.

Interested firms must submit bids for evaluation under an international competitive award process coordinated between the host government and EBRD. Many bids for technical assistance projects are announced in international publications such as the United Nations' *Development Business*, or in EBRD's *Procurement Opportunities*.

Firms may pre-qualify by filing their experience and capabilities with EBRD in advance. EBRD uses its Data on Consultants (DACON) roster to maintain up-to-date information on consulting firms eligible to assist in operations it funds. Firms should ensure that their DACON forms on file with the EBRD are less than two years old, and are encouraged to update their DACON forms to reflect significant new activities that enhance their capabilities.

EBRD maintains field offices in twelve European member countries. (See Appendix F for a listing of these EBRD contacts.) EBRD field offices may assist U.S. companies with business advisory services and project identification.

Contact:
Office of the U.S. Director
European Bank for Reconstruction and Development
One Exchange Square
London EC2A 2EH
United Kingdom
Tel: 011 (44-171) 338-6000
Fax: 011 (44-171) 338-6100

International Finance Corporation

The **International Finance Corporation (IFC)**, a member of the World Bank Group, fosters economic growth by promoting private sector investment in developing member countries. IFC's activities are closely coordinated with and complement development objectives of other World Bank institutions. In addition to project financing services, IFC also offers advisory services and technical assistance in capital market development, corporate restructuring, risk management and project preparation and evaluation.

Firms can contact IFC regional offices for technical assistance on project development in the region. IFC will also advise governments on promoting environmentally sound private enterprise and investment.

Contact:
International Finance Corporation
1850 Eye Street, NW
Room I-3131
Washington, DC 20433
Tel: (202) 473-1926
Fax: (202) 676-0365
See Appendix F for a listing of IFC country offices.

Inter-American Development Bank (IDB)

The **Inter-American Development Bank (IDB),** headquartered in Washington, DC, has been a major lender to its Latin American and Caribbean members since its inception in 1959. The IDB is currently the principal source of external finance for most Latin American countries.

IDB funds technical assistance projects in Latin America, primarily for industrial development or major infrastructure planning. By the end of 1992, IDB had committed $1.9 billion in technical cooperation projects, including $987 million on a grant or contingent-recovery basis and $915 million in reimbursable funds.

Interested firms must submit bids for evaluation under an international competitive-award process coordinated between the host government and IDB. Many bids for technical assistance projects are announced in international publications such as the United Nations' *Development Business.*

Firms may pre-qualify by filing their experience and capabilities with IDB in advance. IDB uses its Data on Consultants (DACON) roster to maintain up-to-date information on consulting firms eligible to assist in operations it funds. Firms should ensure that their DACON forms on file with IDB are less than two years old, and are encouraged to update their DACON forms to reflect significant new activities that enhance their capabilities.

IDB maintains field offices in twenty-five Latin American member countries. (See Appendix F for a listing of these IDB contacts.) IDB field offices may assist U.S. companies with business advisory services and project identification.

Contact:
Headquarters
Inter-American Development Bank
1300 New York Avenue, NW
Washington, DC 20577
Tel: (202) 623-1000
Fax: (202) 623-3096

Japan Development Bank (JDB)

The **Centers for Promotion of Direct Investment in Japan**, located at the Japan Development Bank's headquarters and overseas representative offices, offer several services to encourage the import of manufactured goods into Japan and direct investment by foreign-affiliated companies.

Its functions include:

- Consulting for investment projects in Japan;
- Supplying necessary information on potential project sites, including information on regional and local conditions;
- Providing introductions to a potential project site suitable for the construction of offices, distribution centers, factories, laboratories, etc;
- Extending introductions to research institutes to carry out project-related feasibility studies; and
- Introducing potential partner companies.

Information on research institutes which assist in funding feasibility studies is supplied by the Japan Development Bank through its Centers for Promotion of Direct Investments in Japan. The Centers' offices are designed to encourage the import of manufactured goods and processed foods into Japan and direct investment by foreign-affiliated companies. The Centers can introduce research institutes to carry out project-related feasibility studies.

Contact:
Centers for Promotion of Direct Investment in Japan

Washington, DC
1101 17th Street, NW Suite 1001
Washington, DC 20036
Tel: (202) 331-8696
Fax: (202) 293-3932

New York
575 Fifth Avenue, 28th Floor
New York, NY 10017
Tel: (212) 949-7550
Fax: (212) 949-7558

Los Angeles
601 South Figueroa Street, Suite 4450
Los Angeles, CA 90017-5748
Tel: (213) 362-2980
Fax: (213) 362-2982

Tokyo
International Department
Japan Development Bank
9-1 Otemachi 1 chome, Chiyoda-ku
Tokyo 100, Japan
Tel: 011 (81)-3-3244-1785
Fax: 011 (81)-3-3245-1938

Overseas Economic Cooperation Fund (OECF)

The **Overseas Economic Cooperation Fund (OECF)** is a Japanese governmental financial institution that was established in 1961 to contribute to the economic advancement and stability of developing nations. Working alongside the Japan International Cooperation Agency (JICA), the OECF is one of the main Japanese aid-implementing agencies. In 1989 alone, it extended $4 billion in loans to developing countries. Some of this untied financial assistance results in contracting opportunities for U.S. businesses, especially those involved in high-technology fields, energy production, and infrastructure development.

Contact:

Overseas Economic Cooperation Fund
1900 L Street, NW
Suite 312
Washington, DC 20036
Tel: (202) 463-7492
Fax: (202) 463-7496

Tokyo
Takebashi Godo Building
4-1, Otemachi 1-chome
Chiyoda-ku,
Tokyo 100, Japan
Tel: 011 (81)-3-3215-1311
Fax: 011 (81)-3-3201-5982
Cable: COOPERATIONFUND
Tlx: J28790

Japan International Cooperation Agency

The **Japan International Cooperation Agency (JICA)** is the main Japanese government aid-implementing agency. Along with other forms of technical assistance, JICA finances grant-funded pre-feasibility and feasibility studies. JICA permits participation of non-Japanese companies in its Development Survey program, but only as members of a consulting team comprised of at least 50-percent Japanese nationals.

The U.S. and Foreign Commercial Service representatives (US&FCS) at the U.S. Embassy in Japan will assist U.S. firms interested in JICA projects by providing information on Japanese consulting firms seeking work with U.S. firms. JICA's Development Survey program is important because an estimated 40 percent of all studies performed under the program evolve into untied OECF-financed projects.

Types of studies include:

- Master Plan Study — a formulation of a long-term, integrated development plan in which the development potential of a specific sector or region is studied;

- Feasibility Study — an assessment of the technical, economic and financial feasibility of a project; and

- Resources Survey — a preparation of basic data and information on forestry, fishery or mineral resources.

Contact:
Washington, DC Representative
Japan International Cooperation Agency
900 19th Street, NW
Suite 350
Washington, DC 20006
Tel: (202) 457-0412
Fax: (202) 457-0415

Headquarters
Japan International Cooperation Agency
JICA Shinjuku Mitsui Building 2-1-1
Nishi-Shinjuku, Shinjuku-ku
Tokyo 100, Japan
Tel: 011 (81) 3-3346-5311

U.S. Embassy, Tokyo
APO San Francisco, CA 96503
Tel: 011 (81) 3-3224-5069
Fax: 011 (81) 3-3589-4235

Israel-U.S. Binational Industrial Research and Development Foundation (BIRD)

The **BIRD Foundation** provides conditional grants to teams composed of a U.S. company and an Israeli company. BIRD's grants account for 50 percent of each company's costs on a given project. For a project in which the product is ready for sale in 16 months, the maximum amount granted has been approximately $1 million for the team. For a duration longer than three years, the total for the two companies can equal $3 million. (Shorter duration projects are preferred.) Grants are also available for "mini-projects," where the total budget is $200,000 and the duration is one year or less. For these mini-projects, BIRD may provide up to $75,000 or 50 percent of the total project cost.

Application Procedure:

The team composed of an Israeli company and a U.S. company must submit a proposal that is similar in format to a business plan. BIRD has a handbook to guide companies in preparing the proposal. Each proposal requires the approval of the Foundation's Board members. The Board meets twice a year and proposals must be submitted two months in advance of Board meetings.

Contact:

BIRD Foundation
3 Tevuot Ha'aretz Street
P.O. Box 39104
Tel Aviv 61390, Israel
Tel: (011) 972-3-470710, 485432
Fax: (011) 972-3-498341

Govt. of Israel Investment Authority
Shlomo Hanel
800 Second Avenue
New York, NY 10017
Tel: (212) 560-0600, ext. 258

In 1987, Ready Systems Corporation, a Sunnyvale, California-based software tool producer, acquired Medicom, Ltd., an Israeli high-technology firm. Shortly afterwards, Ready Systems began a project to develop computer-aided, real-time design tools ("CARD-tools"), but needed additional financial assistance to support research and development. The company looked to the BIRD Foundation to obtain the necessary funding. With financial assistance, Ready Systems and its new subsidiary were able to develop, test, and successfully market the new CARDtool product line in Israel.

Business Advisory Service (BAS)

BAS was established under the auspices of the United Nations Development Programme (UNDP) and the IFC serves as the executing agency. Funding and assistance for BAS' activities in the Caribbean and Central America have been provided by a number of international and governmental development agencies. Forms of support include completion of feasibility studies and technical assistance. BAS will prepare the financial plan and project proposal for use by the sponsor in negotiating with financial institutions. The staff facilitates linkages with sources of project finance, both debt and equity, from within and beyond the region.

BAS generally focuses on projects with an estimated investment cost of at least $500,000, but is willing to provide advisory assistance to smaller projects. BAS provides assistance in securing financing for working capital or for refinancing existing businesses (only when such financing is an integral part of a new business or expansion project). Projects that are essentially trading operations or real estate developments are not within the scope of BAS activities. Though BAS does not require project sponsors to have a local majority, some financial institutions that work with BAS prefer projects that foster local ownership.

Contact:
Business Advisory Service
International Finance Corporation
1818 H Street, NW
Washington, DC 20433
Tel: (202) 473-0900
Fax: (202) 334-8855

U.S.-Israel Cooperative Development Research (CDR) Program

The **U.S.-Israel CDR Program** provides funding for scientists from Israel and less-developed countries (LDCs) to cooperate in joint research in the areas of natural sciences and engineering. The focus of this program is on problems that are especially important in developing countries. CDR began in 1985 and was suspended at the end of 1988 after more than 100 grants had been made totalling $16 million. The program was reactivated in 1989 and it is expected that $2.5 million will be available annually for new grants.

LDC and Israeli scientists and institutions are invited to submit joint research proposals. Grants cannot exceed $200,000 and are usually disbursed over a three-, four- or five-year period. Investigators may be from universities, government laboratories or the private sector. Government laboratories are required to provide at least 25 percent matching funds. Priority is given to research collaboration involving Israel and developing countries in Africa, Asia/Near East, Europe and Latin America/Caribbean. Participation of U.S. scientists may be included.

The U.S.-Israel CDR Program emphasizes the following areas: arid lands agriculture, agroforestry, agricultural intensification (including water management and multiple cropping), plant biotechnology, biotechnology related to human and animal health, innovative use of by-products, marine sciences and aquaculture, biological control of insects, energy research and studies of global climate change.

Contact:
U.S.-Israel Cooperative Development Research (CDR) Program
Agency for International Development
Room 320, SA-18
Washington, DC 20523-1818
Tel: (703) 875-4444
Fax: (703) 875-4394

OPIC Project Development Program

To promote U.S. direct investment in South Africa, the Overseas Private Investment Corporation (OPIC) is developing a preinvestment assistance program. OPIC's Project Development Program will partially offset U.S. companies' up-front costs in evaluating investment opportunities by funding a portion of the costs of the preinvestment analyses.

The goal of the preinvestment support provided by OPIC is a detailed investment project analysis in sufficient technical and financial detail to allow sponsors to make an informed investment decision and merit serious consideration by financing institutions.

OPIC's Project Development Program will provide eligible U.S. investors with up to 50 percent of the total costs (75 percent for small businesses) of conducting the following types of evaluations:

- Market entry strategy assessment;
- Business plan development; Prototype "pilot project implementation;
- Feasibility studies; and
- Other preinvestment analyses.

To maximize the use of limited resources, OPIC's total contribution will not exceed $150,000 per project; the U.S. sponsor is required to contribute at least 50 percent of the cost (25 percent for small businesses). As part of the proposal, the sponsor should submit a detailed budget for the proposed preinvestment analysis, which, if approved, will serve as part of the agreement between OPIC and the project sponsor. The terms of this program are subject to change, and potential applicants should contact OPIC for updated information on this program.

Contact:
Investment Development Department
Africa Manager
Overseas Private Investment Corporation
1100 New York Avenue, NW
Washington, DC 20527
Tel: (202) 336-8623
Fax: (202) 408-5145

South Pacific Project Facility

The **South Pacific Project Facility (SPPF)** began operations in August 1990. It is modeled on the African Project Development Facility (APDF) and the Business Advisory Service (BAS). The SPPF has been established to assist in the development of small- and medium-sized private enterprises in the South Pacific island countries. Average project size is about $1 million. SPPF has been authorized to operate for an initial period of 5 years.

Contact:
South Pacific Project Facility
International Finance Corporation
The World Bank
1818 H Street, NW
Washington, DC 20433
Tel: (202) 473-0051
Fax: (202) 676-1513

Technical Support/
Export Assistance Coordination

International Executive Service Corps

The National Association of State Development Agencies (NASDA) and USAID Private Sector Project is a cooperative agreement between NASDA and USAID in cooperation with the **International Executive Service Corps (IESC)**. NASDA works with IESC to help U.S. companies identify joint-venture partners in developing countries. The goals of this program are well-suited to assisting U.S. companies in Asia, where personal contacts among business partners are critical.

Through its Multiple Business Services program, IESC locates international business opportunities in developing countries that can lead to linkage with U.S. companies. NASDA's network of state-level departments of economic development disseminates IESC business opportunities to small- and medium-sized businesses throughout the U.S. NASDA also assists with state-level conferences for business audiences designed to debrief volunteer executives on the opportunities identified in developing-country markets.

Contact:
National Association of State Development Agencies
750 First Street, NE, Suite 710
Washington, DC 20002
Tel: (202) 898-1302
Fax: (202) 898-1312

Central and Eastern Europe
Capital Development Initiative

The **Central and Eastern Europe Capital Development Initiative (CDI)** is a U.S. Agency for International Development (USAID) program designed to assist countries in Central and Eastern Europe (CEE) with their environmental pollution problems through infrastructure projects and local environmental businesses. The program assists U.S. environmental firms which specialize in services and technologies needed in the region and helps them to develop business investments and partnerships in the CEE.

Sanders International, the CDI contractor, has regional offices in Warsaw, Prague, Bratislava and Budapest, which are staffed by U.S. and local personnel trained and experienced in environmental issues and business development. As a potential business partnership begins to materialize, Sanders staff can assist with arranging meetings, identifying local regulatory and legal requirements, and facilitating information exchange among the parties. CDI has funds to sub-contract technical and financial assessments of projects and to assist the parties in developing investment and technical information and materials.

Contact:
Program Manager
Capital Development Initiative
Sanders International, Inc.
1616 P Street, NW, Suite 410
Washington, DC 20036
Tel: (202) 939-3480
Fax: (202) 939-3487

Energy Sector Management Assistance Project

The **Energy Sector Management Assistance Project (ESMAP)** is sponsored by the United Nations Development Programme (UNDP) and the World Bank. ESMAP assists developing countries in managing their energy sectors to promote energy-efficient and environmentally sound development. ESMAP will provide managerial assistance and advice in energy sector planning, institutional and policy development, and technical assistance in subsectoral areas such as natural gas development, power planning and restructuring, energy efficiency, environmental impacts and household energy.

ESMAP is funded by developed donor countries and international development agencies, including UNDP and the World Bank. Staffed with engineers, energy planners and economists, consultants and support personnel, ESMAP provides international energy expertise to developing countries. By emphasizing a country-specific and sectorwide framework, ESMAP carries out energy assessments and pre-investment studies and supplies institutional and policy advice to governments.

The findings and recommendations emerging from ESMAP studies (usually conducted jointly with local counterparts) provide governments, donors and potential private sector investors with the information needed to identify economical and environmentally sound energy projects.

ESMAP recently conducted a study of household energy consumption in the Philippines. Prior to this study, initiatives to increase energy efficiency and diversify fuel sources concentrated on the industrial and power sectors. The study showed that the household sector is the largest energy-consuming sector in the economy, using 48 percent of all energy. Based on these findings, efforts are being refocused to place greater emphasis on household and residential energy efficiency.

ESMAP publishes a quarterly newsletter, *The ESMAP Connection*, which is available free-of-charge. The newsletter covers recent ESMAP publications, technical notes from ESMAP projects, and briefs of ESMAP-sponsored projects.

Contact:
Energy Sector Management Assistance Project
Power Development/Efficiency and Household Fuels Division
The World Bank
1818 H Street, NW
Washington, DC 20433
Tel: (202) 473-3412
Fax: (202) 477-0545

Committee on Renewable Energy Commerce and Trade (CORECT)

The **Committee on Renewable Energy Commerce and Trade (CORECT)** is an inter-agency working group of 14 federal agencies formed in 1984 to advance commerce and trade in renewable energy technologies by bringing together potential users, funding sources and U.S. industry members to ensure that U.S. renewable energy applications are considered for viable applications throughout the world.

CORECT's Southeast Asia Project Identification Effort identified over a dozen geothermal power projects targeted for development by NAPOCOR, the national power utility of the Philippines, and the Philippine National Oil Company. Several of the geothermal fields were slated for project development. ORMAT, Inc., a Nevada-based producer of geothermal power equipment, had placed a bid for one of the projects. In bidding for the project, ORMAT faced stiff competition from other companies with existing contracts. CORECT and DOE mobilized other federal agencies, including Ex-Im Bank, USAID and DOC, to work with ORMAT in producing a $57-million competitive financial package for two geothermal projects. Twenty million dollars in grants from USAID, blended with $37 million in loans from Ex-Im Bank, equalized the financing among the competitors and tilted the balance in favor of ORMAT's superior technology. Winning these projects allowed ORMAT to be recognized as a manufacturer and developer of geothermal power plants and enabled ORMAT to pursue larger projects in Southeast Asia.

Contact:

Committee on Renewable Energy Commerce and Trade
U.S. Department of Energy
1000 Independence Avenue, SW
Washington, DC 20585
Tel: (202) 586-5335
Fax: (202) 586-8134

Training

Renewable Energy Training Institute

The **Renewable Energy Training Institute (RETI)** is a non-profit corporation that promotes the use of renewable energy and energy efficiency by brokering training services and organizing short training courses in developing countries. Courses can last from a few hours to a few weeks and are taught by trainers recruited from the international renewable energy and energy efficiency industries. The services offered by RETI are primarily in the areas of course quality assurance, marketing and facilitation of training.

All logistical aspects of training events are handled by RETI, which has relationships with several developing country institutions to ensure that training programs are relevant to a particular country or project and to develop a sustainable training presence. These local partners are involved in identifying training needs and teaching courses. RETI also has relationships with U.S. industry trade associations, U.S. national laboratories and multilateral organizations to coordinate participation of these training specialists.

Training is available in the following technologies: biomass, demand-side management, geothermal, hydropower, photovoltaics, solar thermal and wind energy, among others. RETI facilitates technology transfer from experts within the renewable energy and energy efficiency industry, including manufacturers, consultants, developers, and representatives from private voluntary organizations.

Trainees or the host country generally pay the cost of the training received. However, RETI can assist countries in locating funding assistance. Under special circumstances, RETI can also solicit sponsorship funding from international development donors. Trainees often include government officials, business leaders, technicians, utility officials, teachers and development workers.

Contact:
RETI Director
Renewable Energy Training Institute
122 C Street, NW
Fourth Floor
Washington, DC 20001
Tel: (202) 383-2550
Fax: (202) 383-2555

U.S. Environmental Training Institute (USETI)

The **U.S. Environmental Training Institute (USETI)** serves as a training forum linking U.S. businesses with private and public sector professionals from developing countries in need of appropriate, effective environmental solutions. Through its comprehensive, short-term training courses, USETI seeks to forge long-term, productive relationships between the private sector, government, international agencies and NGOs in both developing countries and the U.S. USETI offers significant opportunities for energy information and technology exchange.

Training courses at USETI leverage resources from both the federal government and the U.S. business community to provide quality, results-oriented training designed to address environmental needs of industrializing countries.

USETI was initiated as a joint effort between the U.S. environmental industry and the U.S. Government in 1991. Through 1994, more than 700 private and public sector officials from industrializing countries throughout the world have attended courses on topics such as air pollution control, environmental management, wastewater treatment and pollution prevention. These courses were supported by private sector corporations, non-profit organizations, trade associations and U.S. government agencies.

USETI has developed partnerships with academic institutions, U.S. and international private voluntary organizations and multilateral institutions such as the World Bank, the United Nations Development Programme and the International Finance Corporation.

In response to many requests for in-country training, USETI is beginning to increase the number of programs offered at overseas locations. USETI will utilize in-country regional alumni activities to promote networking and information sharing to build on relationships between U.S. environmental experts and USETI alumni.

Participants for courses are selected based on criteria including relevant academic and professional experience and commitment to the course activities and information. Acceptance criteria for all courses are listed in USETI's Prospectus and Catalogue of Courses.

Asians and Pacific Islanders recognize that one way to lessen the environmental impact of energy production is to help communities curb electricity consumption. Following a two-week USETI course in Washington and San Francisco, the 18 participants returned to their respective homes in India, the Philippines, Thailand, Vanuatu, and the Lao P.D.R. to introduce voluntary demand-side management programs. NGO and corporate presenters and course sponsors included the International Institute for Energy Conservation, Pacific Gas and Electric, and the Asia Technical Alternative Energy Unit of the World Bank.

Contact:
United States Environmental Training Institute
1000 Thomas Jefferson Street, NW, Suite 308
Washington, DC 20007
Tel: (202) 338-3400
Fax: (202) 333-4782

United States Telecommunications Training Institute (USTTI)

The **United States Telecommunications Training Institute (USTTI)** is a public/private partnership between the communications industry and the federal government. The goal of this collaborative effort is to share the United States communications and technological advances on a global basis by providing a comprehensive array of free telecommunications and broadcast training courses for individuals from developing nations.

Communications professionals currently employed in the public or private sector of a developing country who are proficient in English are encouraged to apply.

Contact:
United States Telecommunications Training Institute
1150 Connecticut Avenue, NW
Suite 702
Washington, DC 20036
Tel:(202) 785-7373
Fax: (202) 785-1930

American Export Training Institute (AETI)

The **American Export Training Institute (AETI)** offers financial training seminars to U.S. companies and financial institutions involved with exporting. Seminars cover a broad range of export-related topics, including documentation, letters of credit and other methods of payment, exporting risks, and trading procedures and regulations. Structured as a hands-on learning environment, the seminars give practical information on export financing techniques. Individual export counseling is also available to course participants after completing the seminars.

AETI's training courses are taught at regional locations based upon the number of course participants and available sites. In-house training services are also available for financial institutions and corporations.

Contact:
American Export Training Institute (AETI)
3000 K Street, NW, Suite 690
Washington, DC 20007
Tel: (202) 337-6300
Fax: (202) 333-1158

Agribusiness Linkage Program (AgLink)

AgLink is a U.S. Department of Agriculture program designed to promote U.S. trade activities with those countries whose markets have only recently become accessible to U.S. businesses. The program provides access to the agribusinesses of the Newly Independent States (NIS), Poland and the Baltics. AgLink establishes the initial link between small- and medium-sized U.S. businesses and comparable overseas partners by identifying appropriate matching firms. Firms participating in AgLink will be reimbursed for travel and per diem costs associated with an initial trip to the target country. The program also provides financial and administrative support for training of the overseas manager at the U.S. company and for a follow-up visit to the overseas company.

Contact:
Coordinator
Agribusiness Linkage Program (AgLink)
RSED/ICD/FAS, Rm. 3222
U.S. Department of Agriculture
Washington, DC 20250-4300
Tel: (202) 720-8877
Fax: (202) 690-0892

In September, 1994, World-Wide Sires (WWS) of Hanford, California, applied for and received assistance from the U.S. Department of Agriculture's AgLink program. WWS was looking to enhance its presence in the Russian market and had identified a potential distributor in Western Siberia. Through the AgLink program, WWS was able to make two visits to Russia which resulted in the signing of a distributor agreement with a Russian company.

Special American Business Internship Training (SABIT)

SABIT, established in 1990, is managed by the U.S. Department of Commerce. SABIT assists economic restructuring in the Independent States of the former Soviet Union by exposing top-level business executives and scientists to American methods of innovation and management. SABIT places executives and scientists from the Independent States in U.S. firms for one-to-six-month internships to gain first-hand experience in a market economy. SABIT has been well publicized in the region and extensive contact has been made with political and economic leaders, business organizations, and private entrepreneurs. The U.S. Department of Commerce has already amassed a large applicant pool from which companies can select interns.

Any U.S. firm may apply to the program. Participant firms must demonstrate a commitment to the goals of the program and:

- Provide the intern with a hands-on training program in the business skills necessary to operate in the market economy;
- Provide an orientation counselor to help the intern adjust to the United States; and
- Provide the intern with medical insurance, housing and any other daily expenses not covered by the stipend provided by the U.S. Department of Commerce.

SABIT provides a unique marketing tool for U.S. companies interested in doing business in the Newly Independent States because SABIT interns are influential business managers and leading scientists in the same or similar sectors as those of their U.S. hosts. On their return home, interns should be in a position to assist in facilitating and generating a receptive climate for future U.S. exports.

Contact:

Special American Business Internship Training Program
U.S. Department of Commerce
International Trade Administration
Room 3413
Washington, D.C. 20230
Tel: (202) 482-0073
Fax: (202) 482-2443

Partners for International Education and Training (PIET)

PIET is a consortium of four international education organizations, The African American Institute, World Learning Inc., AmidEast, and the Asia Foundation. PIET has a contract with the U.S. Agency for International Development (USAID) to administer a portion of the USAID's Participant Training Program. Through this program, PIET will place individuals from developing and transitional countries into training programs in the United States which can either be short-term technical or academic degree programs. Most candidates are placed in agribusiness, project management, and trade promotion training programs.

Contact:
Partners for International Education and Training
2000 M Street, NW, Suite 650
Washington, DC 20036
Tel: (202) 429-0810
Fax: (202) 429-8764

Eurasia Foundation

The **Eurasia Foundation** is a privately managed grant-making organization established with financing from the U.S. Agency for International Development (USAID). The Foundation supports technical assistance, training, educational, and policy programs in the Newly Independent States (NIS) covering a wide range of activities in economic and democratic reform. Grants are made to American organizations with partners in the NIS and directly to NIS organizations.

The Eurasia Foundation's programmatic focus includes three areas:

- Private Sector Development: Topics include management training, economics education, curriculum development, policy advice and information systems.

- Public Sector Reform: Topics include public administration, public policy advice, and development of a non-governmental sector.

- Media and Communication: Topics involve development and support for print, broadcast and electronic media.

The Eurasia Foundation makes grants for technical assistance, training, educational and implementation activities and policy research totalling approximately $16 million per year. The Eurasia Foundation's general criteria for grant-making are that the grant:

- Support private sector development and/or democratic institution-building;

- Produce a significant and sustained effect on the ground in the NIS; and

- Represent a genuine transfer, adaptation, or creation of skills in the NIS.

The Foundation has field offices in Russia, Ukraine, and Central Asia. The field offices are responsible for carrying out small grant programs on the ground. They also assist the Washington, DC office to evaluate grant proposals and to monitor funded projects.

Contact:
Grants Management Office
Eurasia Foundation
2021 K Street, NW, Suite 215
Washington, DC 20006
Tel: (202) 467-8530
Fax: (202) 467-4924

The World Environment Center (WEC)

The **WEC** contributes to sustainable development by strengthening the management of industry-related environmental, health, and safety practices worldwide. The center achieves this mission by:

- Establishing partnerships among industry, government and non-governmental and international organizations to achieve mutually beneficial goals;

- Enhancing the institutional capacity of developing countries by providing technical assistance and volunteer experts; and

- Organizing business exchanges to address environmental problems and promote cooperative ventures by providing funding for short-term technical assistance activities and short-term internships, seminars and study tours.

Contact:
World Environment Center
419 Park Avenue South
Suite 1800
New York, NY 10016
Tel: (212) 683-4700
Fax: (212) 683-5053

The Asia Foundation: US-AEP Fellowship Program

The **Asia Foundation** is a coalition of Asian and American business community groups and governmental institutions. The coalition enhances environmental protection and promotes sustainable development in Asia and the Pacific by mobilizing U.S. environmental technology, expertise, and financial resources. US-AEP is supported by the U.S. Agency for International Development.

The Foundation fellowship program promotes individual expertise and institutional capability in designing policy, increasing public awareness, and implementing and enforcing public and private measures to address critical environmental issues. The Foundation arranges a professional affiliation of 1 to 4 months for each fellow. The affiliations provide opportunities to work with colleagues in public and private institutions in the U.S. and 31 nations in the Asia-Pacific region, thereby developing professional and institutional networks among participating nations.

Contact:
Asia Foundation Headquarters
465 California Street, 14th Floor
P.O. Box 193223
San Francisco, CA 94119-3223
Tel: (415) 982-4640
Fax: (415) 392-8863

Agricultural Cooperative Development International (ACDI)

Agricultural Cooperative Development International is a non-profit training, technical, and management assistance organization created by leading U.S. agricultural cooperatives and farmer organizations. ACDI provides technical assistance and training for starting and strengthening commercial and credit services to farmers in developing countries and emerging democracies. ACDI activities include the identification, development, implementation, and evaluation of management and technical assistance projects. ACDI works in the following areas:

- Agribusiness and Trade Promotion
- Credit Systems
- Natural Resource Management
- Training and Exchange Programs.

In addition, ACDI leads a consortium that implements the Restructuring Agriculture and Business Private Sector Program (RAAPS) in Eastern Europe. RAAPS introduces U.S. agribusinesses to similar firms in Hungary offering U.S. firms an opportunity to explore trade and other business possibilities with very little risk or cost. The program pays for all direct costs, including airfare, lodging, meals and other incidentals for participating U.S. company executives during the one-week program.

Contact:
Project Coordinator
ACDI
50 F Street, NW, Suite 900
Washington, DC 20001
Tel: (202) 879-0221
Fax: (202) 626-8726

Volunteers In Overseas Cooperative Assistance (VOCA)

VOCA works with local leaders, rural-based enterprises and non-governmental organizations to identify their needs and arranges for U.S. volunteers to provide technical assistance and training. With field offices in 23 countries, VOCA mobilizes specialists to offer technical assistance in three major areas:

- Cooperative Assistance
- Farmer- to-Farmer assistance to small- and medium-scale agricultural enterprises
- Private agribusiness development in emerging democracies.

Contact:
VOCA
50 F Street, NW, Suite 1075
Washington, DC 20001
Tel: (202) 383-4961
Fax: (202) 783-7204

Energy Management Consultation and Training (EMCAT)

The **Energy Management Consultation and Training (EMCAT)** project in India helps improve management efficiency of the energy sector. EMCAT seeks to develop human resources in the energy sector by implementing efficient and renewable technology. The $20-million, seven-year (FY 1991-98) EMCAT project trains Indian energy officials and engineers and helps in modernizing power systems, with the assistance of U.S. private expertise and equipment.

EMCAT receives additional support from the World Bank and the Asian Development Bank. The project has trained energy auditors in the U.S., approved a demand-side management study by the Indira Gandhi Institute, approved plant rehabilitation with participation by the U.S. Department of Energy and the U.S. Environmental Protection Agency, and organized workshops on cogeneration in the sugar industry.

Contact:
General Manager, Technology
Industrial Development Bank of India
IDBI Tower Cuffe Parade
Bombay - 400 005 India
Tel: 011 (91-22) 218-9111
Fax: 011 (91-22) 218-9121

International Environmental Management Training Modules

The **International Environmental Management Training Modules and Training Centers Program** seeks to strengthen the institutional management of environmental issues in countries undergoing economic restructuring. This program consists of a series of stages that addresses: financing environmental investments, chemical emergency preparedness, environmental policy development, economic analysis, risk and environmental impact assessments, and hazardous-waste site ranking and enforcement.

Employees of the U.S. Environmental Protection Agency (EPA) facilitate delivery of these modules to foreign audiences and will prepare foreign facilitators to conduct this training without additional EPA assistance. The modules were developed as part of EPA's technical assistance program for Central and Eastern Europe and were successfully presented in developing countries in Asia. The modules have become core elements in the training programs offered by the Environmental Management Training Centers (EMTCs).

Contact:
Office of International Activities
U.S. Environmental Protection Agency
401 M Street, SW
Washington, DC 20460
Tel: (202) 260-4870
Fax: (202) 260-9653

Energy Training Project

The **Energy Training Project (ETP)** helps prevent and control global climate-change gases, as well as mitigate local environmental impacts, by offering a unique opportunity for qualified energy and environmental professionals from developing countries to receive practical, hands-on training. The enhanced local institutional capability to resolve energy sector problems also contributes to increased potential for economic growth through reliable sources of power. Courses conducted in the U.S. are designed to enable mid-level engineers, planners, managers, economists and other specialists to implement new technologies, policies, or procedures. U.S.-based courses are held in various locations around the U.S. and last between two and four months. Other courses conducted in-country are customized on a country-specific or region-specific basis to enable senior-level policymakers and executives to make informed decisions on new energy and environmental technologies, policies and procedures. In-country courses last between one and two weeks. The U.S.-based and in-country training programs are operated for the U.S. Agency for Development (USAID) by the Institute for International Education (IIE).

ETP also offers a Study Tour Program which brings senior-level developing country energy sector professionals to the U.S. to observe new technologies, policies and procedures first-hand, and to meet with and share information with their U.S. counterparts who design and operate these new technologies. The Study Tour Program is operated for USAID by the U.S. Energy Association.

Contact:
U.S. Agency for International Development
Energy Training Project
Tel: (703) 235-4962
Fax: (703) 235-4964

Institute for International Education
1400 K Street, NW
Washington, DC 20005
Tel: (202) 682-6560
Fax: (202) 682-6576

CHAPTER FIVE

Export Financing

Financing may be the key to any business transaction between U.S. companies and overseas buyers. This chapter describes the numerous sources of funding that are available from the U.S. and foreign governments for exporting goods and services. Government-backed financing ranges from the pre-export working capital needed to fill purchase orders, to short-term (180 days) export receivables financing, to customer financing with terms of ten years or more.

Access to financing can also be an important marketing tool. Consequently, the U.S. Government has recently modified many of its programs to provide indications of support at very early stages in the negotiating process.

The following is a summary of key topics on export financing found in Chapter Five:

- Working Capital
- Fixed-Asset Financing for Export Production
- Accounts Receivable Financing
- Export Term Loans/Guarantees
- Export Credit Insurance
- Lease Financing
- Concessionary Financing
- Forfaiting
- Agricultural Loans/Guarantees.

Export Financing

Access to Export Capital Program

The **Access to Export Capital Program (AXCAP),** operated by the Bankers' Association for Foreign Trade (BAFT), is a national database listing of banks and government agencies which are involved in trade finance and the services they offer. AXCAP matches specific exporter needs with appropriate financial services. For first-time exporters or seasoned exporters looking for new markets, AXCAP helps customize financing options for businesses in global markets. Exporters will reach a trade specialist, via a toll-free number, who will pinpoint the specific trade finance problem and provide the exporter with a list of banks and government agencies that offer the needed services. BAFT has mailed AXCAP registration forms to over 1,000 banks to be listed on this database.

Contact:
Access to Export Capital Program
Bankers' Association for Foreign Trade
1600 M Street, NW - Suite 7F
Washington, DC 20036
Tel: (800) 49-AXCAP
Tel: (202) 452-0952 (Washington, DC metro area)
Fax: (202) 452-0959

Malaysia is bounded by the Straits of Malacca and the South China Sea, which are both major sea lanes subject to significant oil spills that require rapid response. A New Jersey-based international marine-spill training and product specialist contacted AXCAP to identify financing options for the national marine-spill response program the Malaysians are developing. The company, with no prior export experience, was interested in securing $750,000 to $1,000,000 over three to five years to cover the initial five-year start-up phase. An AXCAP database search located a bank in New York that met the needs of this company.

U.S. Small Business Administration

The Small Business Administration (SBA) has an **Export Finance Program** that guarantees short- or long-term loans to help small business increase their export sales. These programs are designed to assist small businesses requiring capital to expand manufacturing for international markets, as well as to meet their working capital needs. Loan proceeds may not be used to establish operations overseas.

Meiller Company is a manufacturer of medical supplies that has successfully defied the myth that small firms cannot compete in the international market. The College Station, Texas-based firm entered the European market with the assistance of the Small Business Administration (SBA) and other federal and state agencies.

With SBA's assistance, Meiller has made exports 25 percent of its total sales and the long-term focus of future growth. In recognition of the company's efforts at promoting small business exports, Meiller Company was named "SBA Exporter of the Year" in 1988.

Export Working Capital Program (EWCP)

EWCP helps small businesses export their products and services. Any number of disbursements and repayments can be made, as long as the dollar limit of the credit line is not exceeded and the disbursements are made within the stated maturity period. Proceeds can be used to finance labor and materials needed for manufacturing, purchasing goods or services, or foreign accounts receivable. Funds may not be used to pay off existing obligations, purchase fixed assets (this applies to the working capital program only), or provide funds to establish international joint ventures.

Eligibility: Applicants must qualify under SBA's size standards and meet the other eligibility criteria applicable to all SBA loans. In addition, an applicant must have been in business (not necessarily international business) for at least 12 months prior to filing an application. The business must be current on all payroll taxes and have a depository plan for the payment of future withholding taxes.

Terms: SBA can guarantee up to 90 percent of a loan up to a limit of $833,000. An applicant may have other SBA loans in addition to loans under this program, as long as SBA's share of the total outstanding balance of all loans does not exceed $833,000. If the borrower has also secured an international trade loan, the limit is $1.25 million. For loans which exceed this amount, the exporter must solicit funding assistance from Ex-Im Bank.

The maturity of an EWCP is based on an applicant's business cycle but cannot exceed 36 months, including all extensions. Borrowers can re-apply for a new credit line when their existing line of credit expires; however, a new credit line may not be used to pay off an existing line of credit. Interest rates are set through negotiations between the applicant and the participating lender. For maturities of 12 months or less, the fee is 0.25 percent of the guaranteed portion of the loan. For maturities exceeding 12 months, the fee is two percent of the guaranteed portion of the loan, and no additional fees are charged to extend the maturity. In addition, the normal fees permitted on all SBA loans may also be assessed on EWCP loans.

Collateral may include accounts receivable, inventories, assignments of contract proceeds, bank letters of credit or appropriate personal guarantees. Only collateral that is located in the U.S. and its territories and possessions—or other assets under the jurisdiction of U.S. courts—is acceptable.

Waste-Tech, Inc. of Libertyville, IL, is a wholesaler and manufacturer of high-tech pollution-control equipment which removes water from sludge deposits, reducing the original volume for easier disposal. This process creates both a positive environmental and economic impact. Waste-Tech has thirty employees and has been in the filtration and pollution-control business for more than 15 years. Waste-Tech has been exporting for nearly three years, with its manufacturing, engineering, and sourcing of components conducted in the United States.

Waste-Tech was recently awarded a contract for nearly $1.3 million to supply an eight-tube Python Pinch Press system to Enirisorce, an Italian mining company. For this first venture into the Italian market, SBA guaranteed 90 percent of an $833,000 loan by First of America Bank. First of America issued a standby letter of credit to support progress payments to be made by Enirisorce to Waste-Tech. According to Robert Manwaring, President of Waste-Tech, "I couldn't have done it without SBA's support... the Export Working Capital Program promotes a can-do attitude."

International Trade Loan Program

The **International Trade Loan Program** provides long-term, primarily fixed-asset financing to help small businesses establish or expand international operations. Loans are made through lending institutions under SBA's Guaranteed Loan Program.

Terms: Under this program, SBA can guarantee up to $1.25 million, less the amount of SBA's guaranteed portion of other loans outstanding under SBA's regular lending program (the guaranteed loan for facilities and equipment is limited to $1 million and the working capital portion is limited to $250,000). Maturities of loans may extend to the 25-year maximum period applicable to most SBA loan programs. The maximum rate for longer maturities is 2.75 percentage points above the New York prime interest rate.

Only collateral located in the U.S., including its territories and possessions, is acceptable for a loan made under this program. The lender must take a first lien position (or first mortgage) on the items financed under this section. Additional credit assurances may be needed, such as personal guarantees and subordinations.

Contact:
Any SBA District Office (Appendix C)

or

U.S. Small Business Administration
409 3rd Street, SW, 6th Floor
Washington, DC 20416

Office of Financial Assistance
Tel: (202) 205-6490
Fax: (202) 205-7522

Office of International Trade
Tel: (202) 205-6720
Fax: (202) 205-7272

State Development and Funding Programs

State programs can often fill financing gaps not covered by federal and private entities. Many offer their own loan guarantee programs similar to those offered by SBA. U.S. firms can access these state programs to complement federal funding options. Some state programs also provide assistance in the form of export counseling or technical assistance, while others offer financial support for international activities.

Many state trade programs work with Ex-Im Bank to help exporters arrange financing, including California, Florida, Maryland, Michigan, Minnesota, Oklahoma, Texas, Virginia and Washington. Maine, New Hampshire and Vermont have cooperative arrangements with Ex-Im Bank to support exports. To learn more about state programs, contact a local International Trade Office (listed in Appendix G) or the National Association of State Development Agencies (NASDA) in Washington, DC, for information regarding available state resources.

Contact:
National Association of State Development Agencies (NASDA)
750 First Street, NE
Suite 710
Washington, DC 20002
Tel: (202) 898-1302
Fax: (202) 898-1312

Export-Import Bank of the United States

The **Export-Import Bank of the United States (Ex-Im Bank)** is an independent U.S. government agency chartered by Congress to facilitate the financing of exports of U.S. goods and services. By neutralizing the effects of export credit subsidies from other governments and by absorbing credit risks the private sector will not accept, Ex-Im Bank enables U.S. firms to compete fairly in overseas markets on the basis of price, performance, delivery, and service.

Ex-Im Bank provides export credit support to either U.S. exporters on a short-term basis, or to foreign purchasers of U.S. products on a longer-term basis (2-12 years). Through loan guarantees and insurance, Ex-Im Bank fosters exports by making working capital available to U.S. exporters. Through similar mechanisms, as well as direct loans (and, on occasion, grants), Ex-Im Bank provides credit at attractive interest rates to foreign buyers to encourage their purchase of U.S. goods and services. Ex-Im Bank's financing programs are as follows:

- **Working Capital Guarantee** -- export-related working capital for U.S. exporters;
- **Credit Insurance** -- accounts receivable financing for U.S. exporters;
- **Direct Loans** -- credit extended to foreign buyers of U.S. goods and services at a fixed interest rate;
- **Guarantees** -- a guarantee of repayment on a fixed-number or floating-rate export loan from a lender to a foreign buyer of U.S. exports; and
- **Grants** -- special funds set aside to counteract credit subsidies offered by other governments.

Ex-Im Bank reviews requests for financing based on the financial and technical aspects of a transaction, as well as the degree of foreign government-subsidized export credit the U.S. exporter faces from competitors. It also considers the impact the transaction will have on the U.S. economy. Because of its mandate to create economic benefits in the U.S., Ex-Im Bank will not support transactions where less than 50 percent of the contract value is of U.S. origin. In all but a few exceptions, Ex-Im Bank is also prohibited from financing military sales.

Business Development Group

In order to improve processing of applications and better assist exporters, Ex-Im Bank has created the Business Development Group. All preliminary inquiries should be directed to this unit, while loan processing actually takes place in the Export Finance Group. Ex-Im Bank is increasing outreach efforts to exporters and to public and private buyers in targeted foreign markets through the Business Development Group. This unit of Ex-Im Bank: creates market-specific financing packages designed to meet the needs of foreign buyers and U.S. exporters; identifies specific, high-potential foreign markets in which to promote the use of Ex-Im Bank financing; and trains a broad range of government, private, foreign and domestic personnel in the use of Ex-Im Bank programs abroad.

Types of Commitment

Depending on the stage of the transaction, Ex-Im Bank can issue a Letter of Interest, a Preliminary Commitment, or a Final Commitment.

Letters of Interest (LI) indicate financial structures offered to exporters by Ex-Im Bank. The LI was developed to greatly improve efficiency and shorten response time. It is used when the U.S. exporter needs a financing indication from Ex-Im Bank in the early stages of negotiations. Engineering, economic, policy and credit analyses are not performed by Ex-Im Bank prior to issuing the LI. However, an LI is normally issued within seven days of a request.

The LI will indicate that Ex-Im Bank is open for business in that foreign market, the maximum repayment term for the potential sale, the assigned risk category for the proposed obligator and/or guarantor, the indicative exposure fee, commitment fee, interest rate, and the program options (loans or guarantees) that may be available. The LI is valid for six months from the date of signing. A request for a Final Commitment (AP) will be considered if the exporter wants the commitment. There is no obligation for Ex-Im Bank to convert the LI to a final commitment.

When the appropriate application is submitted, Ex-Im Bank charges a one-time processing fee of $100 for an LI or final approval.

A **Preliminary Commitment (PC)** outlines the amount, terms and conditions of the financial assistance Ex-Im Bank is prepared to offer; however, it is only offered in exceptional circumstances. It is normally issued for a duration of four months, but this can be extended where appropriate. Prior to expiration, the PC can be converted to a Final Commitment for a loan and/or guarantee. Applications for PCs may be submitted by the foreign buyer, a U.S. exporter, a U.S. or foreign bank involved in the transaction, or any other responsible applicant with an explanation as to why a PC is required as opposed to an LI. The application must include sufficient information to allow Ex-Im Bank to appraise the financial, economic, and technical aspects of the transaction.

Applications for **Final Loan and Guarantee Commitments** must be submitted by the prospective borrower or lender, depending on whether the request is for a direct loan or guarantee. Unlike PC applications, in which Ex-Im Bank may waive some of the informational requirements due to the early stage of the transaction, applications for a Final Commitment must include all appropriate information for Ex-Im Bank to appraise the financial, economic, and technical aspects.

Ex-Im Bank Loan Programs

Working Capital Loan Guarantee

This program gives U.S. exporters access to working capital loans from commercial financial institutions. By providing 90-percent repayment guarantees to lenders on secured short-term loans against inventory and foreign receivables, exporters obtain the necessary working capital to purchase inventory, build products, and extend terms to overseas buyers. This program provides the means for small- and medium-sized companies to more aggressively pursue exports. Working Capital Guarantees can be issued for specific transactions or for a series of transactions in the form of a line of credit.

Eligibility: Ex-Im Bank will issue its guarantee to the lender if, in its judgment, the eligible exporter is creditworthy for the loan or line of credit to be guaranteed and the product being exported has at least 50-percent U.S. content. (The creditworthiness of an exporter is determined by assessing financial information, management, track record and the type of transaction to be financed.) Before Ex-Im Bank will issue a guarantee to a lender with which it has no working experience, it may require a full financial disclosure. The lender must be able to demonstrate the ability to service loans to exporters in accordance with Ex-Im Bank's guarantee. The lender must also certify that the loan would not otherwise be made without the guarantee.

Terms: The terms of the guaranteed loan can be up to 12 months, but may be longer if required. The guarantee is for 90 percent of the principal amount of the loan and interest. Ex-Im Bank requires that the eligible lender be secured with inventory of exportable goods, accounts receivable on goods or services already exported, or other acceptable collateral. Ex-Im Bank will not impose any interest-rate or fee ceiling on the lender for guaranteed loans, although it will monitor rates and fees being charged. Typically the interest rates for these types of loans are based on the prime lending rate, with a spread of between one and three percentage points.

Robotic Vision Systems, Inc. (RVSI), a small high-technology producer of advanced inspection and measurement systems that exports 75 percent of its products to Europe and Asia, attributes its recent success to Ex-Im Bank's support. Founded in 1977, RVSI relied for many years on contracts with the auto industry and the U.S. government as its primary source of revenue. However, by the mid-to-late 1980's these sources began to fade and RVSI was forced to diversify its customer base. Seeing an opportunity to expand by entering the global electronics market place, RVSI converted from domestic government military projects to product sales of related technologies for commercial use. With growing work-in-process and an expanding base of foreign receivables, RVSI found itself in need of additional working capital. A shortage of adequate export working capital threatened to choke off growth and jeopardize the transition to commercial business.

RVSI applied for an Ex-Im Bank Working Capital Loan Guarantee to support its international sales growth. Ex-Im Bank approved a $750,000 Transaction-Specific Guarantee in September 1992 to support the sale of approximately $1.5 million of inspection and measurement systems. With the Ex-Im Bank guarantee, RVIS was able to obtain adequate financing to complete these sales, which, in turn, paved the way to new international orders. With a strong management team and a commitment to export growth, RVSI's expansion continued. In September 1993, Ex-Im Bank provided another $750,000 guarantee, this time on a revolving basis. Ex-Im Bank continues to support RVSI's growing exports.

Fees: Ex-Im Bank charges a $100 processing fee, as well as a guarantee fee of 1.5 percent of the loan amount, payable when the final commitment is issued.

Application Procedure: Ex-Im Bank requires the following types of information for the requested loan guarantee:

- Information on the goods to be financed (e.g., cash flow, terms of payment, etc.);
- A summary of the exporter's business plan and history of activities;
- A recent interim financial statement, including aging of accounts receivable and payable;
- Three years of complete financial statements;
- At least five credit and/or bank references;
- A summary of management's experience in related and non-related fields; and
- For newly formed trading companies or other exporters, an opening balance sheet may be submitted in lieu of this information.

Application forms are available from Ex-Im Bank. From the information provided by the applicant, Ex-Im Bank will decide whether the request meets the program guidelines and offers a reasonable assurance of repayment. If the applicant is the lender, it is required to submit its own credit analysis and describe how it will control disbursement and application of funds, payment procedures, and other related matters.

Ex-Im Bank support was vital for East Hartford, Connecticut-based Scan-Optics, Inc. ("SOI"), a manufacturer of high-end information processing systems used for data capture, document processing, and information management. Since its inception, exports have comprised a significant portion of SOI's sales, climbing to 50 percent of hardware sales in 1992. Given the small size of SOI, cost of high technology, and the international elements of its business, few lenders were willing to provide advances against its foreign receivables and inventory. This lack of export working capital threatened to undermine SOI's export sales, international competitiveness, and overall commercial viability. Because of the relative importance of exports to SOI, it approached its lender in late 1992 and applied for export working capital. The bank agreed, subject to the availability of an Ex-Im Bank guarantee.

In March 1993, Ex-Im Bank approved an application for a $2-million Working Capital Loan Guarantee. Although the export market was generally sluggish, SOI's commitment to international sales paid off. In early 1994, it won a three-year, $1.6-million contract to develop two prototype document scanners for the Japanese Health Department; this contract subsequently grew to $7.5 million. SOI's existing Ex-Im Bank-guaranteed line of credit was not sufficient to support this contract, and SOI once again sought Ex-Im Bank's assistance. In May 1994, Ex-Im Bank responded favorably and approved a $4-million revolving Working Capital Loan Guarantee.

To accelerate the process of obtaining a working Capital Guarantee, Ex-Im Bank has extended Delay and Authority to qualified lenders for up to $2 million per transaction. This permits the lender to commit Ex-Im Bank to a loan with minimal documentation and provides a reduction in guarantee fees.

Under the Primary Lender Program, a qualified bank is assured faster turn-around for loans up to $5 million. Ex-Im Bank has made a commitment to prior lenders that it will make a decision on a pending loan within 10 business days for standard transactions.

Credit Insurance

Ex-Im Bank's Credit Insurance policies provide protection against both the political and commercial risks of a foreign buyer defaulting on a credit obligation. Policies are available for single or repetitive export sales and for leases. They generally cover 100 percent of the principal for political risks and 90 to 95 percent for commercial risks, as well as a specified amount of interest.

Short-term policies are used to support the sale of consumer goods, raw materials and spare parts on terms of up to 180 days and bulk agricultural commodities, consumer durables and capital goods on terms of up to 360 days. Capital goods may be insured for up to five years, depending upon the contract value, under medium-term policies. Exporters may obtain receivables financing more easily, because the proceeds of the policy are assignable to banks.

Medium- and Long-Term Loans/Guarantees/Insurance

U.S. exporters can obtain medium- and long-term loans for their overseas customers for up to 85 percent of the value or 100 percent of the U.S. content of an export transaction, whichever is less. Repayment terms on these Ex-Im Bank loans/guarantees range from between two to ten years with principal and interest scheduled in equal semiannual or quarterly installments based on the type of product being exported. For insurance, which provides for 100 percent coverage, terms are limited to 5 years and amounts less than $10 million. On transactions over $10 million, ten-year terms may be available depending on the type of product being exported.

Medium- and longer-term loans/guarantees/insurance should be viewed as pre-sale marketing tools in addition to after-the-sale financing alternatives. U.S. exporters often face stiff competition from similar products offered by foreign manufacturers; such financing options can enhance the attractiveness of their offer. On larger purchases, financing is not only desirable, it is often a requisite.

Cray Research Inc. (Cray) was founded in 1972 in Chippewa Falls, Wisconsin, by Seymour Cray whose goal was to develop the most powerful computer systems available. Although Cray's position in the world economy is now well-established, new markets in Eastern Europe and the Newly Independent States of the former Soviet Union present both opportunities and challenges. In early 1993, Cray began discussions with the Russian State Committee for Meteorology (Rosgidromet) on the sale of a supercomputer system for weather forecasting (the entire system will include both a large supercomputer and an entry-level supercomputer).

In April 1995, the Cray was approved for a 5-year, $13-million Ex-Im Bank Medium-Term Loan to Rosgidromet for the purchase, installation, maintenance, and security arrangements for the weather forecasting system. This financing will help Cray to establish a presence in the Russian market and effectively face its Japanese competition. The Ex-Im Bank medium-term loan will provide financing for 100 percent of the U.S. content, or 85 percent of the total project, whichever is less.

Eligibility: Any responsible lender or borrower (foreign buyer) is eligible for an Ex-Im Bank loan/guarantee. Only borrowers can qualify for direct loans and only lenders (not necessarily a financial institution) may receive intermediary loans. Evidence of foreign, officially supported export credit competition is required to receive any kind of concessionary financing unless the product is in an industry known to receive frequent government subsidies. The applicant must submit the best information available regarding the existence of foreign, officially supported competition, preferably including the name of the foreign suppliers and the terms and interest rates they are offering. When the identity of the foreign competitor or its financing offer is not known, Ex-Im Bank will employ other means of indirectly establishing subsidized official export credit competition.

Terms: Ex-Im Bank will provide a credit or guarantee/insurance for up to 85 percent of the U.S. export value of each transaction. A 15-percent cash payment must be made to the U.S. seller from the foreign buyer, which may be financed without Ex-Im Bank support. If the U.S. export item contains more than 15-percent foreign-made components, Ex-Im Bank supports 100 percent of the U.S. content as long as it exceeds 50 percent of the contract amount.

U.S. companies can also take advantage of other countries' export credit agencies. Ex-Im Bank has cooperative agreements with many of these organizations which facilitate the financing of goods and services from non-U.S. sources. For a listing of the major export credit agencies in foreign countries, see Appendix I.

Financing Terms: Financing from private lenders may be denominated in dollars or other hard currency. Repayment of principal and interest is scheduled in equal semiannual or quarterly installments, normally beginning six months from the date of product delivery or project completion. Repayment terms usually range between two to ten years based on the type of product or project and the official OECD country classification.

Repayment terms generally follow those which are customary in international trade and usually follow the schedule below:

CONTRACT VALUE	MAXIMUM REPAYMENT TERM
Medium-Term	
Up to $75,000	2 years
$75,001-$150,000	3 years
$150,001-$300,000	4 years
$300,001 or more	5 years (exceptionally up to 7 years)
Long-Term	Over 7 years (usually not to exceed 12 years)

Rates: Ex-Im Bank's guarantee is available for fixed or floating interest rate loans, typically based on the London Inter-Bank Offering Rate (LIBOR). In the event of a claim, Ex-Im Bank guarantees 100 percent of the guaranteed loan's principal and interest. Interest rates for direct loans are based on the lowest rates permitted under OECD guidelines. Under most circumstances, this rate is the OECD Commercial Interest Reference Rate (CIRR), which changes monthly and varies according to the repayment term of the loan as follows:

REPAYMENT PERIOD:	EX-IM BANK'S LENDING RATE (CIRR)
Up to 5 years	3-year Treasury rate + 1%
Over 5 years to 8-1/2 years	5-year Treasury rate + 1%
Over 8-1/2 years	7-year Treasury rate + 1%

Fees: Ex-Im Bank charges an up-front exposure fee to the exporter, assessed on each disbursement of a loan made or guaranteed. Exposure fees vary according to the repayment term of the loan, the classification of the borrower or guarantor (i.e., government, local bank, or private buyer) and the borrower's country. The exposure fee can be financed in the export loan and thereby passed on to the buyer.

Because Ex-Im Bank must always determine reasonable assurance of repayment when extending credit, it typically requires a government, local bank or foreign branch of a large commercial bank to issue a guarantee. For government buyers, a central bank, finance ministry or government development bank will provide this guarantee. If ample high-quality information can be obtained on a foreign enterprise, Ex-Im Bank will entertain a credit application without outside guarantees.

An annual commitment fee of 0.5 percent is charged to the borrower on the undisbursed amount of each direct loan. Ex-Im Bank charges the lender a fee of 0.125 percent for the undisbursed amount of each guaranteed loan. No commitment fee is charged for a medium-term intermediary loan. However, if a medium-term intermediary loan is combined with a guarantee covering the intermediary's loan to the foreign borrower, a 0.5 percent per annum commitment fee is charged on the undisbursed balance of the guaranteed loan.

Environmental Exports Program

To respond to the growing needs of environmental exporters, Ex-Im Bank has developed a special **Environmental Exports Program** that will provide enhanced levels of support for a broad range of environmental-related exports. One of the major features of the program is enhanced medium- and long-term support for environmental projects, products, and services.

These enhancements, which are reflected in Ex-Im Bank loan and guarantee programs include:

- Local Cost Coverage of 15 percent: Makes U.S. exports more attractive by extending support to a greater portion of the sales price, to include installation and civil works costs incurred in the host country.

- Capitalization of Interest During Construction: Rolls interest due on construction loans into the Ex-Im Bank financing package. Responds to requests from many U.S. exporters for a means of deferring interest payments.

- Longest repayment terms allowed by existing international agreements (OECD Guidelines).

Leasing Program

Ex-Im Bank has two types of lease coverage--operating and financing leases. Operating leases are used when the lessor eventually takes repossession of the product and the lease can be underwritten without an advance payment. A financing lease is used for transactions such as medium-term sales, whereby the lessee makes several payments to the lessor and eventually purchases the product. In these cases, Ex-Im Bank requires a 15-percent advance payment. Both types of policies are of the single-transaction type, which requires one application per lease. Definitions of an operating lease, true lease, financing or full-payout lease vary according to the context of accounting, taxes, commercial law, or international trade, but do not affect the choice between the two types of policies.

Operating Lease Policy

Coverage for Stream of Payments during Repossession Efforts:
This insurance policy divides coverage into two distinct parts, the first of which addresses the stream of payments which falls due during a limited repossession-efforts period after default by the lessee. Although the length of the repossession-efforts period will be underwritten on a case-by-case basis, it will generally extend to cover those periodic and approved non-periodic payments which fall due during a maximum period of five months after the default. The intention of this first coverage is to maintain a stream of payments while the lessor takes action to repossess the leased products. Coverage for the stream of payments is usually provided at 100 percent for sovereign lessees and 90 percent for all others.

Coverage for Governmental Prevention of Repossession:
If the insured has elected to purchase this coverage and is unable to effect repossession during the repossession-efforts period, the insured may then claim repayment, but only if repossession is prevented by government confiscation and/or expropriation. Coverage will be limited to the actions of the governments of those countries which the insurers agree to specify in the declarations. Failure by the insured to effect repossession for reasons other than confiscation or expropriation is not covered. The valuation of coverage is 100 percent of the fair market value of the leased products at the time of claim submission.

Financing Lease Policy

Similar to the structure of a medium-term Ex-Im Bank-supported loan, a 15-percent advance payment from the lessee to the lessor on or before the delivery of the leased products is required. Should the lessee default, coverage is provided for the insured percentage of each lease payment as it falls due until the end of the lease term. Coverage is usually provided at 100 percent for sovereign lessees and 90 percent for all others. At the time of claim payments, the insured is obligated to transfer to Ex-Im Bank all remaining obligations of the lease, as well as title to the leased products. The coverage of lease payments as they become due remains effective regardless of failed repossession efforts for any reason, or Ex-Im Bank's own subsequent repossession of a leased product which has lost its market value.

Tied-Aid Capital Projects Fund

The Ex-Im Bank **Tied-Aid Capital Projects Fund** counters a foreign-aid donor's use of trade-distorting tied-aid credits. This fund may be utilized on a case-by-case basis and will only be applied when U.S. exports are directly threatened by foreign tied-aid. The project is being developed along the following guidelines:

- Financing of relatively low concessionality (35 percent);
- Recipient countries of strong and improving creditworthiness; and
- Revenue-generating projects in revenue-generating sectors.

There are additional considerations which may increase the likelihood of tied-aid support. For example, small business exporters as defined by the Small Business Administration (fewer than 500 employees) receive a high priority. Another factor would be the potential for generating future sales where the use of tied-aid could "lock-in" a long-term supply relationship. Ex-Im Bank will support sales which combine substantial follow-on market penetration with strong international competitive advantages. In order to qualify, applicants should have a planning horizon extending beyond the current sale; expect substantial follow-on market penetration, financed in the future on commercial terms; and be willing to engage in energetic price competition against foreign exporters.

Ex-Im Bank has a mandate to meet unfair foreign government financing subsidies. Since many governments subsidize their industries as a matter of policy, low-cost loans or grants are very common in the international arena, particularly on larger projects. Ex-Im Bank programs are subject to Organization for Economic Cooperation and Development (OECD) guidelines for government-supported export financing. Ex-Im Bank is bound by OECD framework agreements; however, it will still attempt to meet foreign competition by offering more attractive terms than would normally be available. Part of the financing offer may be in the form of a grant.

Ex-Im Bank is committed to upholding OECD rules on trade-related aid and supporting the reduction of trade-distorting tied-aid. Ex-Im Bank's tied-aid credit will be structured as low-rate loans for 100 percent of the export value, with a total term of 25 years. The exact interest rate will depend on the concessionality (as defined by the OECD) of the foreign tied-aid credit encountered. The fees are strictly risk-based. Ex-Im Bank's fees will reflect pertinent sovereign risks, the financing of 100 percent of export value and the 25-year term exposure to risk.

Over 100,000 Indonesia communities, many of them slated for development assistance from the government, are not linked to the national power grid. Electrification of these communities by conventional small diesel generators is undesirable due to high operating costs, difficult fuel supply, and excessive requirements for on-site operation and maintenance services.

To help meet and beat foreign competition to supply equipment and services to the Government of Indonesia, Westinghouse, Inc. applied for and received funding through Ex-Im Bank's Tied-Aid Capital Projects Fund. The commitment by Ex-Im Bank to assist with this $20-million pilot project was instrumental in helping Westinghouse prepare an attractive financing package for its Indonesia customer. The success of the pilot project will help Westinghouse participate in future donor agency projects and establishes U.S. leadership in this strategic market.

Operations and Maintenance (O&M)

Ex-Im Bank will finance service contracts which have a duration of at least two years. These activities include start-up and shut-down of production machinery; receiving, storing, and maintaining the flow of raw materials; product quality testing and control; controlling costs; and equipment repair. This program covers the U.S. costs of executing the contract, including salaries for U.S. citizens working at the site, home office costs associated with the work, travel expenses, and the cost of spare parts. Upgrading of old equipment and other rehabilitation work of a capital nature are also covered by Ex-Im Bank. In order to be eligible, the O&M contract must provide a long-term benefit, such as training of local personnel, the owner or the host country.

For additional information on Ex-Im Bank's programs, contact Ex-Im Bank headquarters in Washington, DC, a regional Ex-Im Bank branch, or a U.S. Export Assistance Center (see Appendix B).

Contact:
U.S. Export-Import Bank
Business Development Group
811 Vermont Avenue, NW
Washington, DC 20571
Tel: (202) 565-3900
Tel: (800) 765-3277
Fax: (202) 565-3931

OECD Consensus Agreement: The OECD Consensus Agreement is a consensus agreement adopted in 1978 by members of the Organization for Cooperation and Economic Development (OECD) to limit export-credit competition among the member governments. Export credit agencies like Ex-Im Bank are governed by this agreement. The Guidelines cover cash payment requirements, minimum interest rates, maximum repayment periods, local costs, and procedures for negotiating any deviations from the Agreement.

The Agreement sets out maximum credit periods according to the buyer's country. There are three categories of countries, which are currently being phased into two basic categories. Repayment of the credits must be in equal half-yearly installments. Interest must also be paid at least half yearly and is usually paid on the reducing balance of the outstanding principal. Consensus requires that the buyer must pay at least 15 percent of the contract value before the starting point of credit. At least five percent of the contract value must be paid on or before the date on which the supply contract becomes effective. Interest can be either officially supported or under pure cover at commercial rates. Exporters are able to offer fixed or floating, favorable interest rates to overseas buyers. The minimum officially supported fixed interest rate is laid down by the Consensus on the basis of the three country categories. Category II and III markets are located in a matrix of rates which is revised every six months (January and July). If the weighted average of long-term interest rates for major currencies changes, 0.5 percent or more, rates are adjusted accordingly.

This matrix rate will essentially cease after 1998. A different system based on Commercial Interest Reference Rates (CIRR) is used for Category I countries, which include Japan and most EU members. These CIRR-based rates are sometimes more competitive than the matrix rates. After 1995, all other countries will be in Category II and also be extended for CIRR. CIRRs are calculated each month for almost all of the ECD participants' currencies. Both CIRRs and matrix rates can be held for up to 6 months. The Berne Union has established maximum credit terms for particular goods. For exports of particular goods, or for particular contract values, the payment terms may be shorter than the Agreement would allow. Underwriters will use their commercial judgment to determine appropriate maximum credit terms.

Private Export Funding Corporation

The **Private Export Funding Corporation (PEFCO)** is a consortium of private lenders which acts as a supplemental lender to traditional export financing sources. It works with Ex-Im Bank by using private capital to finance U.S. exports. PEFCO makes loans to public and private borrowers located outside of the U.S. who require medium- and/or long-term financing on purchases of U.S. goods and services. PEFCO also purchases from lenders or noteholders the Ex-Im Bank-guaranteed obligations of foreign importers who have financed the purchase of U.S. goods and services through traditional lenders or suppliers. It also provides funding to exporters who have obtained an Ex-Im Bank Working Capital Guarantee which other financial institutions are unwilling to fund. In all cases, the loans made by PEFCO, or the foreign importer notes purchased from others, must be covered by the comprehensive guarantee of repayment of principal and interest by Ex-Im Bank.

Project and Product Buyer Credits

PEFCO lends funds to foreign buyers of capital equipment or expensive products where the amounts are larger and/or repayment periods are longer than traditional lenders make for their own account.

Eligibility:

- Ex-Im Bank Comprehensive Guarantee must be available
- Amount must exceed $1 million
- Fixed interest rate is required
- Final maturity must be over five years
- Payment net of any local or withholding taxes
- The loan request must come through a commercial bank.

Terms: PEFCO loans have ranged from $1 million to $225 million (with five- to 22-year terms) and have been sponsored by domestic and foreign banks. Occasionally, PEFCO loans have been made to commercial or special-purpose lessors or "borrowers of convenience" with the actual users of the equipment being obligors of the intermediaries. Terms and conditions reflect market conditions and respond to requirements of borrowers.

Application Procedure: PEFCO should be approached through a commercial bank. When contacted, PEFCO will provide a fixed-rate quote (valid for five working days) and an indication of the terms of its potential credit, provided the amount and appropriate disbursement and repayment schedules are known. A firm offer can be made available for a period of up to 45 days. If the offer is accepted, a Credit Agreement will be negotiated with the Borrower, PEFCO, Ex-Im Bank and any other lender or guarantor.

Note Purchase Facility (NPF)

NPFs are designed to provide assured liquidity to traditional lenders who utilize Ex-Im Bank medium-term programs. Under this facility, PEFCO will purchase from lenders, noteholders, or prospective lenders, the Ex-Im Bank-guaranteed notes being used to finance U.S. goods and services.

Eligibility:

- Security: Ex-Im Bank comprehensive guarantee
- Amount: Not in excess of $10 million
- Repayment: Seven years or less
- Interest Rate: Either fixed or floating with Ex-Im Bank guarantee on same basis
- Prepayment: Requires noteholder's consent
- Taxes: Payment net of any and all foreign local or withholding taxes
- Source: Any existing lender or noteholder or potential lender.

Terms: PEFCO offers are based on current market conditions and purchase is without recourse to seller. Offers on existing notes carrying fixed or floating interest rates are available for up to two days pending response. Offers for pending commercial transactions may be made available to commercial banks on fixed- or floating-rate terms for extended periods at an additional cost. PEFCO requires possession of a note and an Ex-Im Bank Guarantee Agreement.

Application Procedure: Any potential lender, lender or noteholders can request an application from PEFCO by letter or telephone.

Lender-of-Last-Resort

The Lender-of-Last-Resort facility provides financing for exporters which Ex-Im Bank has determined cannot obtain financing from other sources, even with an Ex-Im Bank working capital guarantee.

Terms: PEFCO will provide financing for the portion of exports secured with an Ex-Im Bank working capital guarantee. PEFCO cannot finance any portion of the exports not covered by the Ex-Im Bank guarantee.

Eligibility: To be eligible for financing, exporters must have the following:

- An Ex-Im Bank Preliminary Commitment for a Working Capital Guarantee;
- Proof that the exporter cannot obtain financing from other sources even with the Ex-Im Bank guarantee; and
- A referral to PEFCO by Ex-Im Bank.

Contact:
Private Export Funding Corporation
747 Third Avenue
New York, NY 10017
Tel: (212) 826-0710
Fax: (212) 826-1897

Export-Import Bank of Japan

The **Export-Import Bank of Japan (JEXIM)** is Japan's export credit agency which facilitates Japanese and third country exports of goods and services. While most of its projects are designed to support Japanese exports, JEXIM provides financial support to encourage exports from the United States. JEXIM and the Japan Overseas Economic Cooperation Fund (OECF) will consider projects referred by the Joint Committee of Experts, set up by Japan and the United States, eligible for general untied loans for development projects. As part of a joint effort with U.S. Ex-Im Bank to increase exports to Japan, JEXIM will also make available medium- and long-term financing for imports from the United States to Japan.

In March 1992, a U.S. electronics firm received a JEXIM loan for the expansion and improvement of its production facility. The Florida firm which obtained the loan produces electronic anti-corrosion devices used in cars, machinery, and construction. Currently, eighty percent of the company's products are exported to Japan, making the company an obvious choice to receive a JEXIM loan for the promotion of manufactured exports to Japan. This was the first firm to receive such a loan from JEXIM.

Contact:
Export-Import Bank of Japan
The Overseas Investment Consulting Office
Representative Office in Washington, DC
2000 Pennsylvania Avenue, NW
Suite 3350
Washington, DC 20006
Tel: (202) 331-8547
Fax: (202) 775-1990

Additional Addresses:
International Relations Division
Policy Coordination and Planning Department at the Head Office
1-4-1, Ohtemachi 1-chome
Chiyoda-ku,
Tokyo 100, Japan
Tel: 011 (81)-3-3287-9108
Fax: 011 (81)-3-3287-9539

Overseas Private Investment Corporation

The **Overseas Private Investment Corporation (OPIC)** is a U.S. Government agency that encourages mutually beneficial American private business investment in developing countries. Services that are available through OPIC include investment finance by direct loans and loan guarantees, investment insurance against a broad range of political risks, and a variety of investor services. These programs are designed to reduce risks and perceived blocks in international investment.

Lease Financing

This program offers loans and loan guarantees to foreign leasing companies where there is a significant U.S. private business interest. The funds are used to encourage U.S. exports of equipment which will be leased in the host country.

Eligibility: The borrowing company or U.S. sponsor must be an established leasing company with a history of successful leasing operations. Companies must demonstrate the capability to proceed with the proposed leasing plan. Leases should be made to private-sector companies on a medium- to long-term basis. In some cases, OPIC will consider financing a portion of the equipment costs of a single cross-border lease.

Terms: Terms of the guarantees are typically from four to seven years with grace periods. U.S. dollar loans are provided by a U.S. lender under an OPIC guarantee, which covers 100 percent of all the lender's risks. The loans can carry fixed or floating rates pegged to U.S. Treasury rates or the London Inter-Bank Offer Rate (LIBOR). The borrower also pays an annual guarantee fee to OPIC in the range of one-and-one-half to three percent.

Security for the loans may include first liens on the assets financed and/or other collateral or pledges as required to adequately secure OPIC's financing. Direct loans from OPIC are available to leasing companies in which a U.S. small business has a significant interest. A small business is currently defined as a manufacturing firm with revenues of less than approximately $142 million or a non-industrial firm with a net worth of less than $48 million. This definition is subject to annual adjustment. OPIC can lend up to $6 million per project at a fixed rate, priced at prevailing U.S. government agency rates of comparable maturity.

Insurance Leasing

OPIC offers political risk insurance coverage for cross-border operating and capital-lease transactions with terms of at least 36 months. OPIC's insurance for assets leased under an operating lease provides coverage for the original cost of the leased assets (including duties, freight and installation) incurred by the lessor. Insurance for capital leases covers the stream of payments due under the lease agreement. OPIC's insurance provides coverage against the following:

- The inability to convert into dollars local currency received as lease payments;
- Loss due to expropriation, nationalization or confiscation by host government; and
- Loss due to political violence.

Coverage is also available for equity investments in, and loans to, offshore leasing companies, for management and maintenance agreements involving leasing companies, and for consigned inventory.

Eligibility: OPIC may insure an investment by an eligible investor in a project controlled by foreign interests, but it is only the eligible investor's investment that is insured, not the entire project. Eligible investors are U.S. citizens, corporations, partnerships or other associations which are substantially owned by U.S. citizens, created under the laws of the U.S., or of any state or territory of the U.S. Eligible foreign businesses must be at least 95-percent owned by investors eligible under the preceding criteria.

OPIC covers U.S. private investments in over 115 "less developed, friendly" countries. OPIC insures not only new investments, but also those used to expand or modernize existing plants. It may include the cost of acquiring an existing business. The investor should apply for insurance sufficient to cover possible project-cost overruns. Coverage is available for conventional equity investments, loans and for investment of funds and goods or services under various contractual arrangements. To be eligible for insurance, an investor must apply for and receive an OPIC Registration Letter before the investment is made or irrevocably committed. This letter does not commit OPIC to offer insurance, nor does it commit the investor to accept it.

Premiums: Premium rates are determined by the risk profile of a particular project. Annual base rates for leasing insurance are as follows:

Coverage	Current (%)	Standby (%)
Inconvertibility	0.30	0.25
Expropriation	0.60	0.25
Political Violence*	0.60	0.25

* Investors may choose to delete civil strife from coverage; the premium rate is typically lowered by 0.10 percent in this case.

Small Contractor's Guarantee Program

The Small Contractor's Guarantee Program assists small business construction and service contractors. The program is limited to small business contractors.

Terms: OPIC will guarantee an eligible financial institution for up to 75 percent of a standby letter of credit or other form of performance or advance-payment guarantee issued on behalf of a contractor. The contractor may also apply for OPIC's political risk insurance for up to 90 percent of that portion of the letter of credit not guaranteed by OPIC. (OPIC insurance programs are covered at length in Chapter Seven)

Contact:
Overseas Private Investment Corporation
Finance Department
1100 New York Avenue, NW
Washington, DC 20527
Tel: (202) 336-8750
Fax: (202) 408-9866

U.S. Agency for International Development

The **U.S. Agency for International Development (USAID)** sponsors several programs related to export finance. The Forfait Guarantee Program is a non-recourse export financing guarantee program that assists U.S. exporters in obtaining financing for exports to USAID-assisted developing countries. Forfaiting is a method of providing fixed-rate financing for international trade transactions.

In a forfait transaction, the importer's bank usually guarantees a series of promissory notes or bills of exchange which cover repayment of a supplier credit provided by the exporter to the importer. The notes are given to the exporter at the time of shipment and become the exporter's property. The notes represent the unconditional and irrevocable commitment of the importer and/or its guarantor (the importer's bank) to pay the notes at maturity. Once the notes become the exporter's property, the exporter can sell them to a third party (called a forfait house) at a discount for immediate cash payments. USAID assists U.S. companies in negotiating guarantee contracts with U.S. banks. Currently, USAID works with three active forfait houses through which its guarantee can facilitate financing for exports in developing countries.

Eligible Exports: Exports that are eligible for financing under the forfait program are manufactured goods such as machinery, spare parts, tools and durable goods.

Terms: Financing guarantees are available for up to five years with the maximum value for exports of $1 million. The buyers must be 100-percent privately owned, legal entities in the country of import.

Contact:
Center for Economic Growth (CEG)
U.S. Agency for International Development
Washington, DC 20523
Tel: (202) 647-7611
Fax: (202) 647-1805

U.S. Department of Agriculture

Export Enhancement Program

The **Export Enhancement Program (EEP)** is a subsidy program that is designed to challenge unfair trading practices and encourage negotiation on agricultural trade problems; expand U.S. market opportunities for certain commodities to targeted destinations; and provide commodities to exporters as bonuses to make U.S. commodities more competitive in global markets by meeting competition from subsidizing countries. Since EEP's establishment in 1985, 112 initiatives have been announced with 75 countries. Sales pertaining to these initiatives have totaled more than $11.5 billion.

Eligibility:

Eligible exporters are those that have at least three years' experience in exporting an eligible commodity. The company must also have an office and agent in the United States, provide evidence of financial responsibility and provide various financial securities in connection with participation.

Agricultural Export Credit Guarantee

The Commercial Export Credit Guarantee Programs (GSM-102 and GSM-103) of the Commodity Credit Corporation (CCC) are designed to expand U.S. agricultural exports by stimulating U.S. bank financing to foreign purchasers. Financing through these programs is available in cases where credit is necessary to increase or maintain U.S. exports to a foreign market and where private financial institutions would be unwilling to provide financing without a guarantee.

CCC covers the risk that a foreign bank might fail to pay under a letter of credit for any reason. Failure to pay could result from bankruptcy of the bank issuing the letter of credit, from foreign exchange controls imposed by the government or for any other reason. In all cases, CCC requires that the foreign buyer's bank issue a letter of credit in favor of the exporter covering payment for the commodities in U.S. dollars. Payment of interest to the U.S. bank that finances the transaction can be covered either by the letter of credit or by a separate loan agreement between the U.S. bank and the foreign buyer's bank. These guarantees cover 98 percent of the principal and most of the interest on loans extended by guaranteed U.S. banks. No coverage is available for ocean freight under the guarantee.

The Export Credit Guarantee Program (GSM-102) provides the exporter or the exporter's assignee with the guaranteed repayment of six-month to three-year loans made to banks in eligible countries where U.S. farm products are purchased. The 1990 Farm Bill authorized $5 billion in GSM-102 guarantees be made available in each fiscal year through 1995, plus an additional $1 billion over the next five years for emerging democracies. Any agricultural commodity may be covered.

The Intermediate Credit Guarantee Program (GSM-103) provides guarantees for three- to ten-year loans. The 1990 Farm Bill directs that not more than $500 million be made available for intermediate guarantees during fiscal years 1990 through 1995.

Eligibility:

Eligible countries include those for which the guarantees are necessary to secure financing of the exports and where there is enough foreign exchange to make the scheduled payments. Commodities are reviewed on a case-by-case basis to determine eligibility.

Rates:

Normally the rate of interest is a fraction above the prime lending rate or the LIBOR, set on a floating basis.

Buffalo International, Inc., a Clearwater, Florida-based exporter of U.S. lumber products, has relied for many years on a small group of buyers in the French West Indies. In 1995, it won an opportunity to diversify into a new market-Mexico. While this sale presented a tremendous opportunity to Buffalo (nearly a 100 percent increase in sales), the buyer's request for two-year financing posed a daunting problem. Lacking resources to provide the financing itself, Buffalo turned to the U.S. Department of Agriculture for assistance. Through the GSM-102 Program of the Commodity Credit Corporation (CCC) Buffalo was able arrange a guaranteed loan for 98 percent of the contract value with the remaining 2 percent held as a receivable from the Mexican buyer. Separately; Buffalo was able to obtain financing for this receivable through an export line of credit backed by credit insurance from the Export-Import Bank of the United States and a working capital guarantee from the Small Business Administration.

Contact:
CCC Operations Division
FAS/USDA
14th Street and Independence Avenue, SW
Washington, DC 20250-1000
Tel: (202) 720-6211
Fax: (202) 720-0938

Facility Guarantee Program

Expected to be operational in late 1995, USDA's Facility Guarantee Program will provide a credit guarantee to U.S. exporters of agricultural equipment to support activities in emerging markets. Although the program criteria have not yet been finalized, USDA expects that the program will provide a 90% guarantee of the U.S. content, following a 15 percent downpayment. In the event of a default, USDA will pay the U.S. exporter and assume title to the accounts receivable.

Contact:
CCC Operations Division
FAS/USDA
14th Street and Independence Avenue, SW
Washington, DC 20250-1035
Tel: (202) 720-1537
Fax: (202) 720-0938

CHAPTER SIX

Investment & Project Financing

Financing for projects in Western Europe and Japan is available from many sources. However, in the developing world, project financing can be difficult to obtain. The federal government and several multilateral organizations can help by extending loans, guarantees, equity, and grants to viable projects. Financing support can fund new projects or expansions of existing operations.

Repayment of project financing is based on the economic viability of the venture. Generally, this financing is offered to project sponsors on a limited, or non-recourse basis: the lender does not look to the project sponsors as the ultimate source of repayment. To facilitate development projects, grace periods may be as long as three years with amortization of up to fifteen years.

Special government-supported investment funds have also been established to complement private and public sources of capital. In most cases, these funds have specific development goals which permit them to assume a higher level of risk without charging unreasonable rates of return. Typically, these funds should be seen as passive equity investors which will exercise limited management control. This chapter details the critical government resources that can be accessed for project financing in primarily the developing world.

The following is a list of key topics on project financing found in Chapter Six:

- U.S. Government Sources of Project Financing
- Multilateral and Foreign Sources Project Financing
- Regional Development Sources of Financing
- Government-Backed Equity Funds.

Loans: U.S. Government Sources of Finance

Overseas Private Investment Corporation

The **Overseas Private Investment Corporation (OPIC)** is an independent U.S. Government agency that encourages mutually beneficial direct U.S. investment in developing countries. In recent years, this role has been expanded to include newly emerging democracies and the fledgling free-market economies.

OPIC assists U.S. investors through three programs: (1) financing investments through direct loans and loan guarantees; (2) insuring investments against a broad range of political risks; and (3) providing a variety of investor services, including advisory services, investment missions and outreach. All of these programs are designed to mitigate the risks associated with overseas investment.

Project Financing

OPIC's loans and loan guarantees are extended in the form of project financing. Project evaluations are based primarily on the economic, technical, marketing and financial soundness of the project. The project must have an adequate cash flow to pay all operational costs, to service all debt and to provide the investment owners with an adequate return. To the extent that such project financing is appropriate, sponsors are not required to pledge their own general credit. For ventures in which project financing is impractical, OPIC will consider more conventional secured lending techniques.

OPIC can provide a significant portion of medium- and long-term funds for financing in countries where conventional financial institutions are frequently reluctant or unable to lend. OPIC programs support private-sector investments in financially viable projects; however, OPIC does not offer concessional terms often associated with government-to-government lending, nor does it finance export sales unrelated to direct investment.

Under certain circumstances, OPIC may purchase equity in a project, including convertible notes and certain other debt instruments with equity participating features. The terms and conditions of such participation are decided on a case-by-case basis.

Eligibility: All projects considered for OPIC financing must be commercially and financially sound. They must be within the demonstrated competence of the proposed management, which must have a proven record of success in the same or closely related business, as well as a significant, continuing financial risk in the enterprise. Investments in which OPIC's share includes equity and/or equity participation are subject to more selective application of these criteria. In addition, any OPIC commitment for a guaranteed loan must be approved by the host country in which the project borrower is located. Eligible enterprises include manufacturing, agricultural production, fishing, forestry, mining, energy development, storage, processing and certain service industries that convey to the host country exceptional developmental benefits. Special emphasis is placed on projects in poorer developing countries and those involving smaller U.S. firms or cooperatives as sponsors.

OPIC's participation in a project is typically limited to $200 million. The minimum project size in generally in the $2-$4 million range.

Financing Plan: Investors must be willing to establish sound debt-to-equity relationships that will not jeopardize the success of the project through insufficient equity or excessive leverage. Although the financial structure may vary with the nature of a specific business and be affected by such factors as the existence of long-term sales contracts, experience indicates that a ratio of 60 percent debt to 40 percent equity is generally satisfactory.

The financing plan should provide funds to meet all costs including feasibility studies, organizational expenses, land, construction, machinery, equipment, training, market development, interest payments during construction, start-up expenses including initial losses, and adequate working capital.

OPIC Participation: The amount of OPIC's commitment varies, taking into consideration the contribution of the project to the host country's development, the financial requirements and the extent to which the financial risks and benefits are spread among the investors and the lenders.

OPIC will assist in designing the financial plan and in coordinating it with other lenders and investors. OPIC will participate in up to 50 percent of the total costs of a new venture; up to 75 percent of total project costs may be considered in the case of the expansion of a successful existing business. OPIC may consider investing in up to 30 percent of the project's equity securities as well. Project sponsors are encouraged to arrange for additional participation from other local and international sources.

Quasi-Equity and Equity Participating Investments: In addition to providing debt capital, OPIC also provides permanent capital through capital stock investments and the purchase of a project's debentures convertible to stock. In these cases, owners share their equity in a project with OPIC, which permits them to reduce their risk exposure and obtain substantially more debt capital for the project.

Making equity investments involves greater investor risk than being a secured creditor of a project. As such, OPIC is very selective in its equity investments, investing only in those projects with highly qualified and experienced management; efficient, strongly competitive operations; and established, market-tested products or services.

OPIC does not seek to acquire a majority stake in any company, to participate in its day-to-day management, or to remain an investor beyond the first few years of operation. An OPIC investment will generally be in the $2 million range, but may be higher in exceptional circumstances. While projects sponsored by U.S. companies of any size are eligible, OPIC will give preferential consideration to projects which include significant involvement by U.S. small businesses or cooperatives.

Application Procedures: Potential project sponsors interested in obtaining financing should provide OPIC with a copy of the business plan for the proposed project. The business plan should establish general eligibility and give OPIC the basis on which to respond to the amount and terms of the requested financing, including:

- A general description of the project;
- Identity, background and the audited financial statements of the project's proposed principal owners and management;
- Planned sources of supply, anticipated output and markets, distribution channels, competition, and the basis for projecting market share;
- Summary of project costs and sources of procurement of capital goods and services;
- Proposed financing plan, including the amount of the proposed OPIC participation and financial projections; and
- Brief statement of the contribution the business is expected to make to local economic and social development.

The sponsors may be asked to provide additional economic, financial and technical information in the formal application for financing; the requested information will vary by project type. The time required to review an application and to commit and close a loan or equity investment varies from three to six months, or longer. Investors are encouraged to consult with OPIC early in the investment process; to coordinate the requirements of other investors, lenders, and host country officials; and to satisfy as many of the requirements as possible.

Contact:
OPIC InfoLine
Overseas Private Investment Corporation
1100 New York Avenue, NW
Washington, DC 20527
Tel: (202) 336-8498
Fax: (202) 408-9859 -- Main fax

Export-Import Bank of the United States

The **Export-Import Bank of the United States (Ex-Im Bank)** is an independent U.S. Government agency that helps finance exports of U.S. goods and services. Ex-Im Bank has also co-financed projects with the U.S. Agency for International Development (USAID), the World Bank and regional development banks to support sound projects. While Ex-Im Bank is not a foreign aid or development agency, its programs can help U.S. exporters participate in development projects.

Project Financing

Through project financing, Ex-Im Bank seeks to assume or share risks to mobilize scarce capital that might otherwise not be available. With this type of financing, Ex-Im Bank provides loans or guarantees for new projects (not expansions) and relies for repayment, wholly or in part, on the cash flow from the project. Project financing does not provide Ex-Im Bank with full recourse to a third-party guarantor such as a government, bank or investor in the project. Ex-Im Bank limited-recourse transactions should involve at least $25 million of U.S. content. They may be structured as BOT (Build-Operate-Transfer), BOOT (Build-Own-Operate-Transfer), BOO (Build-Own-Operate), or variations of these arrangements. The approach excludes asset-based aircraft financing and financing for an existing company.

Ex-Im Bank will consider project financing in any country in which it is not prohibited by U.S. law from doing business. Special criteria may apply in certain markets, depending on Ex-Im Bank's assessment of country risk. Applications are to be submitted by project sponsors and investors, not intermediaries, financial advisors or proposed guaranteed lenders, unless such entities have the written mandate of the project sponsors or investors. Applicants must also complete the standard application form for Ex-Im Bank loans and guarantees.

Application Criteria: Applications to Ex-Im Bank should include a detailed description of the project and be accompanied by completed independent feasibility studies. The projects must involve commercially proven technology and highly competent, experienced contractors. Ex-Im Bank may need to negotiate a government-to-government bilateral agreement (also referred to as an executive agreement) when political risk coverage or comprehensive coverage is being provided. This can be structured as a one-time agreement, referenced by Ex-Im Bank for each subsequent project risk application.

There is a minimum capital requirement for a project finance structure. Equity should be related to the construction-cost cycle of the project. The source of equity for cost overruns must be established. Spread of risk and diversity of equity/debt providers is encouraged. Participation of international institutions and co-lenders, such as official export credit agencies, multilateral development institutions such as the International Finance Corporation, or regional development banks and commercial banks with Ex-Im Bank greatly enhances a proposal.

Ex-Im Bank generally will cover only political risks during the construction/pre-completion stage. It will provide political risk or comprehensive (political and commercial) coverage during the post-completion stage. Repayment terms and grace periods are in accordance with OECD guidelines. Ex-Im Bank's standard commitment fees apply. Applicants should consult the country loan officer concerning commitment fees for split coverage, pre- and post-completion, and exposure fees for project financing applications.

Contact:

Business Development Group
Export-Import Bank of the United States
811 Vermont Avenue, NW
Washington, DC 20571
Tel: (202) 565-3946
Tel: (800) 765-3277
Fax: (202) 565-3931

In May 1990, Ormat, Inc. of Sparks, Nevada, applied for and received a $98 million commitment for a geothermal project in the Philippines from Ex-Im Bank. Because of critical timing, Ex-Im Bank staff processed this application in only four weeks. Although Ormat did not prevail against entrenched international competition from Japan, Italy and France, U.S. Government support for the project gained attention in the Philippines.

Soon after, the U.S. Agency for International Development and Ex-Im Bank announced a Mixed Credit Program (grant and loan) for the region. Ormat was one of the first firms to take advantage of this financial instrument and secured an agreement for a small (almost $30 million) project at Mak Ban in the Philippines. Using the same program, Ormat was also awarded a similar project of an equal dollar amount for the development of the Bacon Manito power center.

Having gained a foothold for an American equipment supplier, Ormat was well positioned to bid on larger projects the following year. In the Spring of 1993, Ormat faced intense competition from Japanese equipment suppliers. Largely thanks to the strong advocacy efforts of the U.S. Department of Commerce and U.S. Embassy personnel in the Philippines, Ormat was awarded a substantial contract for what has become the Upper Mahiao project. In less than six months, Ex-Im Bank approved a critical $162-million project-financing guarantee to finance the export of U.S. geothermal power equipment and services.

U.S. Agency for International Development

The **U.S. Agency for International Development (USAID)** is the government agency responsible for managing U.S. foreign economic and development assistance. USAID economic assistance comes in one of two forms:

- The Commodity Assistance Program (CAP) which is a direct loan or grant to a foreign government or private sector to purchase necessary goods and services

- Project-specific loans or grants requiring the procurement of goods and services for project implementation.

Under both programs, USAID does not oversee or manage the distribution of funds, procurement of goods and services, or project implementation. USAID funding recipients work through private sector organizations and businesses, such as Winrock International or the Pragma Corporation, which are responsible for disbursing funds for procurements and supervising development projects.

With the support of a $5-million, three-year grant from USAID's New Business Development program, the Russian Telecommunication Development Corporation (RTDC), a subsidiary of USWest, will establish three Russian Centers for Business Skills Development. Located in Moscow, St. Petersburg, and Nizhny, these centers will conduct market-based business skills training in a comprehensive fashion, beginning with a "business core" curriculum which will expand into specialized skill areas, cross-functional training, and industry-specific training programs.

The USAID grant will be used primarily to fund the program start-up and leverage the contributions of other Western companies and participants. These training centers will provide affordable training to small and independent Russian business people. RTDC anticipates these centers will become a valuable source of skilled manpower invaluable to business development in the emerging Russian market. Based upon the success of the initial three centers, RTDC plans to establish as many as twelve centers in the next five years.

Center for Economic Growth

The **Center for Economic Growth (CEG),** a division of the Bureau for Global Affairs at USAID, will consider market-term financing for projects in developing countries through its Private-Sector Revolving Fund. Projects in a number of industry sectors are eligible. For loans or loan guarantees, the CEG will consider only private enterprises with substantial local ownership. Sponsors must be either host-country nationals, U.S.

firms or U.S. citizens. Projects must have a substantial developmental impact, provide sound sustainable development, generate net employment opportunities, earn net foreign exchange, develop managerial and technical skills, and/or transfer technologies.

Loans may be used to capitalize a new enterprise and/or expand an existing enterprise. Revolving fund managers give priority to innovative and financially viable projects benefiting mainly smaller businesses in developing countries which can serve as models for replication in other countries. Increasingly, financing is offered in conjunction with USAID Mission financing.

Terms: CEG has flexibility in negotiating terms and conditions depending on the nature, risk and developmental impact of the project. Financing is available for up to $3 million, with emphasis in the range of $250,000 to $1 million, but never more than 25 percent of total project cost. The maximum term of the loan is 10 years with a negotiable grace period for principal repayment. There are no fixed or minimum requirements for collateral. Repayment is on a semi-annual or annual basis.

Prospective sponsors must demonstrate that they meet the given criteria and submit a business plan to CEG. The plan should include:

- Project description;
- Financing requirements (from all sources);
- Technical, marketing, and financial plan;
- Legal requirements; and
- Management and implementation plan.

As much detail as possible should be included under each of the major topic areas described above. Any other factors or commitments critical to project success should be included as well.

Small Business Loan Portfolio Guarantee (LPG)

The **Small Business Loan Portfolio Guarantee (LPG) Program** under USAID's Center for Economic Growth features a loan guarantee program that allows financial institutions throughout the world to increase their level of small business lending to both new and existing customers. The LPG Program allows for credit guarantees of up to 50 percent of the principal amount of new small business loans.

Terms: Guarantees are available for up to $3 million on loan portfolios of $6 million. The initial guarantee period is three years and is renewable for a total of up to nine years.

Eligibility: The LPG program is available to selected private banks and financial institutions engaged in or wishing to expand their small business lending in USAID-assisted countries.

Eligible Loans: Guarantees cover small business loans made to finance any productive or commercial activity, subject to limited restrictions. Maximum loan size to a small business is $150,000. Guarantees may include credit issued through loans, lines of credit, finance leases, overdrafts, commercial letters of credit and other instruments.

Fees: A commitment fee to contract loan guarantee coverage is required. (The standard fee is 0.5 percent of the U.S. Government contingent liability.) Competitive annual utilization fees are based on the level of guarantee coverage actually used. Rates are comparable those for similar letter of credit facilities.

Contact:
Center for Economic Growth
U.S. Agency for International Development
Bureau of Global Affairs
320 21st Street, NW
Washington, DC 20523
Tel: (202) 663-2660
Fax: (202) 663-2670

Housing Guaranty Program (HGP)

Through its **Housing Guaranty Program (HGP)**, USAID provides loan guarantees tosupport debt financing for housing and related municipal and infrastructure projects (e.g.,water and wastewater treatment, etc.) in emerging markets around the world. The HGP involves collaboration with a host-country housing institution acting as borrower, including government ministries, national housing banks, housing development corporations, or similar public and private institutions. Local development and commercial banks can also be used as the obligor. Based upon the USAID guaranty, the borrower seeks the most favorable terms and pricing for the loan from U.S. capital markets.

USAID typically seeks to arrange a total facility for each country under which several sub-loans may be made for individual projects. The term of each sub-loan can be up to 30 years, with up to a 10-year grace period on principal. Interest rates are typically priced at a spread above U.S. government borrowing costs of a similar maturity. Also, USAID requires that projects in most countries generally provide affordable housing (i.e., housing that is affordable to a local buyer whose income is equal to the median income for that particular market).

Contact:
Director, Office of Housing and Urban Programs
U.S. Agency for International Development
320 21st Street, NW
Washington, DC 20523
Tel: (703) 875-4903

Multilateral and Foreign Sources of Finance

International Bank for Reconstruction and Development (World Bank)

The **World Bank** extends between $21 billion and $24 billion in loans and credits to developing countries each year. A portion of this financial and technical assistance generates contracting opportunities for U.S. suppliers of goods and services.

U.S. companies have traditionally fared well in World Bank procurement. In 1992, U.S. suppliers to World Bank- and International Development Association-financed projects received contracts amounting to $1.3 billion. However, as World Bank assistance programs have expanded and developed, so has foreign competition for project-related bids.

The World Bank's mission falls into four general investment and development goals:

- To lend funds to developing countries
- To provide advice and technical assistance
- To serve as a catalyst to stimulate investment in developing countries
- To create an atmosphere for development.

The World Bank finances projects in developing countries by making large loans with long maturities (15 to 20 years) and grace periods (five years). Loans must be made for productive purposes and must stimulate economic growth. Loans are made to or guaranteed by the borrowing government. The World Bank's decision to lend must be based on economic considerations alone. The use of loans cannot be restricted to purchases in any particular member country.

Typically, the Bank finances about 40 percent of total project costs. Supplemental funding is provided by the borrowing country, other agencies and commercial bank enterprises. To illustrate, the Bank's 1992 lending commitments of $21.7 billion generated between $50 and 60 billion in total project investment.

The Bank lends funds for a variety of carefully selected and clearly defined projects. These projects, which generally require the borrowing country to buy goods, civil works, and services in the international marketplace, offer many business opportunities. About 30,000 contracts are awarded to firms annually by borrowers of Bank funds. Approximately 70 percent are for goods and equipment, 20 percent for civil works, and 10 percent for consulting services.

There are two basic categories of lending activities -- investment loans and adjustment loans. Investment loans, by far the most common type of lending, account for more than 75 percent of the Bank's total annual commitments. These loans finance individual projects and segments of a country's investment program in a specific sector, such as transportation or agriculture.

Adjustment lending includes structural adjustment loans (SALs) and sector adjustment loans (SECALs). SALs help countries reform economic and fiscal policies and address balance of payments problems. SECALs support more narrowly focused reforms in a particular sector.

Any Bank member country with an annual per capita income below the borrowing threshold level -- $4,095 in FY 1991 -- may apply for loans or credits. The borrower may be a government, a government agency, or a private enterprise or institution that can obtain the government's guarantee.

International Development Association

The **International Development Association (IDA)** was formed in 1960, to complement World Bank activities in lesser developed countries. IDA provides low-cost, long-term loans and technical assistance to eligible borrowers. The funds are used for basic investments in infrastructure and social development which could not be funded on reasonable terms by private capital markets. IDA is a combined banking institution and development agency in the World Bank Group, providing credit to countries with annual per capita incomes of less than $1,235.

Since 1960, IDA has lent more than $75 billion to promote development. Currently, 70 countries are eligible to borrow from IDA. Most of IDA's lending goes to countries with annual per capita incomes of $765 or less, nearly half of which are in Africa. The remainder of IDA funds go to poor countries in Asia, Latin America, Eastern Europe and the Middle East. IDA projects focus on peace and national security, international trade, environmental protection, illegal immigration and global and regional problems.

IDA funding is provided by contributions from 34 donor countries, an occasional contribution from IBRD profits, and repayment of IDA credits. Loans have a 10-year grace period and must be repaid in 35 or 40 years. IDA concessional credits are administered by the same World Bank staff which processes and monitors IBRD market-term loans. Unlike IBRD lending, IDA credits may only be extended to governments or government agencies.

Based on donor contributions and expected revenues from loan repayment, IDA expects to make concessional loans amounting to $22 billion between 1993 and the year 2000. The seven largest donors to IDA are: the United States, Japan, Germany, France, the United Kingdom, Italy, and Canada.

Contact:
International Bank for Reconstruction and Development
1818 H Street, NW
Washington, DC 20433

General Project Procurement Information Contact:
Tel: (202) 458-4090
Fax: (202) 477-0623

International Finance Corporation

The **International Finance Corporation (IFC)**, a member of the World Bank Group, invests in private ventures in developing countries by providing equity financing and loans without government guarantees in collaboration with other investors. Always a minority partner, IFC seeks project sponsors from industrial and developing countries around the world with which it can form joint enterprises. IFC investment projects range from $4 million to several hundred million dollars and are carried out with the cooperation of its 154 member countries.

IFC does not require government guarantees for its financing. In its project financing role, IFC provides loans and makes equity investments. Like a private financial institution, IFC prices its finance and services in line with the market as much as possible, taking into account the cost of its funds and seeking profitable returns. IFC shares full project risks with its partners.

IFC will finance up to 25 percent of a project's cost in a variety of forms depending on the needs of the project. IFC offers technical and advisory services, assembles financing packages, unites investors and arranges syndications with banks. IFC staff and consultants can assist in designing a project, appraise its prospects and help to secure cost savings and efficient management. The staff will assess the technical and market aspects of the project, but will not conduct feasibility studies. All projects are reviewed to ensure compliance with World Bank and local environmental policies and guidelines.

IFC seeks to identify projects suitable for financing and works closely with project sponsors to develop bankable projects. It also performs a preliminary assessment of the project's viability. Projects that are satisfactory in these respects are carefully tracked and IFC assists the sponsors, if necessary, to strengthen the project.

The International Finance Corporation (IFC) recently provided a financing package worth over $62 million to support the establishment of a joint venture in Thailand involving National Medical Enterprises (NME) of the United States. The IFC's investment consists of a direct loan of $25 million, a syndicated loan of $35 million, and an equity/subordinated debt component of $2.2 million. The project, estimated to be worth over $111 million, will pay for the construction of 530-bed hospital in Bangkok, to meet a growing demand for medical services.

IFC's financial involvement was instrumental in allowing NME and its Thai partner to build an appropriately-sized hospital. Consequently, the hospital will be more competitive and better able to deliver higher-quality service to the local population.

There is no standard IFC application form. IFC requires certain preliminary information to make an initial determination of project viability: a description of the project; information on sponsorship, management and technical assistance; environmental impact; general market information; technical feasibility; an estimate of investment requirements, project financing and expected returns; and an anticipated timetable for project preparation and completion.

In addition to its investment role, other IFC international support activities include:

- Providing advice to the private sector and public sector on the institutional setting needed to attract foreign/local investment in projects;

- Country-wide studies to assess the role of the private sector in providing goods and services, to identify specific market opportunities and to promote this market; and

- Participation in the Global Environment Facility, through the development and co-financing of investment projects as well as technical assistance and research related to the protection of biological diversity, global warming, pollution of international waters and the depletion of the stratospheric ozone layer.

Contact:
International Finance Corporation
1850 Eye Street, NW
Room I-10157
Washington, DC 20433
Tel: (202) 473-0661
Fax: (202) 676-9495

Asian Development Bank

The **Asian Development Bank (ADB)** helps to accelerate economic and social growth in the Asia/Pacific region by providing financial and technical assistance for projects that will help developing member countries. The technology representative focuses on energy and environmental infrastructure projects in the region. In public sector projects, ADB follows strict International Competitive Bid (ICB) guidelines. ADB's experience with private sector projects has been limited to small projects with indigenous entrepreneurs, where its participation has not exceeded $5 million. The recent reorganization of ADB allows substantial resources to be committed to major capital projects, particularly those using the Build-Operate-Transfer (BOT) format. ADB's program criteria dictate that proposed projects must be targeted to member countries. The project must have the approval of the principal planning and financial authorities of the host government, which will be confirmed through ongoing discussions between ADB and host-government personnel.

ADB is a major lender for infrastructure and agricultural development in Asia. As a result of the recent wave of privatization of industry throughout the region, ADB's relatively small private-sector investment arm has become more widely used in ADB's operations. This reorganization is expected to make ADB a significant force in Build-Operate-Transfer (BOT) type projects.

For direct loans made by ADB, the loan agreement sets out the terms and conditions of the loan, including those relating to payment of principal, interest and other charges, maturities and dates of repayment. Interest charged by ADB on loans from ordinary capital resources (OCR) and the service charge on loans from Special Funds are computed on the outstanding amount of the loan. ADB also charges a commitment fee on loans made from OCR.

The borrower is normally permitted to draw on the loan only to meet expenditures in connection with the project as they are incurred. In the interest of economy and efficiency, the ADB generally requires that borrowers seek competitive bids from potential suppliers in ADB member countries; engineering plans and specifications be drawn up independently of the suppliers; and, if appropriate, independent consulting engineers be retained by borrowers.

Except in special circumstances, ADB requires that loan proceeds or other financing by ADB be used only for procurement of goods and services produced in member countries. ADB adjusts its variable lending rate in January and July of each year.

Financing Policies: ADB lends to public and private entities. Projects will not be supported without approval from the host country. In 1992, Bank lending co-financed 22 projects and programs worth $3.15 billion in loans, or roughly 34 percent of all loans ADB approved that year. ADB will take equity interests to encourage the financing of private-sector sources in developing member countries. ADB will also participate in sector and cross-country loans and equity financing.

ADB determines loan terms based on the type of loan made. Loans from the Bank's ordinary capital resources carry variable rates that are adjusted every six months. Loans to poorer developing countries from special funds have a fixed repayment period of 40 years and have a 10-year grace period. Ordinary capital loans have a maturity period between 10 and 30 years, with grace periods ranging from three to seven years. Program loans are over 15 years, including a three-year grace period. Private-sector loans have maturities of up to 12 years, with suitable grace periods, and carry either a fixed-rate or a floating rate above the London Inter-Bank Offer Rate (LIBOR).

Application Information: No application form exists for project financing. To submit a potential project for consideration for financing, contact the appropriate industry and geographic section of ADB. The following information is generally required to evaluate most projects:

- The proposed borrower's business history;
- Project description and project operation plans;
- Feasibility studies, pre-investment surveys, and other technical and financial feasibility information;
- Amount of loan requested and estimates of project cost;
- Financial performance estimates and cash-flow projections; and
- Volume and value of annual sales.

ADB will pay particular attention to the economic viability, technical feasibility and financial stability of the proposed project in the application review. The amount financed from ADB varies between 40 and 80 percent.

Contact:

Headquarters
Asian Development Bank
P.O. Box 789
1099 Manila, Philippines
Tel: 011 (63-2) 711-3851
Fax: 011 (63-2) 741-7961, 632-6816

Senior Commercial Officer
#6 ADB Avenue
Mandaluyong Metro Manila
Tel: 011(63) 2-632-813-3284/6054
Fax: 011(63) 2-632-816-7684/4003

Asian Development Bank Liaison
Office of Multilateral Development Bank Operations
U.S. & Foreign Commercial Service
U.S. Department of Commerce
14th Street and Constitution Avenue, NW
Washington, DC 20230
Tel: (202) 482-4333
Fax: (202) 273-0927

African Development Bank

The **African Development Bank (AfDB)**, headquartered in Abidjan, Côte d'Ivoire, has committed more than $22.3 billion for over 1,600 loans and grants to 51 African countries since it began operations in 1966. AfDB is the major source of external public financing on the continent, having committed nearly $3 billion in new loans and grants in 1992.

Project Finance

AfDB assists financially viable projects which have significant economic merit and catalyze the flow of domestic and external resources. Bank assistance is provided directly to private enterprises and financial institutions and is also available indirectly through private financial institutions such as development, commercial and merchant banks. The AfDB may use a number of financial instruments, including equity and term loans. The nature, terms and conditions of the Bank's investment in a particular venture depend on the risks and expected returns of the venture, as well as the characteristics of the entity receiving the financing.

The total amount of AfDB assistance to an enterprise, including loans and equity investment, will not normally exceed one third of the total cost of the project. The size of an AfDB loan will generally be in the range of $100,000 to $10 million. The Bank encourages growth of private enterprise in Africa and does not wish to compete with private sources of finance. Its role is to stimulate and support initiatives by private entrepreneurs, investors, and bankers, and to provide direct financial support for eligible projects.

An AfDB equity investment will not normally exceed 25 percent of the share capital of the enterprise and will normally not be smaller than $100,000. AfDB will not agree to be the largest single shareholder in a venture.

Eligibility: Financial assistance may be considered for specific projects and investment programs and investment programs to establish, expand, diversify, rehabilitate and modernize productive facilities in a variety of sectors. Privately owned and managed enterprises eligible for financing may be partly foreign owned. For AfDB to be involved in a project, it must be satisfied that the project is consistent with the country's economic and development objectives and possesses sufficient comparative advantage to be likely to succeed.

Contact:

African Development Bank
P.O. Box 1387
Abidjan 01
Côte d'Ivoire
Private Sector Development Unit
Tel: 011 (225) 20-41-68
Fax: 011 (225) 20-49-64

US&FCS - AfDB
AfDB Liaison Officer
U.S. Embassy Abidjan
5 Rue Jesse Owens
01 B.P. 1712
Abidjan 01, Côte d'Ivoire
Tel: 011 (225) 22-24-37
Fax: 011 (225) 21-46-16

European Bank for Reconstruction & Development

The **European Bank for Reconstruction and Development (EBRD)** lends and invests exclusively for projects and investment programs in the countries of Central and Eastern Europe, including the former Soviet Union. In 1993, EBRD approved 91 investment projects, bringing the total number of projects approved since its inauguration to 156. The total amount of approved financing reached 2.27 billion ECU (approximately $4.0 billion).

Project Finance

The EBRD generally does not finance the total cost of an operation. Rather, it plays a catalytic role in stimulating capital and investment from other sources, both public and private. With limited resources relative to the scale of need in the region, the EBRD emphasizes the quality of its projects and the added value it brings to them. The EBRD requires that its projects have a "multiplier effect," such as demonstration value, mobilization of co-financing, or relief of infrastructural bottlenecks that constrain private-sector development. The EBRD assists projects that encounter difficulty in securing financing by sharing and minimizing investor risk; promoting foreign direct investment; encouraging co-financing by reducing risk through its preferred creditor status; enabling mobilization of domestic capital; and complementing the efforts of other lenders. In many cases, co-financing commercial banks are willing to participate only on the condition of EBRD involvement. Foreign joint ventures are a major component of EBRD lending, accounting for 28.5 percent of the total portfolio and 45.8 percent of private-sector investments.

Terms: EBRD funding is on market terms, rather than on subsidized or concessionary terms, although it has a substantial number of Technical Cooperation grant funds to provide appropriate advisory or training services. EBRD raises most of its funds through the sales of AAA-rated bonds on international capital markets.

Eligibility: Public sector requests for financing are normally submitted to the EBRD by the host government or public authority sponsoring the project; proposals by private enterprises operating in the public sector are also considered. These proposals are reviewed by the EBRD's Development Banking Vice Presidency. Private-sector requests are usually submitted directly to the EBRD by the commercial enterprises seeking finance. These enterprises can be from one of the countries in which the Bank operates or from elsewhere in the world. Proposals are reviewed by EBRD's Merchant Banking Vice Presidency, involving a full assessment of project merits and a timely processing of credit decisions. The EBRD maintains strict confidentiality on private-sector funding proposals and does not publish operational, procurement or other general information about such transactions.

Contact:
Headquarters
Office of the U.S. Director
European Bank for Reconstruction and Development
One Exchange Square
London EC2A 2EH
United Kingdom
Tel: 011 (44-171) 338-6000
Fax: 011 (44-171) 338-6100

Inter-American Development Bank

The **Inter-American Development Bank (IDB)**, headquartered in Washington, DC, has been a major lender to its Latin American and Caribbean members since its inception in 1959. Its cumulative lending and technical cooperation amounted to $56.8 billion by the end of 1992. The IDB is currently the principal source of external finance for most Latin American countries.

Project Finance

The IDB finances projects up to a certain percentage, ranging from 50 percent for the more economically developed countries to 80 percent for the poorer countries. The borrower finances the remainder with local resources. For the least developed member countries, the Bank may use its concessional resources to finance up to 90 percent of a project.

Terms: The terms and conditions of loans depend on the resources used. Amortization periods of loans provided with ordinary capital resources range from 15 to 25 years. Interest rates charged on these loans reflect the costs incurred by the IDB in borrowing funds on the world's capital markets. The interest rate for loans approved after January 1990 is adjusted semi-annually and is applicable to outstanding balances, not solely to future disbursements. The IDB uses the different currencies derived from the subscriptions and contributions of all of its member countries and from borrowings in the world's capital markets. Freely convertible currency is used by the IDB to finance the direct and indirect foreign-exchange costs of a project; domestic currencies are used to finance local costs.

Eligibility: Public and private entities in the Latin American member countries, including national and regional authorities, are eligible to borrow from the IDB. However, the IDB does not finance projects if the host government objects to such financing. The IDB generally requires that loans to private entities be guaranteed by the government.

Special Programs

In order to promote infrastructure projects in Latin American and Caribbean countries, the IDB recently introduced a new program to support private-sector involvement in such projects. Under this program, the IDB can provide loans, loan guarantees, and credit enhancements for private-sector infrastructure projects. Loans and loan guarantees are available up to the lesser of 25 percent of the project cost or $75 million. What makes this program attractive is that unlike the rest of IDB's programs, these loans and loan guarantees do not require a government counter-guarantee.

Separately, many such private-sector infrastructure projects are unable to raise financing because they are dependent on the performance of a para-statal organization (e.g., a state utility company buying power under a take-or-pay arrangement with a private power generator). Many such organizations do not have the financial or operating track record to satisfy potential project lenders and investors. Because of ongoing privatization and decentralization trends, many governments are unwilling to provide explicit guarantees to the lenders/investors to cover the risks of their para-statals. Under this new program, the IDB can also provide credit enhancements to private lenders. Such enhancements can either extend the terms of the loan (e.g., from 12 to 15 years) or cover certain obligations of the government, such as the performance of a para-statal, the right of the project to convert local currency, etc. Under this structure, the local government would provide its guarantee to the IDB, which would typically be less explicit than one provided to private lenders, and the IDB in turn would provide its guarantee to the lender. There are no dollar limits on these credit enhancements.

This program will focus on water/wastewater, roads and ports, power, and telecommunications projects. All eligible projects must meet the IDB's lending and developmental criteria for the appropriate host country. The majority of shareholders in the project must be IDB members. (IDB members include all of Latin America, the Caribbean, the United States, Canada, Western Europe, Israel, and Japan.)

Contact:
Headquarters
Inter-American Development Bank
1300 New York Avenue, NW
Washington, DC 20577
Tel: (202) 623-1000

Inter-American Investment Corporation

The **Inter-American Investment Corporation (IIC)**, an affiliate of the Inter-American Development Bank (IDB), provides financing for private-sector investment projects in Latin America and the Caribbean. IIC was capitalized in 1986 with $200 million. A primary objective of IIC is to promote the development of private enterprise in IDB's regional member countries. To ensure that projects comply with international standards, home-country laws, and Inter-American Development Bank criteria, the IIC screens all projects for environmental sustainability as well as economic viability.

IIC provides loans, including subordinated and convertible loans, and makes capital investments. Additional support may be provided in the form of guarantees or surety bonds to back loans or the placement of shares and obligations. IIC will provide between $2 million and $10 million per project. In 1993 alone, the Board of Executive Directors approved financing for 31 transactions totaling $123.7 million. In addition to funding, IIC offers financial counseling for preparation of feasibility studies.

Eligibility: Although all economic sectors are eligible, only small- and medium-sized companies may qualify for IIC financing. In addition, a minimum of 51-percent local ownership is required. The IIC considers partners from other Latin American and Caribbean member countries as local ownership. Eligible projects must meet one or more of the following feasibility and economic efficiency criteria:

- Assist in the promotion and use of material and human resources in IIC member countries;
- Provide incentives for job creation;
- Promote savings and the use of capital in productive investment;
- Assist in the generation and/or savings of foreign exchange;
- Stimulate management skills and the transfer of technological know-how; and
- Mobilize broader public participation in company ownership, through participation of the greatest possible number of investors in the capital stock of such companies.

Terms: IIC loans are denominated in U.S. dollars for maximum amortization periods of 12 years, including up to a five-year grace period. Loans may be granted at a fixed rate based on U.S. Treasury bonds rates plus a margin; or a variable rate based on six-month London Inter-Bank Offer Rate (LIBOR) plus a margin.

Financing for new projects in the region can cover up to 33 percent of total project costs and up to 50 percent for expansion of existing projects. Financing is not contingent upon government guarantees or the procurement of goods and services in any given country, and may be used for both local and foreign currency costs, including fixed assets, working capital and pre-operating expenses.

Application Procedures: The sponsor of a potential project should provide the IIC with the following preliminary information:

- Description of the project;
- Brief history of the company and its management;
- Market studies and anticipated output and sales for the project;
- Technical viability and summary of operating expenses;
- Proposed financing plan, including the amount of IIC participation anticipated and financial projections;
- Information about environmental impact of the production process; and
- Brief statement on the project's contribution to local economic and social development, government policies relevant to industry, and government controls of exchange or use of foreign currency.

Contact:
General Manager
Inter-American Investment Corporation
1300 New York Avenue, NW
Washington, DC 20577
Tel: (202) 623-3902
Fax: (202) 623-2360

The involvement of the Inter-American Investment Corporation (IIC) in Hidroelectrica Platanar, S.A., of Costa Rica reflects the new trend toward privatization of electric power generation. The Inter-American Development Bank referred the company to IIC for help in obtaining long-term financing. IIC will lend $6 million of the $20 million project to construct a 15-megawatt hydroelectric plant in northeast Costa Rica. IIC involvement has helped to attract other financial institutions to the project. No governmental guarantees are contemplated in the financial plan. The project design was reviewed for negative impact on water, land, people, and forests, and for seismic risk. It complies with environmental standards as set by the Costa Rican Ministry of Natural Resources and Mines and involves a substantial reforestation program. Projects such as Hidroelectrica Platanar, by creating a new energy source based on a natural renewable resource, are the key to Costa Rica's energy growth and conservation strategy. By lessening Costa Rica's dependence on imported fossil fuels, the project will also help conserve scarce foreign exchange.

Regional Development Sources of Finance

North American Development Bank (NADBank)

The **North American Development Bank (NADBank)**, which was created following the ratification of the North American Free Trade Agreement (NAFTA), is dedicated to financing border development, environmental improvement projects, and providing support for community adjustment and investment for the United States and Mexico. NADBank was created to ease environmental concerns and questions of trade dislocation on the part of the United States following the rapid industrialization and development of the Mexican border region. Established with a capital base of $450 million, the NADBank will be further capitalized by $2.55 billion of callable capital from the United States and Mexico. In contrast with other development banks, the NADBank will provide project-related loans, equity participation, and credit enhancement for a focused type of development project. At this stage, the NADBank has not fully defined its mandate in Mexico beyond border environmental-remediation projects. Projects that seek NADBank financing must first be approved by the Border Environment Cooperation Commission (BECC), a bi-national organization which requires that projects observe environmental laws and that project goals are in the local and national interest. Co-financing with the World Bank and Inter-American Development Bank (IDB) will also be an important aspect of NADBank's financing strategy for environmental projects.

Contact:
Office of the Assistant Secretary for International Affairs
U.S. Department of the Treasury
15th Street and Pennsylvania Avenue, NW
Washington, DC 20220
Tel: (202) 622-1850
Fax: (202) 622-0417

Japan Development Bank (JDB)

The **Japan Development Bank (JDB)** has over 100 loan programs for a wide variety of capital investments and R&D expenditures. It also has established a Loan Division in the International Department to serve foreign-owned corporations. The loans are used for the acquisition of property, plant equipment, and specified non-capital expenditures in Japan.

Lending conditions, such as interest rates, for a particular project depend on the degree of policy relevance of the given project.

Terms & Conditions:

- **Interest Rate:** The maximum rate is set as the standard rate, equal to the long-term prime rate provided by long-term credit banks. Several preferential rates, described as Level 1-5, are available below the standard rate, depending on the priority attached to the project in terms of policy relevance. Although the rates are revised according to current financial conditions, the rates applied are fixed at the time that funds are disbursed and remain fixed throughout the loan period. For the latest rate levels, contact the nearest JDB office.

- **Amounts:** In principle, the upper limit of the loan is approximately 40 to 60 percent of the project's total required funds. The percentage can vary subject to the availability of JDB resources. There is no upper limit on the amount of the loan.

- **Loan Term:** The loan term is based on the project's profitability, durability and other factors; the average loan term is 15 years. Grace periods of up to three years may be offered with loans.

- **Repayment:** Repayment of principal shall be made in regular installments. Interest accrued between each repayment shall be paid at the end of the accrual period on the stipulated payment day, together with the payment of the principal.

- **Collateral:** Required in principle; guarantor is occasionally required.

Nippon R-M Co., Ltd., a manufacturer specializing in automobile refinishing paint, was created as a 50-50 joint venture between Germany's BASF AG and Japan's NOF Corp. in 1971. In April 1994, through the use of JDB's "Import Facilities Loan Programme," Nippon R-M completed construction of a new, three-story building to be used as corporate headquarters and a staff training center. Automobile dealerships and body painters are the targeted users of the training center where Nippon R-M will introduce new color-matching technologies and environmentally sound paints to their customers. Through these activities, Nippon R-M plans to expand their customer base and increase import sales of company products.

For Import Facilities Enhancement:

The interest rate level for this loan programme is up to 0.5% reduction from level 5. Level 5 is based on the government 10-year bond rate and the most preferential rate in the JDB's interest structure.

(For the lowest rate levels, please contact the nearest JDB office.)

PROMOTION OF FOREIGN DIRECT INVESTMENT IN JAPAN

Eligible Companies	Importers, wholesalers or retailers of manufactured goods and processed foods listed in sections 0,1,5,6,7 and 8 of the Standard International Trade Classification.
Eligible Projects	Investment projects in Japan for promoting imports involving the purchase or construction of facilities with the following functions: Inspection, quality improvement and adjustment of products to meet local standards and specifications; expediting distribution, collection of cargo, storage, repacking and package processing; after-sale service; display, exhibition and sales of goods and samples; leasehold facilities for the above mentioned purposes.
Interest Rate	The interest rate level for this loan program is level 5, which is the most preferential rate in the JDB's interest rate structure. In addition, as a part of an emergency financial package announced by the Japanese government in August, 1993, this rate level will be lowered by March 31, 1994. The lower rate changes according to the fluctuation of interest rate level 5 within a 0.4 to 0.5 percent range. (For the lowest rate levels, please contact the JDB office nearest you.)

OTHER PROGRAMS

In addition to these two programs, JDB provides funds for wide variety of capital investments and R&D expenditures. Some of the loan programs utilized by foreign corporations are:

- Special research for high-technology fields
- Projects involving newly developed technology
- Intelligent buildings
- Regional development
- Technopolis
- Promotion of Technology in Areas Suitable for Industry

Development of Industry in Specified Regional Areas
- Upgrading reliability of information devices
- Telecommunications
- Biotechnology
- Software, information processing

Eligibility:

Foreign companies and foreign-affiliated companies are eligible for all of JDB's loan programs.

For Import Facilities Enhancement:

<u>Eligible Companies</u>

Importers, wholesalers or retailers of manufactured goods and processed foods listed in sections 0, 1, 5, 6, 7 and 8 of the Standard International Trade Classification.

<u>Eligible Projects</u>

Investment projects in Japan for promoting imports involving the purchase or construction of facilities with the following functions:
- Inspection, quality improvement and adjustment of products to meet local standards and specifications.
- Expediting distribution, collection of cargo, storage, repacking and package processing.
- After-sale service.
- Display, exhibition and sales of goods and samples.
- Leasehold facilities for the above-mentioned purposes.

For Promotion of Direct Investment in Japan:

<u>Eligible Companies:</u>

Any company of any nationality.

For Promotion of International and Joint R&D Projects

<u>Eligible Companies</u>

Foreign companies or foreign-owned companies (whose foreign capital ratio is 50% or more) and Japanese companies.

Eligible Projects

A project must meet the following qualifications:

- R&D expenditure for the joint development of new technology conducted in Japan by Japanese and foreign companies;

- The technology shall be related to high-technology fields (such as electronics and fine chemicals); and

- The funds or talents needed for the R&D shall be shared by Japanese and foreign companies.

Contact:
International Cooperation Department
Japan Development Bank
9-1, Otemachi 1-chome
Chiyoda-ku, Tokyo 100, Japan
Tel: 011 (81) 3-3244-1785
Fax: 011 (81) 3-3245-1938
Telex: J24343 DEVEBANK
Cable: DEVEBANK TOKYO

Additional Addresses:
Washington
Chief Representative
Japan Development Bank
1101 17th Street, NW
Washington, DC 20036
Tel: (202) 331-8696
Fax: (202) 293-3932

New York
Chief Representative
Japan Development Bank
575 Fifth Avenue, 28th Floor
New York, NY 10017
Tel: (212) 949-7550
Fax: (212) 949-7558

Los Angeles
Chief Representative
Japan Development Bank
601 South Figueroa Street, Suite 4450
Los Angeles, CA 90017-5748
Tel: (213) 362-2980
Fax: (213) 362-2983

Applied Materials, Inc. of Santa Clara, California, is a top U.S. firm in the semi-conductor fabrication equipment industry. In 1983, Applied Materials Japan (AMJ), a wholly owned subsidiary, needed to modify systems and begin development work in Japan. Specifically, AMJ wanted a new, massive technology center in Japan. At that time, no wholly non-Japanese-owned firm had received funding from the Japan Development Bank. Due to the support of the local prefecture government (in which the AMJ wanted to build) and because of the presence of Japanese executives and negotiators at AMJ who understood Japanese business practices and reflected a long-term commitment by AMJ, JDB granted the loan. AMJ also received further funding from the JDB for research and development activities.

Overseas Economic Cooperation Fund

The **Overseas Economic Cooperation Fund (OECF)**, a development finance institution funded by the Japanese government, principally assists developing countries in their self-help efforts by supplying low-interest, long-term loans. Established in 1961, the OECF provides approximately $9.4 billion a year in various types of Official Development Assistance (ODA) loans to foreign governments, plus about $94 million per year in non-ODA loans and equity investment to projects of (primarily Japanese) corporations operating in developing countries. OECF also finances development projects with other financial institutions such as the Asian Development Bank and the World Bank. The majority of OECF loans and services are extended in accordance with untied international competitive bidding procedures.

Over the past decade, Japan has become increasingly involved in global development projects. Japanese ODA to developing countries totals more than $10 billion per year. At the 1992 Global Climate Change meeting in Rio de Janeiro, Japan pledged to spend $9 billion over the next five years to tackle global environment issues.

Eligibility: OECF loans are provided only to governments (or public entities guaranteed by government). Eligibility for private sector loans and equity investment depends principally on two factors: difficulty obtaining funds on normal commercial terms from traditional financial institutions, and the project must be intended to promote the economic development and welfare of developing countries.

Terms: The repayment period of OECF loans is 25 to 30 years, with an average of 28 years. This includes a grace period, which varies from seven to ten years. The average interest rate is about 2.5 percent. OECF loans are generally denominated in Japanese yen, but may be in currencies other than yen.

Contact:
Overseas Economic Cooperation Fund
Headquarters
Takebashi Godo Building
4-1, Otemachi 1-chome, Chiyoda-ku
Tokyo 100, Japan
Tel: 011 (81) 3 215-1311
Fax: 011 (81) 3 201-5982, 201-8309

Washington, DC Office
2100 Pennsylvania Avenue, NW
Suite 535
Washington, DC 20037
Tel: (202) 463-7492
Fax: (202) 463-7496

Andean Development Corporation

The **Andean Development Corporation (Corporacion Andina de Formento-CAF)**, headquartered in Venezuela, began operations in 1970. CAF provides technical and financial support for a variety of industry sectors in the Andean countries of Bolivia, Colombia, Ecuador, Peru and Venezuela.

CAF's authorized capital amounts to $2.1 billion, $900 million of which represents subscribed capital consisting of $453 million of paid-in capital and $448 million of guarantee capital. In addition to its capital resources, CAF conducts fund-raising activities with international public and private financial institutions, including the Inter-American Development Bank, the U.S. Agency for International Development, and private international banks.

Short- to long-term financing is available through various CAF operational programs, including Technical Cooperation, Pre-Investment Loans, Project Execution Loans, Equity Participation in Andean Multinational Corporations, and Trade Financing.

Project Execution Loans

Project Execution Loans can be utilized to finance most implementation aspects of a specific project. This loan mechanism cannot be used for land acquisition or payment of taxes.

Loans available through this mechanism for projects in Colombia, Peru, and Venezuela are a maximum of 70 percent of total project costs and a minimum of $500,000. For projects in Bolivia and Ecuador, loan amounts can range from $250,000 up to 80 percent of the total project cost. Interest rates are established according to the actual cost of CAF resources which are based on London Inter-Bank Offer Rate (LIBOR). Repayment terms range from up to three years for working capital to up to 12 years, including a grace period for fixed-asset loans.

Equity Participation in Andean Multinational Corporations

CAF may subscribe shares in new or established corporations within the Andean region with ownership by investors from two or more CAF member countries. CAF will only consider a project in which the paid-in shareholder's capital, excluding CAF, is at least 40 percent of the total project cost. CAF's equity participation is limited to a maximum of 20 percent of an eligible company's capital stock and up to a maximum amount of $200,000. CAF may make its participation subject to the appointment of a representative on the company's board of directors, and once it has performed the promotion task, it may transfer its shares or interest to subregional investors.

Eligibility: CAF financing is available to nationally owned companies located in the Andean Pact member countries of Bolivia, Colombia, Ecuador, Peru and Venezuela.

Application Process: Eligible companies interested in accessing financing through CAF programs must apply through their local CAF representative office, which in turn will forward the application to CAF headquarters. The time frame for CAF consideration for Project Financing applications is approximately three months.

Contact:

Andean Development Corporation
Av. Luis Roche-Altamira
Edificio Torre Central, Pisos 4 as 10
Apartado Postal Carmelitas 5086
Altamira 69011-69012
Caracas, Venezuela
Tel: 011 (58-2) 285-55-55
Fax: 011 (58-2) 284-5754

Bolivia Office
Av. Arce, Pasaje Esmeralda, No. 4
Casilla de Correo No. 550
La Paz, Bolivia
Tel: 011 (591-2) 363-934
Fax: 011 (591-2) 391-032

Colombia Office
Carrera 7 a, No. 26-20
Edificio Seguros Tequendama, Piso 15
Apartado Aereo 17826
Bogota, Colombia
Tel: 011 (571-2) 287-9584
Fax: 011 (571-2) 288-2517

Peru Office
Av. Camino Real, No. 456,
Of 801-802
Torre Real, San Isidro, Lima 27
Casilla Postal 18-1020, Lima 18
Lima, Peru
Tel: 011 (51-14) 402790
Fax: 011 (51-14) 400491

Ecuador Office
Av. 18 de Septiembre 332 y Juan Leon Mera
P.O. Box 259
Quito, Ecuador
Tel: 011 (593-2) 549-814
Fax: 011 (593-2) 564-246

Multilateral Investment Fund (MIF)

The **Multilateral Investment Fund (MIF)**, administered jointly by the Inter-American Development Bank (IDB) and the Inter-American Investment Corporation (IIC), is a market-based tool for assisting in the economic and social costs of privatization in Latin American and Caribbean countries. This $1.3-billion fund is dedicated to broadening participation in the private economy, especially by those people left out of the economic mainstream. Accordingly, MIF participates in projects as both a development institution and as a venture-capital fund. MIF will focuses on start-up companies, innovations, and activities with demonstration value throughout the region. MIF funding will be provided to companies primarily in the form of grants.

Contact:
Director of MIF - A1103
Inter-American Development Bank
1300 New York Avenue, NW
Washington, DC 20577
Tel: (202) 942-8211
Fax: (202) 942-8291

Global Environment Facility

The **Global Environment Facility (GEF)** provides grants for investment projects, technical assistance and research for the incremental costs of activities with global environment benefits. GEF is a joint program funded by the World Bank, United Nations Development Programme (UNDP) and United Nations Environment Programme (UNEP). GEF differs from traditional World Bank programs in two fundamental ways:

- The facility finances projects targeted solely at global environmental problems, while many existing World Bank investments tend to support national action plans to improve resource management and control local degradation; and

- GEF allows middle-income countries that have significant environmental problems (e.g., Hong Kong) to borrow money at low interest rates.

GEF became operative in 1991 as a three-year pilot project to address environmental problems that transcend national boundaries and whose solutions provide global benefits. It funds low- and middle-income countries with investments and technical assistance in four focal areas: global warming (reducing greenhouse-gas emissions);

biodiversity (international ecosystem preservation); international waters (prevent dumping of solid and liquid wastes into oceans and seas); and ozone depletion (reduce emissions of CFC and other ozone-depleting gases). GEF funds investment and technical assistance projects which benefit the global environment as opposed to the local environment. Projects financed by GEF must be innovative and demonstrate the effectiveness of a particular technology or approach.

GEF-sponsored projects must also contribute to development, knowledge creation and dissemination. Projects that are economically viable on the basis of benefits to the recipient country are not normally eligible. Projects must have substantial global benefits which are unlikely to materialize without GEF support. The funds are provided on grant terms and are in addition to ongoing multilateral and bilateral assistance programs.

Contact:
GEF Administrator
The World Bank
1818 H Street, NW
Washington, DC 20433
Tel: (202) 473-1053
Fax: (202) 522-3240

Caribbean Financial Services Corporation (CFSC)

Established in 1984, the **Caribbean Financial Services Corporation (CFSC)** works in cooperation with the U.S. Agency for International Development (USAID) and the European Investment Bank (EIB) to provide financing and assistance for development projects in the English-speaking Caribbean. With capital resources of $21 million, the CFSC provides medium- and long-term financing and equity for projects and institutions that enhance the region's foreign-exchange earning capability.

Terms and Conditions:

CFSC loans range from $100,000 to $600,000, and arrangements can be made for co-financing with other financial institutions. Terms are generally from five to fifteen years with a two-year grace period. The CFSC also requires that projects maintain a debt-to-equity ratio of 60:40. For equity participation, the CFSC provides between $100,000 and $300,000, and eligible projects must expect to have at least a 15-percent internal rate of return.

Eligible projects include manufacturing, agribusiness, tourism, and enterprises that enhance foreign-exchange earnings. There are no restrictions on investors in projects, but eligible projects must be beneficiary states of the Caribbean Basin Initiative (CBI): Antigua and Barbuda, Barbados, Belize, Dominica, Grenada, St. Kitts-Nevis, and St. Lucia.

Contact:
Managing Director, Caribbean Financial Services Corporation
Rendezvous Court
Rendezvous Christchurch
Christchurch, Barbados
Tel: (809) 436-1960
Fax: (809) 426-1869

Central American Bank for Economic Integration (CABEI)

The **Central American Bank for Economic Integration (CABEI)** is a source of financial assistance for member governments of the Central American Common Market (CACM) (Costa Rica, El Salvador, Guatemala, Honduras, and Nicaragua) to support regional development projects.

CABEI's Industrial Reactivation Program provides financing and technical assistance for industrial development projects. Since 1963, the program has disbursed more than $245 million in loans for projects.

Loans are distributed through central banks of the CACM member states.

Eligibility:

Eligible projects include industrial development initiatives that contribute to regional and extra-regional trade, utilize regional inputs, and generate employment. Financing is available for feasibility studies, working capital, technical assistance, and procurement of inputs.

Contact:
Central banks and major lending institutions in CACM member states.

Colombian Private Investment Fund

The **Colombian Private Investment Fund** provides medium- and long-term financing with working capital and fixed investments for industrial development projects.

Terms and Conditions:

Loans are available for terms of up to 10 years with a three-year grace period for fixed capital and terms of up to three years for working capital. Interest is based on the cost of a 90-day certificate of deposit plus six percent. The maximum financing available is $1 million and financing can cover up to 60 percent of total project costs.

Application Procedures:

Applicants for financing must seek a Colombian-based bank or finance corporation which will solicit the financing on its behalf.

Contact:

Applicants should contact a Colombian-based bank or finance corporation.

Costa Rica Private Investment Corporation (PIC)

Working in cooperation with the U.S. Agency for International Development, the German Finance Corporation, and the United Kingdom's Commonwealth Development Corporation, the **Costa Rica Private Investment Corporation (PIC)** provides financing and equity for projects which improve regional exports. With $45 million in resources, the PIC provides medium- and long-term financing and equity participation for eligible projects throughout Central America, although primarily in Costa Rica.

Terms and Conditions:

Loans for eligible projects may range from $150,000 to $3 million and terms are variable at London Inter-Bank Offer Rate (LIBOR) plus four percent with a minimum five-year repayment period. Equity may be provided for up to 20 percent of the projects and financing may cover up to 60 percent of the total project cost.

Eligibility:

There are no restrictions upon nationality for eligible projects and sponsors; however, financing is not available for land purchases, real estate, citrus, palm oil, or refinancing.

Contact:

Managing Director
Private Investment Corporation
P.O. Box 8609-1000
San Jose, Costa Rica
Tel: 011 (506) 33-6422
Fax: 011 (506) 33-6544

Caribbean Basin Projects Financing Authority (CARIFA)

Caribbean Development Program

Established in 1986, Puerto Rico's **Caribbean Development Program (CDP)** provides financial assistance for projects in Puerto Rico and beneficiary states of the Caribbean Basin Initiative by taking advantage of Section 936 of the U.S. Internal Revenue Code. Under Section 936, U.S. corporations receive partial tax exemption on income earned in Puerto Rico provided that profits are reinvested in projects in Puerto Rico. In 1986, the U.S. Congress extended this tax exemption to beneficiary states of the Caribbean Basin Initiative (CBI).

The **Caribbean Basin Projects Financing Authority (CARIFA)** is an additional source of CDP financing for medium- and large-scale projects in eligible CBI states.

Terms and Conditions:

CARIFA provides loans at lower-than-market rates for approved projects requiring more than $10 million in funds. The CDP offers loans with rates one to two points below market rates for qualified projects. Terms are generally from five to ten years.

Eligibility:

Eligible projects for funding include manufacturing, agricultural, tourism, and infrastructure projects. There are no eligibility restrictions on applicants for funding. Funds are obtained through commercial and investment banks in Puerto Rico.

U.S. Government restrictions dictate that only states which have signed a Tax Information Exchange Agreement (TIEA) with the United States are eligible. These states include Barbados, Costa Rica, Dominica, Dominican Republic, Grenada, Honduras, Jamaica, St. Lucia, and Trinidad and Tobago.

Application Procedures:

Projects must be approved by the Commissioner of Financial Institutions in Puerto Rico. In addition, the Economic Development Administration must verify that the project will have a positive economic impact, and that the project conforms to the U.S. Department of the Treasury regulations supporting economic development in the Caribbean Basin.

Contact:

Caribbean Development Program
U.S. Department of State
Commonwealth of Puerto Rico
P.O. Box 3271
San Juan, Puerto Rico 00902-3271
Tel: (809) 721-1751
Fax: (809) 723-3304

Additional Addresses:
U.S. Department of the Treasury
Internal Revenue Service
Office of Associate Chief Counsel (International)
1111 Constitution Avenue, NW
Washington, DC 20224
Tel: (202) 622-3810
Fax: (202) 566-3368

Bahamas Development Bank (BDB)

The **Bahamas Development Bank (BDB)** provides medium- and long-term financing for public and private development projects. Financing includes loans, guarantees, and equity participation. Technical assistance is also available for project development.

Terms and Conditions:

BDB financing is available for terms up to 10 years with a grace period which varies according to the specific project. BDB generally limits its participation in nonagricultural projects to 70 percent of the total project costs with the remaining 30 percent consisting of borrower equity; BDB will finance up to 80 percent of agriculture projects. Equity positions are available only if no other financial sources are available. Guarantees can be provided for loans from other sources for approved projects.

Contact:
Bahamas Development Bank
Managing Director
P.O. Box N3034
Nassau, Bahamas
Tel: (809) 332-8721
Tlx: DEVBANK NASSAU

Caribbean Development Bank (CDB)

The **Caribbean Development Bank (CDB)**, working in association with the Caribbean Common Market (CARICOM), provides long-term financing for development projects in the Caribbean. With $210 million in capital resources, the CDB provides loans and letters of credit for private-sector projects in manufacturing, forestry, fishing, tourism, and mining. Since 1970, the CDB has provided over $350 million in loans and $78 million in letters of credit for these sectors. Financing for pre-feasibility and feasibility studies is also available.

Terms and Conditions:

CDB loans range from $750,000 up to a maximum of 40 percent of the project total cost. Loans are available for 10- to 15-year terms with an additional five-year grace period. Since all loans are in local currency, the borrower must assume all currency risk. The CDB can issue loan guarantees, but prefers to handle only direct loans.

Eligibility:

Only projects in CARICOM member states are eligible for CDB financing, including Antigua and Barbuda, Bahamas, Barbados, Belize, British Virgin Islands, Dominica, Grenada, Guyana, Jamaica, Montserrat, St. Kitts and Nevis, St. Lucia, St. Vincent and the Grenadines, and Trinidad and Tobago. Priority will be given to applicants from CARICOM member states, but non-CARICOM nations may receive financing for export development projects, projects requiring technology transfers or use of local raw materials, and projects that allow local ownership by CARICOM nationals. Projects involving retail or wholesale trade, or office or condominium-type construction are ineligible.

Contact:

Vice-President, Corporate Services and Bank Secretary
Caribbean Development Bank
P.O. Box 408, Wildey
St. Michael, Barbados
Tel: (809) 431-1600
Fax: (809) 426-7269

Sources of Equity

Africa Growth Fund

The **Africa Growth Fund** is owned by a select group of major U.S. corporations and was created with Overseas Private Investment Corporation (OPIC) support. This fund can provide the critical equity component to complete the financial structure of a new project or a planned expansion. Investments can be made in a wide range of industry sectors in Sub-Saharan, OPIC-eligible African countries.

Terms: Every project must be supported by OPIC political risk insurance or similar risk-mitigation measures. The Africa Growth Fund may not invest in military projects or in companies which are viewed as controlled by local governments or government agencies.

This fund seeks investment opportunities in which it can provide between 20 percent and 45 percent of a project's total equity capital. Eligible investments include newly organized ventures, privatization of government holdings or the expanded capitalization of existing enterprises seeking to increase their current level of activity. Typically, total project costs range between $5 million and $50 million.

Application Process: The Africa Growth Fund requires no formal application. However, complete information must be provided on any proposed investment before its final review. Sponsors must submit a complete business plan, financing proposal and feasibility analysis, prepared according to international standards.

Contact:
Headquarters
The Africa Growth Fund, L.P.
35 Glastonbury Blvd.
Glastonbury, CT 06033
Tel: (203) 633-9999
Fax: (203) 633-6799

Washington, DC Office
1850 K Street NW, Suite 390
Washington, DC 20006
Tel: (202) 293-1860
Fax: (202) 872-1521

Asia Pacific Growth Fund

Hambrecht and Quist Asia Pacific (HQAP) manages the OPIC-supported, $75-million Asia Pacific Growth Fund, which invests in rapidly growing companies in the ASEAN countries, Taiwan, and Micronesia. The partnership is primarily interested in making equity and equity-related investments in private companies. This fund will not invest in companies located in Hong Kong, Japan, North and South Korea, the People's Republic of China, or Vietnam.

The Asia Pacific Growth Fund provides expansion capital for established Asian companies that may not yet have the levels of sales and profitability required for an initial public offering, but have clearly demonstrated the ability to successfully develop projects.

HQAP will submit company and investment information on prospective investments to OPIC for criteria qualification. Projects supported by HQAP are not screened by OPIC for investment soundness but strict adherence to OPIC criteria, including environmental impact assessment and benefit to the host country. HQAP local professionals are responsible for completing initial project requirements. If the project is acceptable, a project summary is sent to HQAP headquarters in San Francisco.

Part of this fund's regional strategy is to cultivate partnerships with local institutions and industrial companies throughout Asia. Funds managed by HQAP have largely been raised from local investors who play an active role in managing each fund. Many of these investors are leading industrial corporations in the region, which provides the local investment teams with key regional contacts, access to investment opportunities, and critical industry expertise.

In addition to HQAP headquarters in San Francisco, the Asia Pacific Growth Fund maintains offices in Taiwan, the Philippines, Singapore, and Thailand.

Contact:
H&Q Asia Pacific G.P.
One Bush Street
San Francisco, CA 94104
Tel: (415) 576-3300
Fax: (415) 576-3621

Global Environment Fund

The **Global Environment Fund (GEF)** is managed by the Global Environment Fund Management Corporation in Washington, DC, and is partially capitalized by the proceeds from notes guaranteed, at maturity, by OPIC. This fund makes equity or equity-related investments in private companies or projects operating in emerging market countries in Asia, Latin America, Europe, Russia and the NIS, the Middle East and Africa. GEF targets environment-oriented industries. This fund seeks significant minority positions in financially sound firms that meet these criteria. GEF especially seeks co-investment opportunities with established U.S. companies engaged in joint venture or other operational partnerships with local firms. Submission of a completed business plan or offering memorandum, including relevant financial data and a cover letter on company stationery, is sufficient to initiate the investment review process.

Contact:
Global Environment Fund Management Corporation
1201 New York Avenue, NW
Suite 220
Washington, DC 20005
Tel: (202) 789-4500
Fax: (202) 789-4508

ENTERPRISE FUNDS

The Enterprise Funds are privately managed equity pools designed to foster development of small- and medium-sized enterprises in Central and Eastern Europe (CEE) and the Newly Independent States (NIS) of the former Soviet Union. Initially funded by the U.S. Agency for International Development (USAID), the Enterprise Funds can provide capital to commercially viable projects in the form of equity capital and/or extended credit for start-up or expansion. The Enterprise Funds are expected to raise additional capital from private and public sources. Loans range from $500,000 to $2 million and are offered directly or in conjunction with commercial banks acting as intermediaries. These funds offer equity investment support, technical assistance and training related to actual or potential investments and loans.

Central Asian-American Enterprise Fund

The **Central Asian-American Enterprise Fund** will promote the creation and expansion of small- to medium-sized businesses in Kazakhstan, the Kyrghyz Republic, Uzbekistan, Turkmenistan, and Tajikistan. This fund serves as a catalyst for additional foreign investments in the region. The Fund plans to open branch offices in Ashgabat, Bishkek, and Tajikistan.

Central Asian-American Enterprise Fund

595 Madison Avenue, Suite 300   01, Turab Tula Street
New York, NY 10022   Tashkent, Uzbekistan 700066
Tel: (212) 826-2100   Tel: 011 (7-371) 245-5756
Fax: (212) 826-8844   Tel: 011 (7-371) 245-6248
    Tel: 011 (7-371) 245-5747
    Tel: 011 (7-371) 245-5751
531 Seyfullina Street   Tel: 011 (7-371) 245-5740
Almaty, Kazakhstan   Fax: 011 (7-371) 244-3183
Tel/Fax: TBA   Fax: 011 (7-371) 244-2603

Czech-American Enterprise Fund

Formed after the dissolution of the Czech and Slovak Federal Republic in 1993, the **Czech-American Enterprise Fund (CAEF)** promotes the development of small- to medium-sized private businesses in the Czech Republic. This fund has capital of $65 million and is supported by the U.S. Agency for International Development (USAID) pursuant to the Support for East European Democracy Act (the "SEED Act"). The primary focus of this fund is on support of private enterprises in the manufacturing, food processing, energy, and fabrication sectors of the Czech Republic. The Czech-American Enterprise Fund invests through loans and equity capital. Offices are located in Prague and Washington, DC.

Contact:
Czech-American Enterprise Fund

U.S. Office
1620 Eye Street, NW Suite 703
Washington, DC 20006
Tel: (202) 467-5480
Fax: (202) 467-5466

Czech Office
Blanicka 28/1008
120 00 Prague 2, Czech Republic
Tel: 011 (42-22) 424-7046
Fax: 011 (42-22) 424-6048

Defense Enterprise Fund

The **Defense Enterprise Fund** is a venture capital fund created to make equity or debt investments in joint ventures between Russian, Ukrainian, Kazakh, or Belarussian companies and Western companies. The primary focus of this fund is to assist these ventures in converting industrial resources from defense production to civilian production.

Contact:

Defense Enterprise Fund
104 Crofton Road
Waban, MA 02168
Tel: (617) 527-3307
Fax: (617) 527-2722

Environmental Enterprises Assistance Fund

The **Environmental Enterprises Assistance Fund (EEAF)** was created in 1990 to provide long-term risk capital management assistance to environmentally beneficial businesses in developing countries. This fund focuses on environmentally beneficial companies which have been most active in the alternative energy, energy efficiency, or ecotourism sectors. Eastern European countries and republics of the former Soviet Union will be the main target areas for the investments ranging from $100,000 to $2.5 million. EEAF will utilize senior loans, subordinated loans, convertible debt, preferred stock, and common stock instruments. EEAF maintains offices in Costa Rica and Indonesia, and is headquartered in Arlington, Virginia.

Contact:
Environmental Enterprises Assistance Fund
1901 N. Moore Street, Suite 1004
Arlington, VA 22209
Tel: (703) 522-5928
Fax: (703) 522-6450

Apdo 1581-2050
San Pedro de MO, Costa Rica
Tel/Fax: 011 (506) 257-4717

Gedung Graha Purna Yudha, 11th Floor, Room 1108
Jalan Jendral Sudirman Kav. 50
Jakarta, Indonesia 12930
Tel: 011 (62-21) 520-3313 x1406
Fax: 011 (62-21) 525-4305

Hungarian-American Enterprise Fund

The **Hungarian-American Enterprise Fund (HAEF)** is a U.S. Government-supported fund that invests in small- to medium-sized private enterprises which are engaged in manufacturing, retail and wholesale trade, agriculture, construction, communications, pharmaceuticals, and real estate. This fund develops existing Hungarian enterprises by managing risk capital which is used for privatizations, growth, turn-arounds, and start-up of new ventures. Capitalized at $70 million, HAEF provides equity-type capital in the form of share-capital as well as in the form of long-term loans for small investments. This fund is currently seeking to increase its capital base by an additional $70 million from institutional investors and the U.S. Government.

Contact:
Hungarian-American Enterprise Fund
666 Steamboat Road
Greenwich, CT 06830
Tel: (203) 869-3114
Fax: (203) 869-3556

East-West Business Center
Rákóczi út 1-3, 6th Floor
H-1088 Budapest, Hungary
Tel: 011 (36-1) 266-7175
Tel: 011 (36-1) 266-7230
Fax: 011 (36-1) 266-7086

Polish-American Enterprise Fund/Polish Equity Fund

The **Polish-American Enterprise Fund** and the **Polish Equity Fund** collectively represent capital of $340 million for investment in small- to medium-sized businesses in Poland. These two funds focus on private sector development through investments--in the form of loans and equity capital--in businesses which are undergoing privatization. USAID and EBRD support these funds, which maintain offices in Warswaza, Poland, and New York City.

Contact:
Polish-American Enterprise Fund/Polish Equity Fund

375 Park Avenue, Suite 1902   Ul. Nowy Swiat 6/12
New York, NY 10152   00-400 Warswaza, Poland
Tel: (212) 339-8330   Tel: 011 (48-2) 625-1921, 625-2017
Fax: (212) 339-8359   Fax: 011 (48-2) 625-7933

The U.S. Russia Investment Fund

This U.S. Russia Investment Fund was created through the merger of the Russian American Enterprise Fund and the Fund for Large Enterprises in Russia. Combining the capital resources of both grounds, the U.S. Russia Investment Fund is capitalized at $440 million.

The fund operates as a private, non-profit corporation, committed to helping develop privatized or privatizing Russian enterprises by providing equity investments and loans, as well as technical assistance and training, Russian companies. The new fund will maintain a focus on enterprises that are emerging from the mass privatization programs currently underway in Russia and will dedicate a significant amount of resources to small- and medium-sized enterprises. Priority will given to investments in companies considered too risky by other private investors due to either a lack of track record or the fluid political and economic environment in Russia.

Contact:
U.S. Russia Investment Fund

Tsvetnoy Boulevard, 25/3   17 State Street, 33rd Floor
103051 Moscow, Russia   New York, NY 10004
Tel: 011(7-095) 929-9810   Tel: (212) 504-0400
Fax: 011 (7-095) 929-9809   Fax: (212) 668-0770
Satellite: 011 (7501) 929-9809

Slovak-American Enterprise Fund

The **Slovak-American Enterprise Fund (SAEF)**, similar to the CAEF, was formed in 1993, following the break-up of the Czech and Slovak Federal Republic. USAID supports this fund through $65 million in donated capital. The SAEF targets small- to medium-sized private businesses in the manufacturing, food processing, energy, and service markets of the Slovak Republic. This fund is based in Washington, DC, and also maintains an office in Bratislava.

Contact:
Slovak-American Enterprise Fund

U.S. Office	Slovak Office
1620 Eye Street, NW Suite 703	Radlinskeho 27
Washington, DC 20006	P.O. Box 66
Tel: (202) 467-5480	Bratislava, Slovak Republic 810 05
Fax: (202) 467-5466	Tel: 011 (42) 732-6544
	Fax: 011 (42) 736-2530

Western NIS Enterprise Fund

The **Western NIS Enterprise Fund** is a $150-million fund targeting small- to medium-sized enterprises in Ukraine, Belarus, and Moldova. This fund seeks to develop economically viable private enterprises in the region. There are plans to open offices in Minsk and Chisinau in 1995.

Contact:
Western NIS Enterprise Fund

15 West 39th Street, 11th Floor	#4 Muzeyny Lane, 3rd Floor
New York, NY 10018	Kiev, Ukraine 252001
Tel: (212) 906-1215	Tel: 011 (38-44) 240-0243
Fax: (212) 751-4864	

GOVERNMENT-BACKED EQUITY FUNDS

Agribusiness Partners International Fund

The **Agribusiness Partners International Fund**, which is scheduled to begin operations in 1995, was formed to promote a wide range of agricultural enterprises. This fund will focus primarily on improving production, packaging, and distribution of food in the Russian Federation. This fund is supported by OPIC, which will provide an investment guarantee for up to $75 million of the debt portion of the fund. Agribusiness Partners L.L.C., in Omaha, NE, manages this fund which will be capitalized at $100 million.

Contact:
Agribusiness Partners L.L.C.
1004 Farnham Street
Omaha, NE 68102
Tel: (402) 444-1630
Fax: (402) 345-8966

Alliance ScanEast Fund

Alliance ScanEast Fund is a venture-capital fund that will invest principally in Hungary, Poland, and the Baltic states. Its focus is primarily in telecommunications, construction materials, pulp and paper equipment, power generation, environmental technology, petrochemicals and plastics, and oil and gas. A principal element of the fund's investment strategy is the integration into the investment process of its four Finnish industrial partners - A. Ahlstrom Corp., Nestle Corp., Nokia Corp., and the Metra Group. Eligible investment candidates will be private-sector enterprises or public-sector enterprises soon to privatized. Project proposals other than from the industrial partners will be presented to the partners for co-investment opportunities.

Contact:
Alliance ScanEast Fund
Alliance Capital Management Corporation
1345 Avenue of the Americas
New York, NY 10105
Tel: (212) 969-1050
Fax: (212) 969-2221

Bancroft Eastern Europe Fund

The Bancroft Eastern Europe Fund will make direct equity investments in private or privatizing companies in almost all of the Eastern European countries and Newly Independent States. This fund will also invest in manufacturing services in a variety of sectors. Capitalized at $100 million, this fund will be managed by the Bancroft Group, a Washington, DC-based investment consulting company, and Arnhold and S. Bleichroeder Inc., a New York-based investment bank.

Contact:
Bancroft Eastern Europe Fund
Bancroft Group
607 14th Street, NW, Suite 800
Washington, DC 20005
Tel: (202) 434-1600
Fax: (202) 434-1646

Central and Eastern European-NIS Property Fund

The **Central and Eastern European-NIS Property Fund (CEE-NIS Fund)** is the first fund that will develop industrial parks for manufacturing, warehouses, and distribution centers in Central and Eastern Europe and the Newly Independent States. This Fund will be capitalized with $240 million and will begin operation in 1995.

Contact:
Central and Eastern European-NIS Property Fund
372 Washington Street
Wellesley, MA 02181
Tel: (617) 431-2600
Fax: (617) 431-7749

Central Environmental Protection Fund (CEPF)

Founded in 1971, the **CEPF** was formed to utilize fines and subsidies for businesses who engage in environmental protection activities. Re-regulated in 1992 by the Hungarian Ministry of Environment and Regional Policy (KTM), the fund assists public and private business organizations involved environmental protection, commercial solutions concerning the marketing of environmentally friendly products, and actions which strengthen environmental awareness. CEPF disburses funds in the form of grants, loans, interest subsidies, or loan guarantees.

Contact:
Central Environmental Protection Fund
Central Environmental Fund Secretary
Ministry of Environment and Regional Policy
H-1011 Budapest, Fo u. 44-50
P.O.B. 35, Budapest 1394, Hungary
Tel: 011 (36-1) 201-4572/201-4617/201-4133
Fax: 011 (36-1) 22-4879/22-4870

Central European Telecom Investment Fund

The **Central European Telecom Investment Fund** is managed by the former principal economist of the IFC's telecommunications division. The primary activity of this fund is to invest in viable telecommunications projects. Capitalized at $40 million, with an ultimate goal of $100 million, investments will be made in projects in the Czech Republic, Hungary, and Poland. The Central European Telecom Investment Fund is headquartered in Budapest, Hungary.

Contact:
Central European Telecom Investment Fund

Veres Palne	u.7, Iem
Budapest, Hungary	Budapest, Hungary
Tel: 011 (36-1) 118-9594	Tel: 011 (36-1) 118-9823
Fax: 011 (36-1) 266-6484	Fax: 011 (36-1) 266-6484

Czech National Environmental Fund

The Czech Republic created this fund to assist in financing environmental projects. It will be capitalized through money from fines and fees levied at the local level. Funds are awarded as direct grants, low-interest loans, or guaranteed loans from state banks.

Contact:
Czech National Environmental Fund
Czech Ministry of the Environment
Attn: Manager, Environmental Fund
Tel: 011 (42-2) 738-859
Tel: 011 (42-2) 731-452

Ministry of Industry & Trade
Ing. Vokrohlik
Tel: 011 (42-2) 285-2202
Fax: 011 (42-2) 231-1970

East Europe Development Fund

Capitalized at $161 million, the **East Europe Development Fund** manages both private and public equity investments in Eastern Europe and the NIS. In addition to investments in light manufacturing, foods, beverages, health care and distribution, this fund supports construction projects and is open to viable projects in all industries with a preference for projects that offer growth in the targeted regions. Investment opportunities are sought both in privatization and in the rapidly growing private sectors. The East Europe Development Fund will evaluate investments in the $500,000 to $6 million range.

Contact:
East Europe Development Fund
Invesco
11 Devonshire Square
London, England EC2M 4YR
Tel: 011 (44-71) 454-3545
Fax: 011 (44-171) 782-0499

EBRD Regional Venture Funds (Russia)

The EBRD expects to provide equity for the creation of three to five regional venture funds in Russia. The first fund, **The Smolensk Regional Venture Fund**, managed by Simparex (France), will be capitalized with about $12 million of equity (smaller than future funds). The purpose of this fund is to facilitate the modernization, expansion and/or restructuring of privatized enterprises in the Smolensk region by providing new equity capital combined with technical assistance. The typical investment will range from $300,000 to $1.5 million. This fund will target medium-sized companies (about 1,000 employees) in varying sectors. It will focus on enterprises with good growth prospects and not in need of substantial restructuring. Strong management is essential, but U.S. partners are not a requirement, nor is it a prerequisite to have currency earnings.

Contact:
Smolensk Regional Venture Fund
Simparex
139 rue Vendome
69477 Lyon Cedex 06
France
Tel: 011 (33-78) 52 41 07
Fax: 011 (33-78) 52 61 63

EBRD-Small Business Fund

The **Small Business Fund (SBF)** will provide newly created small and micro enterprises in Russia with access to needed capital. The SBF will also provide equity capital, loans, and loan guarantees for purchase of fixed assets or for general working capital needs. The fund will be capitalized at $300 million.

Contact:
Russia Country Team
European Bank for Reconstruction & Development
One Exchange Square
London EC2A 2EH
United Kingdom
Tel: 011 (44-1) 71 338-6298
Fax: 011 (44-1) 71 338-6487

Ecofund

The **Ecofund** was created following the Paris Club agreement to reduce 50% of Poland's debt, which also included a provision that allowed a 10% reduction in exchange for environmental protection. This fund is disbursed in the form of grants, which are limited to 30% of total project costs for commercial projects.

Contact:
Ecofund
Fund Manager
Tel: 011 (48-2) 240-0901
Tel: 011 (48-2) 240-0942
Fax: 011 (48-2) 240-0950

First NIS Regional Fund

The **First NIS Regional Fund**, which has not been launched yet, will have $100 million in capital. This fund will target investments in the natural resources, telecommunications, light manufacturing and consumer products sectors in the $2-to-$10 million range. While these investments will be primarily equity, although convertible debt or warrants may also be purchased.

Contact:
First NIS Regional Fund
Sovlink-American Corporation
1221 Avenue of the Americas, 24th Floor
New York, NY 10020
Tel: (212) 730-4868
Fax: (212) 730-2871

Framlington Investment Fund for Russia

The European Bank for Reconstruction and Development (EBRD) has invested 14 million ECU in the **Framlington Fund**, which is only providing equity investment of up to 20 percent in small- and medium-sized companies in Russia. This fund, capitalized at $65 million as of January 1994, focuses projects in the range of $500,000 to $7 million. Eighty percent of the funds invested will go to companies with largely Western control.

Contact:
Framlington Investment Fund for Russia
155 Bishopsgate
London EC2M 3FT
United Kingdom
Tel: 011 (44-71) 374-4100
Fax: 011 (44-71) 382-9116
(Moscow office: Tel: 011 (7-095) 924-5496)

National Fund for Environmental Protection & Water Management

This fund provides support for environmentally linked projects either as a joint-venture partner or through loans, grants, bonds issuances and related activities.

Contact:
National Fund for Environmental Protection and Water Management

Fund Manager	Fund Manager
Tel: 011 (48-2) 225-0503	Tel: 011 (48-2) 225-2982
Fax: 011 (48-2) 225-4599	Fax: 011 (48-2) 225-4599

First Hungary Fund

Incorporated in 1989, the **First Hungary Fund** is a $122-million fund targeting industries that are expected to grow substantially faster than the Hungarian economy as a whole. This fund will invest in a broad range of projects including start-ups, formerly state-owned enterprises, and telecommunications projects. The equity fund takes positions in the range of $2 to $15 million.

Contact:
First Hungary Fund

Postal Address:	*Office Address:*
1386 PF 906/82.	V. 9 Kristóf tr 6. IV. 10.
Budapest, Hungary H-1052	Budapest, Hungary
	Tel: 011 (36-1) 266-4021
	Tel: 011 (36-1) 137-8720
	Fax: 011 (36-1) 117-7182

Global Environment Emerging Markets Fund

The **Global Environment Emerging Markets Fund** was created to provide investments in environment-oriented industries, especially those engaged in developing, financing, operating, or supplying infrastructure projects related to delivering clean energy and potable water. This fund is capitalized at $70 million and offers equity or equity-related investments in emerging markets around the world.

Contact:

Global Environment Emerging Markets Fund
Global Environment Management Corporation
1201 New York Avenue, NW
Suite 220
Washington, DC 20005
Tel: (202) 789-4500
Fax: (202) 789-4508

New Europe East Investment Fund

The **New Europe East Fund** is a $150-million fund supported by the EBRD which focuses on projects in Eastern and Central Europe as well as the former Soviet Union. This fund will consider investing in new or existing large joint ventures with reputable Western industrial partners.

Although this fund invests primarily in equities, it may also hold convertible and debt instruments. The fund will take no more than a 15-percent equity stake in any enterprise. The average project size will range from $2-10 million not to exceed $15 million for any one project.

Contact:

New Europe East Investment Fund
Capital International
25 Bedford Street
London WC2E 9HN, UK
Tel: 011 (44-71) 236-3514
Fax: 011 (44-71) 257-6767

Pioneer Poland Fund

The **Pioneer Poland Fund**, which is not yet in operation, will have $50 million in capital and will invest principally in medium sized private companies as well as privatizations. Priority sectors include food processing, textiles and construction; and developing industries such as telecommunications, environmental services, distribution, retailing, and software. Investments are intended to be significant minority positions and will range from $500,000 to $5 million, including follow-on investments.

Contact:
Pioneer Poland Fund
ul. Stawki 2
00-193 Warzawa, Poland
Tel: 011 (48-2) 635-9908
Fax: 011 (48-2) 635-6976

Poland Partners Fund

Founded in 1994, the **Poland Partners Fund** is a $60-million, OPIC-supported venture capital fund. Focusing on enterprises that are start-ups, expansions, and privatizing companies, this fund offers capital investments in the $2 to $4 million range. The focus of the Poland Partners Fund is primarily on small- to medium-sized companies that are experiencing rapid development in the food-processing, pharmaceuticals, home-improvement product manufacturing, financial services, packaging, and plastics-molding industries.

Contact:
Poland Partners Fund
Poland Partner's Management Company
1215 19th Street, NW
Washington, DC 20036
Tel: (202) 293-7205
Fax: (202) 296-7844

Poland Partners Management Company
Attn: Managing Director
Ul. Podwale 13
00-950 Warsaw, POLAND
Tel: 011 (48-2) 635-7690
Tel: 011 (48-2) 635-8650
Fax: 011 (48-2) 231-7920

Renaissance Partners Fund

The **Renaissance Partners Fund**, based in Boston, MA, offers investments to start-ups covering a broad range of industries. Capitalized at $40 million, this fund is targeting projects solely in Poland, and expects to support twenty investments with its initial capital.

Contact:
Renaissance Partners Fund
Attn.: Managing Director
Tel: 011 (48-2) 222-8234/35
Fax: 011 (48-2) 222-2224

Russia Partners Fund

This fund, capitalized at $155 million, will provide equity and quasi-equity securities in the $2 to $10 million range to both new and expanding enterprises in Russia, including newly privatized ventures. The Russia Partners Fund will invest in the telecommunications, manufacturing, natural resource processing, pharmaceuticals, and consumer goods industries in the Newly Independent States, Estonia, Latvia, and Lithuania.

Contact:
Russia Partners Fund
Drew Guff
Paine Webber Incorporated
1285 Avenue of the Americas
New York, NY 10019
Tel: (212) 713-3214
Fax: (212) 713-1087

Slovak National Fund

The Republic of Slovakia established the **Slovak National Fund** which is designed to assist with financing environmental projects. Similar to the Czech National Fund, the Slovak National Fund receives money from fines and fees levied at the local level. Money from the fund is awarded as direct grants, low-interest loans, or guaranteed loans from state banks.

Contact:
Slovak National Fund
Slovak Ministry for the Environment
Bratislava
Tel: 011 (42-7) 492-532
Fax: 011 (42-7) 311-368

Slovak Fund for the Environment
Mr. Vozar
Tel: 011 (42-7) 724-909
Fax: 011 (42-7) 311-368

Urals Regional Venture Fund

The **Urals Regional Venture Fund** will be capitalized at about $30 million. Other regional funds will be established for Yekaterinburg, Chelyabinsk, St. Petersburg, Western Siberia and Perm. This fund is scheduled to begin operations in 1995.

Contact:
Russia Country Team
European Bank for Reconstruction & Development
One Exchange Square
London EC2A 2EH
United Kingdom
Tel: 011 (44-1) 71 338-6298
Fax: 011 (44-1) 71 338-6487

CHAPTER SEVEN

Covering the Deal: Insurance

International business involves a certain amount of risk. The insurance programs described in this chapter are designed to protect U.S. firms against commercial and political risks involved with international business. This insurance can cover export sales as well as equity investments in overseas operations. While insurance is an obvious risk-mitigation technique, it also provides an important vehicle for financing development projects and investments. Given the appropriate protection, lenders are more willing to make loans and investors are more likely to invest in international projects.

The following is a list of key topics that can be found in Chapter Seven:

- Political Risk Insurance
- Export Credit Insurance

Investment Coverage

Overseas Private Investment Corporation

The **Overseas Private Investment Corporation (OPIC)** offers political risk insurance to U.S. investors, contractors, exporters, and financial institutions involved in international business in industrializing countries. Insurance is available for new ventures or expansions of existing enterprises and can cover equity investments, loans, technical assistance agreements, and other long-term exposures. The insurance department in OPIC is broken down by regions, with Latin America in Region I, Eastern Europe and the NIS in Region II, and Asia/Africa in Region III.

Traditional Insurance Programs

OPIC offers a number of insurance programs designed to encourage U.S. private investment in projects in developing countries by protecting the investment from political risk. Policies can cover up to 90 percent of investments in qualified projects in eligible countries against loss due to certain political occurrences including the following:

- Inability to convert profits denominated in local currency into dollars or return on the original investment;
- Loss due to expropriation, nationalization or confiscation by action of a foreign government;
- Loss due to political violence such as war, revolution, insurrection or civil strife; and
- Loss of business income due to interruption of the business caused by political violence or expropriation.

Eligible Investors: OPIC may insure an investment by an eligible investor in a project controlled by foreign interests; however, cover is limited to the amount of the eligible investor's investments. Eligible investors are: U.S. citizens; corporations, partnerships or other associations created under the laws of the U.S. or of any state or territory of the U.S. which are substantially owned by U.S. citizens; or a foreign business that is at least 95-percent owned by investors eligible under the preceding criteria.

OPIC recognizes a corporation organized under the laws of the U.S. or of any state or territory of the U.S. to be substantially owned by U.S. citizens if more than 50 percent of each class of its issued and outstanding stock is owned by U.S. citizens.

Eligible Countries: OPIC covers U.S. private investments in over 115 "less developed, friendly" countries. OPIC insurance in high-income LDCs is subject to certain restrictions. In countries with a high per-capita GNP, insurance is available for investments sponsored by U.S. small businesses, projects using OPIC's letter of credit or contractors coverage and other projects that OPIC's Board of Directors determines to merit insurance, such as those offering exceptional developmental or trade benefits.

Eligible Investments: OPIC insures both new investments and expansions to modernize existing plants. This may include the cost of acquiring an existing business. The investor should apply for insurance sufficient to cover possible project-cost overruns. Coverage is available for conventional equity investments and loans and for investment of funds and goods or services under various contractual arrangements. To be eligible for insurance, an investor must apply for and receive an OPIC Registration Letter before the investment is made or irrevocably committed. This letter does not commit OPIC to offer insurance, nor does it commit the investor to accept it.

Other Criteria: Investors are required to supply data on a project's developmental effect on the host country, including information relating to environmental impact, job creation, skills development, balance of payments effects, taxes and host-government revenues, and contribution to basic human needs.

OPIC will not cover investments that would have a negative effect on U.S. domestic employment. It may also refuse coverage for investments in projects that are likely to have adverse effects on the U.S. balance of payments and those used primarily to finance the procurement of goods or services for a project from other industrialized countries. OPIC's bilateral agreements with the governments of OPIC-eligible countries require that the foreign government approve each project for purposes of OPIC's insurance of investment in the project. Insurance coverage cannot take effect until OPIC receives an acceptable Foreign Government Approval (FGA) of the investment.

Inconvertibility

Coverage assures that earnings, capital, principal and interest, and other eligible remittances, such as payments under service agreements, can continue to be converted into U.S. dollars. The insured will be compensated for currency blockage whether it is active (when host-country authorities deny access to foreign exchange through regulations) or passive (when monetary authorities fail to act within a specified period on an application for foreign exchange--usually 60 days). In either case, OPIC makes dollar payments upon receipt of the local currency.

Expropriation

OPIC insurance contracts define expropriatory action to include direct seizure of property as well as a variety of situations that might be described as "creeping expropriation." An action taken by the host government which has a specified impact on either the properties or operations of the foreign enterprise or on the rights or financial interests of the insured investor may be considered expropriatory. For an action to be considered expropriatory, it must continue for at least one year for most investments and three months or less for contracts covering institutional loans. OPIC compensation for expropriatory actions is based on the net book value of the investor's insured interest in the foreign enterprise.

War, Revolution, Insurrection and Civil Strife

Coverage extends to losses from actions taken to hinder, combat or defend against hostile action during war, revolution, insurrection or civil strife. Civil strife includes politically motivated violent acts by a group or individual, including acts of terrorism and sabotage. A loss caused by an individual or group acting primarily to achieve demands of labor or students would be excluded from the coverage.

Business Income Coverage

OPIC covers loss of profits and continuing normal operating expenses when operations are interrupted due to political violence. Losses are covered for a period of up to one year or until the damaged property could reasonably have been repaired or replaced, whichever is sooner. OPIC also compensates for expenses incurred if those expenses reduce the business income loss that would otherwise be payable.

Terms: OPIC insurance contracts require the annual insurance premium to be paid in advance. Premiums are computed for each type of coverage on the basis of a maximum insured amount chosen by the investor on a yearly basis. The insured amount represents the insurance actually in force during any contract year. The difference between the current insured amount and maximum insured amount for each coverage is called the standby amount. The major portion of the premium is based on the current insured amount; a reduced premium rate applies to the standby amount.

Premiums: Annual base rates for manufacturing, agribusiness, and services projects are given below. These rates vary for different industries.

Coverage	Current (%)	Standby (%)
Inconvertibility	0.30	0.25
Expropriation	0.60	0.25
Political Violence*		
Business Income	0.45	0.25
Assets	0.60	0.25

* Investors may choose to delete civil strife from coverage; the premium rate is typically lowered by 0.10 percent in this case.

Rates for natural resource and hydrocarbon projects, or very large projects, may vary by more than one-third of the base rates. OPIC insurance contracts (except for those covering institutional loans and certain service contracts) contain provisions that allow for an increase in the initial current coverage rate by up to 50 percent during the first 10 years of the contract period and an additional 50 percent during the second 10 years of the contract period.

In 1993, Galaxy Group, Ltd, a Polish-American joint venture, was preparing to implement a $3.5-million project to provide parking control systems for the Polish cities of Gdansk and Sopot. The project, providing parking and traffic management systems under license to these cities, would serve as a model that could be replicated in other cities throughout Poland. In addition, the project was to provide an important foothold in the Eastern European market for Galaxy investors who were developing similar projects in neighboring countries.

To secure their investment, two U.S. investors applied to the Overseas Private Investment Corporation for Political Risk Investment Insurance to cover their investment in the project against political risks. Cover was secured, and the project has gone forward successfully.

Minerals Insurance Program

OPIC offers specialized coverage for investments in mineral exploration and development (including processing where it is an integral part of a development project). OPIC will cover up to 90 percent of the initial investment plus an equal amount of retained earnings. The percentage of investment and retained earnings insured will depend on OPIC's assessment of risk factors in the project, including the extent of multinational equity and/or debt participation.

Exploration: Insurance will be provided against all four covered risks (described earlier) during the exploration phase for intangible costs as well as tangible assets.

Breach of Specified Government Contractual Obligations:

Special additional coverage may protect against losses resulting from the breach of certain host-government obligations identified by the project sponsor at the outset as vital to the successful operation of the project. Such special coverages will be individually rated.

Political Violence: In addition to standard political violence coverage, insurance may be offered to cover consequential loss due to closing of operations for a period of at least six months. This loss may be directly caused by political violence in the project country or by specified political violence in another country.

Premiums: Annual base rates for natural resource projects, other than oil and gas, are:

Coverage	Current (%)	Standby (%)
Inconvertibility	0.30	0.25
Expropriation	0.90	0.25
Political Violence*		
Business Income	0.45	0.25
Assets	0.60	0.25

*   Investors may choose to delete civil strife from coverage; the premium rate is typically lowered by 0.10 percent in this case.

Energy Insurance Program

OPIC provides insurance for most types of investment in energy exploration, development and production. This includes investments made pursuant to traditional concession agreements, production-sharing agreements, service contracts, risk contracts and other agreements with host-country governments.

Coverage: Coverage is available for up to 90 percent of the investment and generally does not exceed $100 million per project. OPIC's insurance for energy investments includes coverage against inconvertibility, expropriation, political violence and interference with operations due to political violence.

Coverage for oil and gas projects is issued for a maximum term of 12 years with an extension of 8 years after the original insured period at OPIC's discretion. Insurance covering the construction period, plus ten years, may be issued for coal mining projects, while projects involving the development of alternative energy sources may be insured for up to 20 years.

OPIC insurance is not available for investments in oil and gas exploration, development and production projects in member countries of the Organization of Petroleum Exporting Countries (OPEC). However, projects in OPEC countries involving investments in petroleum service operations and downstream petrochemical projects, as well as investments in other energy and mineral sources, may be eligible.

Premiums: Premium rates are determined by the risk profile for a particular project. The annual base rates for oil and gas projects are as follows:

Development/Production:

Exploration Coverage	Current (%)	Standby (%)
Inconvertibility	0.30	0.30
Expropriation	0.40	1.50
Political Violence (Assets)*	0.75	0.75
Interference with Operations	0.40	0.40

*   Investors may choose to delete civil strife from coverage; the premium rate is typically lowered by 0.15 in this case.

The rates are applied to sums actually invested, beginning with the quarter in which each incremental investment is made. Coverage can be assured for future investments in the project by the payment of the modest standby premiums. The base rates for other types of projects vary in accordance with the type of project and the method of investment.

Contractors & Exporters

OPIC provides cover for U.S. companies acting as contractors in international construction, sales, or service contracts, as well as for U.S. exporters of capital goods, including computers, heavy machinery, turbines, and medical equipment. Cover is available for exporters holding a contract with a foreign government buyer and includes protection against the following risks:

- Wrongful calling of bid, performance or advance payment guarantees, customs bonds, and other guarantees. OPIC requirements state that cover is available only if the underlying contract contains a dispute-resolution procedure and if the insured fulfills its contractual obligations.

- Loss of physical assets and bank accounts due to civil strife, confiscation, or inconvertibility of proceeds from the sale of equipment used at the project site; and/or

- Losses due to unresolved contractual disputes with a foreign buyer. The export contract must have a dispute-resolution procedure to be eligible for cover, and the foreign buyer or project must have secure, adequate financing.

Premiums: Premium rates are determined by the risk profile for a particular project. The annual base rates for cover for contractors and exporters projects are as follows:

Coverage	Current (%)	Standby (%)
Assets		
Inconvertibility	0.30	0.25
Expropriation	0.60	0.25
Political Violence	0.60	0.25
Bid Bonds	0.50	0.25
Performance,		
Advance Payment &		
Other Guarantees	0.60	0.25
Disputes	0.70	0.25

Contact:
Regional Manager
Overseas Private Investment Corporation
1100 New York Avenue, NW
Washington, DC 20527

Region I, Latin America
Tel: (202) 336-8583
Fax: (202) 408-5142

Region II, Eastern Europe
Tel: (202) 336-8617
Fax: (202) 408-5145

Region III, Asia/Africa
Tel: (202) 336-8601
Fax: (202) 408-5142

Multilateral Investment Guarantee Agency (MIGA)

The **Multilateral Investment Guarantee Agency (MIGA)** was formed by the World Bank to facilitate foreign investment in developing member countries and to complement the activities of national investment insurance programs, private insurance companies, and the International Finance Corporation (IFC). MIGA offers long-term political risk insurance and provides advisory and consultative services.

MIGA requires that insured projects are environmentally sound, following either the more stringent of the host country's requirements or the World Bank Group's environmental guidelines for each project. The IFC's Technical and Environmental Department serves as MIGA's environmental adviser. In FY 1993, MIGA provided insurance for financial institutions to expand and diversify financial resources available for investment.

MIGA works with host-country governments to create a conducive investment climate and to advise investors of opportunities in developing countries. MIGA is the newest member of the World Bank Group and more than 80 countries have ratified the MIGA Convention. MIGA's Guarantee Program is designed to encourage investors to take advantage of commercially attractive foreign opportunities despite potential political risks. The MIGA guarantee is typically available for a 15-year term but it can be extended to up to 20 years in some cases.

The types of risk that MIGA will cover include:

- War, Revolution and Civil Disturbance;
- Breach of Contract;
- Currency Transfer; and
- Expropriation.

Eligibility: MIGA limits insurance coverage to new investments between member countries where the investment project is located in a developing country. MIGA has 120 member countries; 25 additional countries are in the process of fulfilling membership requirements.

Investments associated with the expansion, modernization or financial restructuring of an existing enterprise are also eligible, including equity loans and loan guarantees made by equity holders. Some non-equity forms of direct investment may also be covered, such as technical contracts, franchising and licensing agreements. Only new investments on a medium- to long-term basis in commercial enterprises are eligible. Investments must also be sound, contribute to the host country's development, comply with local laws and be consistent with development priorities. MIGA will only consider investments that have not been made or committed prior to the filing of the Preliminary Application for Guarantee. Potential investors are encouraged to investigate MIGA services while their investment is still in the planning stage.

Terms: MIGA insures up to 90 percent of the investment amount for long-term periods (15 to 20 years). There is additional cover for up to 180 percent of earnings attributable to the investment with a ceiling of $500 million. There is no minimum investment requirement, although there is a current ceiling of $50 million per project coverage. Premiums are determined separately for each project, and are based upon MIGA's assessment of several variables, including the type of guarantee requested and the structure of the project to be insured.

Contact:
Multilateral Investment Guarantee Agency
1818 H Street, NW
Washington, DC 20433

Regional Manager, Asia/Latin America
Tel: (202) 473-6165
Fax: (202) 522-2630

Regional Manager, Africa/Eastern Europe
Tel: (202) 473-5419
Fax: (202) 522-2630

Export Transactions

Export-Import Bank of the United States (Ex-Im Bank)

The **Export-Import Bank of the United States (Ex-Im Bank)** provides export credit insurance to protect U.S. exporters of goods and services against the failure of foreign buyers to meet their payment obligations. Ex-Im Bank insures a wide variety of American exports to global markets, with special emphasis on stimulating small business transactions and expanding U.S. exports. Ex-Im Bank's Credit Insurance policies protect against both the political and commercial risks of a foreign buyer defaulting on a credit obligation. Policies are available for single or repetitive export sales and for leases. They generally cover 100 percent of the principal for political risks and 90 to 95 percent for commercial risks, as well as a specified amount of interest.

Short-term policies are used to support the sale of consumer goods, raw materials, and spare parts on terms of up to 180 days; and bulk agricultural commodities, consumer durables, and capital goods on terms of up to 360 days. Exports of most capital goods may be insured for up to five years, depending upon the contract value, under medium-term policies. Coverage is also available for pre-shipments and services policies. Under the Service Sale policy, companies can be protected against customers who fail to pay for services provided due to commercial or specified political reasons.

As a result of this credit protection, exporters may obtain receivables financing because the proceeds of the policies are assignable to financial institutions. This is particularly attractive since it is often difficult to finance export receivables.

Credit insurance is also available through insurance brokers and Ex-Im Bank's five regional offices (Chicago, New York, Miami, Houston and Los Angeles) (See Appendix B for a listing of U.S. Export Assistance Centers).

Small Business Policy

The Small Business Policy covers the repayment risks on short-term export sales by U.S. companies that have had a relatively small volume of exports (less than $3 million) over the previous two years. For the first two years, the policy insures 100 percent of specified political risks and 95 percent of all other risks (commercial risks) that might lead to default by the buyer, subject to policy conditions. Interest, if any, is covered at a specified rate up to a limited time after the due date. The exporter must agree to include in the policy all its eligible sales. This policy insures short-term credit sales of goods and services. With prior written approval, exporters can assign the rights to the accounts receivable to a financial institution as collateral for obtaining financing. Ex-Im Bank will "hold-harmless" the lender who finances the transactions.

Umbrella Policy

The Umbrella Policy encourages U.S. firms with limited exporting experience to expand their export sales. The policy insures all of an eligible company's export credit sales against loss due to administrative, political and commercial reasons and relieves exporters of the paperwork burden associated with obtaining and administering the insurance. Both political and commercial risks are insured directly by Ex-Im Bank.

Short-Term, Single-Buyer Policy

This policy is custom-written for a specific sales contract. Since the policy is structured for single-sale transactions, the standard policy period during which shipments can be made is three months. Ex-Im Bank can issue a policy for up to 12 months to accommodate multiple shipments under a sales contract. Under the policy there is no requirement to insure a spread of business, thus allowing exporters to selectively insure transactions with or without linking them to bank financing. However, payment of a minimum premium is required.

Coverage applies to credit sales to a foreign buyer, export letters of credit opened by a foreign buyer, or export letters of credit opened by a foreign issuing bank, for U.S. goods produced and shipped from the U.S. during the policy period. Cover is provided for credit terms of up to 180 days. On a case-by-case basis, agricultural commodities, capital equipment and quasi-capital equipment may be insured on terms of up to 360 days. Percentages of cover are equalized for commercial and political risks: for sovereign obligers, 100 percent; private-sector and other non-sovereign obligers, 90 percent; letter of credit transactions, 95 percent; bulk agricultural transactions, 98 percent.

Short-Term, Multi-Buyer Policy

This policy is generally written to cover shipments during a one-year period and insures a reasonable spread of an exporter's eligible overseas sales. It provides coverage at lower premiums, helps the exporter to make quicker credit decisions (providing faster service to international buyers) and reduces paperwork. The exporter can obtain financing and can offer competitive credit terms to attract and retain buyers around the globe, even in higher-risk markets. This policy insures short-term sales with repayment terms generally of up to 180 days. At the inception and at each annual renewal of the Short-Term Multi-Buyer Policy, the exporter may choose to cover 90 percent of commercial risks and 100 percent of political risks, or choose equalized cover at 95 percent for both commercial and political risk. For short-term transactions, this coverage applies to the gross invoice amount and, in many cases, to interest at specified rates.

Rimage, a Minneapolis-based corporation, has grown into the second largest designer and manufacturer of diskette-duplication equipment in the world. The company was founded in 1987, and has grown into one of the most recognized names in duplication equipment. Expecting international sales to grow from 25 percent to 30 percent, Rimage saw the need to limit some of the risks inherent to foreign sales while increasing its ability to borrow against its foreign receivables. Rimage filed an application for Ex-Im Bank Credit Insurance to support its overseas sales of diskettes and microcomputer-based products for image-scanning systems.

Ex-Im Bank approved an $800,000 Credit Insurance Policy. The Ex-Im Bank insurance protected Rimage's receivables against both political and commercial risk, along with the risk of default by the foreign distributors. With the help of Ex-Im Bank Credit Insurance, Rimage was able to expand its share of the $80-million diskette-duplication market without substantially increasing its risk.

Medium-Term Policy

The Medium-Term Policy covers capital and quasi-capital goods of U.S. manufacture sold in international markets on terms from six months to five years. Policies are written on a case-by-case basis. The exporter may insure either a single sale or repetitive sales to the same buyer and is not required to insure all medium-term transactions. The amount insured is limited to $10 million.

The foreign buyer must make a 15-percent cash payment on or before the due date of the first installment. The remaining financed portion is covered by a promissory note requiring payment in approximately equal installments on a monthly, quarterly or semiannual basis.

The policy generally covers interest charges up to specified limits as well as principal due. Coverage is for 100 percent of political and commercial loss.

Floor-Plan Coverage

A Combination Medium-Term Policy is utilized mainly to protect exporters in transactions with international distributors in three areas:

- Parts and accessories on terms of up to 180 days;
- Inventory financing, where the exporter may ship goods under a floor-plan arrangement and coverage is for up to 270 days with no down-payment required; and
- Accounts receivable financing, with terms typically up to three years following the minimum cash payment upon resale by the dealer, or at the end of the inventory period.

For medium-term transactions, the buyer must make a 15-percent cash payment and coverage is on the remaining financed portion, plus interest.

Contact:
Export-Import Bank of the United States
811 Vermont Avenue, NW
Washington, DC 20571
Tel: (202) 565-3471
Fax: (202) 565-3486

EID/MITI Overseas Untied Loan Insurance

The **Export-Import Insurance Division of the Japanese Ministry of International Trade and Industry (EID/MITI)** manages Japan's Trade and Investment Insurance System under the Trade and Investment Insurance Law. This insurance covers losses resulting from political risk, such as war or inability to repatriate profits from the host country, and commercial risk, such as bankruptcy or default by the foreign party. Although EID/MITI does not offer direct loans, it insures many types of trade and investment transactions. The availability of such insurance can be instrumental in obtaining outside financing.

EID/MITI developed the Overseas Untied Loan Insurance Program to facilitate international cooperation in funding and implementing projects in developing countries. Under this program, Japanese and non-Japanese companies with subsidiaries in Japan can obtain insurance for long-term loans to foreign companies or governments for projects outside Japan. However, coverage is not extended for loans that are primarily used for the purchase of Japanese exports, or transactions in which there is an equity relationship (or similar relationship) between the lender and the foreign borrower.

Under this program, the loans are specifically defined as:

- Establishing long-term credit necessary for the implementation of a project;
- Acquiring corporate bonds, sovereign bonds or corresponding debentures issued by a foreign company or government to raise capital for a project; and
- Accepting guarantee obligations for a long-term loan obtained by a foreign company or government for a project.

EID/MITI covers losses resulting from inability to recover loans due to political or commercial risks, which are defined as follows:

Political risks are restrictions or an embargo imposed by law on foreign-exchange transactions by a host government; war, revolution or civil disturbance in the host country; or other occurrences in the host country for which neither the lender nor the foreign party is responsible. Political risk is covered up to 95 percent. Loans to projects that enhance trade and sustainable development in the host country may be eligible for coverage up to 97.5 percent, including: those producing exports which earn foreign currency (such as oil or gas) or produce goods to be substituted for imports, such as construction of plants which process raw materials.

Commercial risks are defined as bankruptcy of the foreign borrower. Claims payment is limited to cases in which the bankruptcy is registered with the foreign government and the Japanese embassy in the country confirms it, or default by the foreign party. The foreign party is considered in default if a scheduled repayment is delayed by six or more months after the due date. Commercial risk is covered to a maximum amount of 90 percent.

Terms for this insurance typically exceed three years, since this program is aimed at long-term lending. EID/MITI coverage begins either from the date of establishing long-term credit, or from the date of signing the insurance contract, whichever comes later, and expires on the final due date of the loan. The premium rate is generally determined on a case-by-case basis: the premium for political risk insurance depends on the country's political situation; the premium for commercial risk insurance depends upon the creditworthiness of the borrower, or the security measures that are provided. The premium rate is also affected by term and method of payment. In typical transactions where political and commercial risk is covered under adequate security measures and the country risk factor is average, the annual premium rate will be approximately 0.88 percent.

Contact:
JETRO New York
EID/MITI - New York Office (EID/MITI NY)
1221 Avenue of the Americas
44th Floor
New York, NY 10020
Tel: (212) 819-7769
Fax: (212) 819-7796

Appendix A

Department of Commerce, State, & U.S. Agency for International Development Country Desk Officers

All telephone numbers are in area code (202)

COUNTRY	COMMERCE	STATE	USAID	USDA
Afghanistan		647-9552	647-6967	
Albania	482-2645	647-3298		
Algeria	482-1860	647-4680	647-7462	720-7053
Andorra		647-1414		
Angola	482-4228	647-8434	647-0863	
Anquilla	482-2527	647-2130		
Argentina	482-1548	647-2401	647-4359	720-3221
Aruba	482-2527	647-2621		
ASEAN	482-3877			
Antigua/Barbuda	482-2527	647-2130		
Armenia	482-4655	647-9370	736-4317	
Australia	482-4958	647-9691		720-2690
Austria	482-2920	647-2005		720-3080
Azerbaijan	482-4655	647-9370	736-4317	
Bahamas	482-5680	647-2621		
Bahrain	482-5545	647-6572		
Balkan States	482-2645			
Bangladesh	482-2954	647-9552	647-9631	720-2690
Barbados	482-2527	647-2130		
Belarus	482-4655	647-9370	736-7646	
Belgium	482-5401	647-6027		720-2144
Belize	482-2527	647-3381	647-4105	
Benin	482-5149	647-3066	647-9207	
Bermuda		647-8027		
Bhutan	482-2954	647-1450		
Bolivia	482-2521	647-3360	647-4410	
Bosnia-Hercegovina		736-7024		
Botswana	482-4228	647-9429		
Brazil	482-3871	647-9407	647-4359	720-3221
Brunei	482-4958	647-1221		
Bulgaria	482-2645	647-3298		720-3080
Burkina Faso	482-4388	647-3066	647-7986	
Burma (Myanmar)	482-4958	647-7108	647-4528	720-2690
Burundi	482-4388	647-3139	647-8267	
Cambodia	482-4958	647-3133		
Cameroon	482-5149	647-1707	647-6154	

COUNTRY	COMMERCE	STATE	USAID	USDA
Canada	482-3103	647-3135		720-3221
Cape Verde	482-4388	647-1596	647-6154	
Cayman Islands	482-2527	647-2621		
Central African Republic	482-4388	647-1707	647-8124	
Chad	482-4388	647-1707	647-7986	
Chile	482-1495	647-2401	647-4359	720-3221
Colombia	482-1659	647-3023	647-4365	720-3221
Comoros	482-4564	647-8852	647-8288	
Congo	482-5149	647-3139	647-8124	
Costa Rica	482-5680	647-3381	647-9541	720-3221
Côte d'Ivoire	482-4388	647-3066	647-8100	720-7053
Croatia		736-7361		
Cuba	482-5680	647-9272		
Cyprus	482-3945	647-6113		
Czech Republic	482-2645	647-3052		720-3080
Denmark	482-2841	647-5669		720-2144
D'Jibouti	482-4564	647-7369	647-8288	
Dominica	482-2527	647-2130		
Dominican Republic	482-5680	647-2620	647-4106	720-3221
Ecuador	482-1659	647-3338	647-4410	720-3221
Egypt	482-1860	647-2365	647-7463	720-7053
El Salvador	482-2528	647-3505	647-9535	720-3221
Equitorial Guinea	482-4388	647-1707	647-8124	
Eritrea	482-4564	647-6485	647-9060	
Estonia	482-2645	647-5669	736-7646	
Ethiopia	482-4564	647-6485	647-9063	
European Union	482-5276	647-1708		
Finland	482-3254	647-5669		
France	482-6008	647-1412		720-3080
Gabon	482-5149	647-3546	647-8124	
Gambia	482-4388	647-2865	647-9206	
Georgia	482-4655	647-9370	736-4317	
Germany	482-2435	647-2005		720-2144
Ghana	482-5149	647-1596	647-7465	
Greece	482-3945	647-6113		720-3080
Grenada	482-2527	647-2130		
Guatemala	482-2528	647-3381	647-9967	720-3221
Guinea	482-4388	647-2865	647-6162	
Guinea-Bissau	482-4388	647-1596	647-6049	
Guyana	482-2527	647-2130	647-4106	
Haiti	482-5680	647-4707	647-4106	
Honduras	482-2528	647-4980	647-9555	720-3221
Hong Kong	482- 3932	647-9141		720-3080
Hungary	482-2645	647-4136		720-3080
Iceland	482-2920	647-5669		
India	482-2954	647-9559	647-9668	720-2690

COUNTRY	COMMERCE	STATE	USAID	USDA
Indonesia	482-3877	647-3276	647-4518	720-2690
Iran	482-1860	647-6111		
Iraq	482-1860	647-9448		
Ireland	482-2177	647-8027		720-2144
Israel	482-5506	647-3672	647-2727	720-3080
Italy	482-2177	647-3476		720-3080
Jamaica	482-5680	647-2621	647-4105	
Japan	482-2425	647-3152		720-3080
Jordan	482-5506	647-1022	647-2668	720-7053
Kazakhstan	482-4655	647-9370	647-6920	
Kenya	482-4564	647-6479	647-7885	720-7053
Kiribati		647-0108		
Korea	482-4390	647-7717		720-3080
Kuwait	482-1860	647-6571		
Kyrgyz Republic	482-4655	647-9370	647-6920	
Laos	482-4958	647-3133	647-4528	
Latvia	482-2645	647-5669	736-7646	720-2144
Lebanon	482-1860	647-1030	647-2727	
Lesotho	482-4228	647-8434	647-2944	
Liberia	482-4388	647-2865	647-5581	
Libya	482-5545	647-4674		
Lithuania	482-2645	647-5669	736-7646	
Luxembourg	482-5401	647-6027		
Macau	482-4681	647-9141		
Macedonia		647-7478		
Madagascar	482-4564	647-8852	647-8288	
Malawi	482-4228	647-8432	647-3464	
Malaysia	482-2522	647-3276		720-2690
Maldives	482-2954	647-2351	647-8288	
Mali	482-4388	647-3066	647-5997	
Malta	482-3748	647-3746		
Marshall Isands		647-0108		
Mauritania	482-4388	647-2865	647-8288	
Mauritius	482-4564	647-8852	647-8288	
Mexico	482-0300	647-9894	647-4359	720-3221
Micronesia		647-3546		
Moldova	482-4655	647-9370	736-7646	
Mongolia	482-4681	647-9141	647-4515	
Montserrat	482-2527	647-2130		
Morocco	482-5545	647-4675	647-7462	720-7053
Mozambique	482-4228	647-9429	647-4328	
Namibia	482-4228	647-9858	647-4327	
Nepal	482-2954	647-2351	647-9630	
Netherlands	482-5401	647-6027		720-2144
Netherlands Antilles	482-2527	647-2621		
New Zealand	482-4958	647-9691		720-2690
Nicaragua	482-5680	647-2205	647-8125	720-3221
Nigeria	482-5149	647-4567	647-8834	

COUNTRY	COMMERCE	STATE	USAID	USDA
Norway	482-4414	647-5669		720-2144
Oman	482-1860	647-6572	647-0916	
Pacific Islands	482-4958	647-3546	647-4515	
Pakistan	482-2954	647-9823	647-6967	720-2690
Panama	482-2528	647-4982	647-9541	
Papua New Guinea		647-3546	647-4515	
Paraguay	482-1548	647-2296	647-4359	
People's Republic of China	482-3583	647-9141		720-3080
Peru	482-2521	647-3360	647-4365	720-3221
Philippines	482-4958	647-1222	647-4507	720-2690
Poland	482-2645	647-4136		720-2144
Portugal	482-4508	647-1412		720-3080
Qatar	482-1860	647-6558		
Romania	482-2645	647-3052		720-3080
Russia	482-4655	647-9370	736-4627	720-2144
Rwanda	482-4388	647-3139	647-8267	
Sao Tome & Principe	482-4388	647-1707	647-8124	
Saudi Arabia	482-1860	647-7550		720-7053
Senegal	482-4388	647-2865	647-6049	
Seychelles	482-4564	647-8852	647-8288	
Sierra Leone	482-4388	647-2865	647-8124	
Singapore	482-4958	647-1221		720-2690
Slovak Republic	482-2645	647-3052		
Somalia	482-4564	647-7369	647-9062	
South Africa	482-5148	47-8433	647-4289	720-7053
Spain	482-4508	647-1412		720-3080
Sri Lanka	482-2954	647-2351	647-9630	
St. Kitts-Nevis	482-2527	647-2130		
St. Lucia	482-2527	647-2130		
St. Martin	482-2527	647-2620		
St. Vincent-Grenadines	482-2527	647-2130		
Sudan	482-4564	647-6475	647-9062	
Suriname	482-2527	647-2621		
Swaziland	482-4228	647-8434	647-2944	
Sweden	482-4414	647-5669		720-2144
Switzerland	482-2920	647-2005		720-3080
Syria	482-5506	647-1131		720-7053
Taiwan	482-4390	647-7711		720-3080
Tajikistan	482-4655	647-9370	647-6920	
Tanzania	482-4228	647-8852	647-6331	
Thailand	482-4958	647-7108	647-4528	720-2690
Togo	482-5149	647-3066		
Trinidad & Tobago	482-2527	647-2130		
Tunisia	482-5506	647-3614	647-7462	

COUNTRY	COMMERCE	STATE	USAID	USDA
Turkey	482-1860	647-6114		720-7053
Turkmenistan		647-9370	647-6920	
Uganda	482-4564	647-6479	647-7886	
Ukraine	482-4655	647-9370	736-7646	720-2144
United Arab Emirates	482-1860	647-6558		720-7053
United Kingdom	482-3748	647-8027		720-2144
Uruguay	482-1495	647-2296	647-4359	
Uzbekistan	482-4655	647-9370	647-6920	
Venezuela	482-4303	647-3023	647-4359	720-3221
Viet Nam	482-4958	647-3132	647-4528	
Virgin Islands	482-2527			
Yemen	482-5545	647-6562	647-0916	720-7053
Former Yugoslavia		647-1072		
Zaire	482-4388	647-1707	647-6162	
Zambia	482-4228	647-8432	647-4327	
Zimbabwe	482-4228	647-9429	647-4228	

Appendix B:

Department of Commerce District Offices

In 1994, the Department of Commerce, in coordination with the Small Business Administration, the Export-Import Bank of the United States and the Department of Agriculture, opened four **U.S. Export Assistance Centers (USEACs)** across the United States. Throughout this appendix, these "one-stop shops" have been designated with an asterik (*).

Alabama
Birmingham
(205) 731-1331

Alaska
Anchorage
(907) 271-6237

Arizona
Phoenix
(602) 640-2513

Arkansas
Little Rock
(501) 324-5794

California
*Long Beach USEAC
(310) 980-4550

Los Angeles
(310) 575-7104

Newport Beach
(714) 660-1688

Santa Clara
(408)970-4610

San Diego
(619) 557-5395

San Francisco
(415) 705-2300

Colorado
Denver
(303) 844-6622

Connecticut
Hartford
(203) 240-3530

Delaware
Serviced by Philadelphia, PA

District of Columbia
Serviced by Gaithersburg, MD

Florida
*Miami-USEAC
(305) 526-7425

Clearwater
(813) 461-0011

Orlando
(407) 648-6235

Tallahassee
(904) 488-6469

Georgia
Atlanta
(404) 452-9101

Savannah
(912) 652-4204

Hawaii
Honolulu
(808) 541-1782

Idaho
Boise
(208) 334-3857

Illinois
*Chicago-USEAC
(312) 353-8040

Wheaton
(312) 353-4332

Rockford
(815) 987-4347

Indiana
Indianapolis
(317) 582-2300

Iowa
Des Moines
(515) 284-4222

Kansas
Wichita
(316) 269-6160

Kentucky
Louisville
(502) 582-5066

Louisiana
New Orleans
(504) 589-6546

Maine
Augusta
(207) 622-8249

Maryland
*Baltimore-USEAC
(410) 962-4539

Gaithersburg
(301) 975-3904

Massachusetts
Boston
(617) 565-8563

Michigan
Detroit
(313) 226-3650

Grand Rapids
(616) 456-2411

Minnesota
Minneapolis
(612) 348-1638

Mississippi
Jackson
(601) 965-4388

Missouri
St. Louis
(314) 425-3302

Kansas City
(816) 426-3141

Montana
Serviced by Boise, ID

Nebraska
Omaha
(402) 221-3664

Nevada
Reno
(702) 784-5203

New Hampshire
Portsmouth
(603) 334-6074

New Jersey
Trenton
(609) 989-2100

New Mexico
Santa Fe
(505) 827-3050

New York
Buffalo
(716) 846-4191

Rochester
(716) 263-6480

New York City
(212) 264-0634

North Carolina
Greensboro
(910) 333-5345

North Dakota
Serviced by Minneapolis, MN

Ohio
Cincinnati
(513) 684-2944

Cleveland
(216) 522-4750

Oklahoma
Oklahoma City
(405) 231-5302

Tulsa
(918) 581-7650

Oregon
Portland
(503) 326-3001

Pennsylvania
Philadelphia
(215) 962-4980

Pittsburgh
(412) 644-2850

Puerto Rico
San Juan (Hato Ray)
(809) 766-5555

Rhode Island
Providence
(401) 528-5104

South Carolina
Columbia
(803) 765-5345

Charleston
(803) 727-4051

South Dakota
Serviced by Omaha, NE

Tennessee
Knoxville
(615) 545-4637

Nashville
(615) 736-5161

Memphis
(901) 544-4137

Texas
Dallas
(214) 767-0542

Austin
(512) 482-5939

Houston
(713) 229-2578

Utah
Salt Lake City
(801) 524-5116

Vermont
Montpelier
(802) 828-4508

Virginia
Richmond
(804) 771-2246

Washington
Seattle
(206) 553-5615

West Virginia
Charleston
(304) 347-5123

Wisconsin
Milwaukee
(414) 297-3473

Wyoming
Serviced by Denver, CO

Alabama
Birmingham
(205) 731-1344

Alaska
Anchorage
(907) 271-4022

Arizona
Phoenix
(602) 379-3732

Arkansas
Little Rock
(501) 378-5871

California
San Francisco
(415) 744-6801

Los Angeles
(213) 894-7173

Santa Ana
(714) 836-2494

Fresno
(209) 487-5189

San Diego
(619) 557-5440

Colorado
Denver
(303) 844-3984

Connecticut
Hartford
(203) 240-4700

Delaware
Wilmington
(302) 573-6295

District of Columbia
(202) 634-1500

Florida
Coral Gables
(305) 536-5521

Jacksonville
(904) 443-1900

Georgia
Atlanta
(404) 347-4948

Hawaii
Honolulu
(808) 541-2990

Idaho
Boise
(208) 334-1696

Illinois
Chicago
(312) 353-5429

Indiana
Indianapolis
(317) 226-7269

Iowa
Cedar Rapids
(319) 399-2571

Des Moines
(515) 284-4422

Kansas
Wichita
(316) 269-6273

Kentucky
Louisville
(502) 582-5971

Louisiana
New Orleans
(504) 589-6685

Maine
Augusta
(207) 622-8242

Maryland
Baltimore
(301) 962-4392

Massachusetts
Boston
(617) 451-2047

Michigan
Detroit
(313) 226-6075

Minnesota
Minneapolis
(612) 370-2343

Mississippi
Jackson
(601) 965-5337

Missouri
Kansas City
(816) 374-6762

St. Louis
(314) 539-6600

Montana
Helena
(406) 449-5381

Nebraska
Omaha
(402) 221-4691

Nevada
Las Vegas
(702) 388-6611

New Hampshire
Concord
(603) 225-1400

New Jersey
Newark
(201) 645-2434

New Mexico
Albuquerque
(505) 766-1879

New York
New York City
(212) 264-1495

Syracuse
(315) 423-5377

Buffalo
(716) 846-4301

North Carolina
Charlotte
(704) 371-6563

North Dakota
Fargo
(701) 239-5131

Ohio
Cleveland
(216) 522-4194

Columbus
(614) 469-5548

Oklahoma
Oklahoma City
(405) 231-4494

Oregon
Portland
(503) 326-5203

Pennsylvania
Philadelphia
(215) 962-3750

Pittsburgh
(412) 644-2780

Puerto Rico
Hato Ray
(809) 766-5001

Rhode Island
Providence
(401) 528-4584

South Carolina
Columbia
(803) 765-5376

South Dakota
Sioux Falls
(605) 330-4231

Tennessee
Nashville
(615) 736-5881

Texas
Dallas
(214) 767-0495

San Antonio
(512) 229-4550

Houston
(713) 660-4401

El Paso
(915) 540-5560

Utah
Salt Lake City
(801) 588-3209

Vermont
Montpelier
(802) 828-4422

Virginia
Richmond
(804) 771-2617

Washington
Spokane
(509) 353-2800

West Virginia
Clarksburg
(304) 623-5631

Wisconsin
Madison
(608) 264-5542

Wyoming
Casper
(307) 261-5765

Appendix D:

U.S. Embassies Abroad

AFGHANISTAN
Wazir Akbar Khan Mina
Kabul 62230

ALBANIA
Elbansanit 103
PSC 59, Box 100 (A)
APO AE 09624
Tel: 011 (355) 42-32875
Fax: 011 (355) 42-32222

ALGERIA
4 Chemin Cheikh Bachir El-Ibrahimi
B.P. Box 549, Algiers 16000
Tel: 011 (213) 2 601-425
Fax: 011 (213) 2 603-979

ANTIGUA AND BARBUDA
St. Johns
FPO Miami 34054
Tel: (809) 462-3505/06
Fax: (809) 462-3516
Telex: 2140/USEMB

ARGENTINA
4300 Colombia
1425 Buenos Aires
APO Miami 34034
Tel: 011 (54) 1 774-7611
Fax: 011 (54) 1 775-6040
Telex: 18156 AMEMBAR

ARMENIA
18 Gen. Bagramian
Tel: 011 (7-8852) 151-144
Fax: 011 (7-8852) 151-138
Telex: 243137 AMEMY

AUSTRALIA
Moonah Place
Canberra, A.C.T. 2600
APO San Francisco 96404
Tel: 011 (61) 6 270-5000
Fax: 011 (61) 6 270-5970
Telex: 62104 USAEMB

AUSTRIA
Boltzmanngasse 16, A-1091
Vienna
APO NY 09108-0001
Tel: 011 (43) 1 313 39
Fax: 011 (43) 1 310 6917
Telex: 114634

AZERBAIJAN
Hotel Intourist
Tel: 011 (7-8922) 92-63-06/07/07/08/09,
ext 441/2/6/7/8, 450
Telex: 142110 AMEMB SU

BAHAMAS
Mosmar Building
Queen Street
P.O. Box N-8197, Nassau
Tel: (809) 322-1181
Fax: (809) 328-7838
Telex: 20138 AMEMB NS138

BAHRAIN
Shaikh Isa Road
P.O. Box 26431, Manama
FPO NY 09526-6210
Tel: 011 (973) 273300
Fax: 011 (973) 272594
9398 USATO BN

BANGLADESH
Dhaka
Adamjee Ct. Bldg., 5th Fl.
Motijheel Commercial Area
G.P.O. Box 323, Ramana
Tel: 011 (880) 2 237161

BARBADOS
Canadian Imperial Bank
 of Commerce Building
Broad Street, P.O. Box 302;
Box B, Bridgetown
FPO Miami 34054
Tel: (809) 436-4950
Fax: (809) 429-5246
Telex: 2259 USEMB BG1 WB

BELARUS
Starovilenskaya 46
Minsk
Tel: 011 (7-0172) 34-65-37

BELGIUM
27 Boulevard du Regent
B-1000 Brussels
APO NY 09667-1000
Tel: 011 (32) 2 513-3830
Fax: 011 (32) 2 512-6653
Telex: 846-21336

BELIZE
Gabourel Lane and Hutson Street,
P.O. Box 286
Belize City
Tel: 011 (501) 2 77161
Fax: 011 (501) 2 30802

BENIN
Rue Caporal Anani Bernard
B.P. 2012, Cotonou
Tel: 011 (229) 300650
Fax: 011 (229) 301974

BERMUDA
Consulate General
Crown Hill, 16 Middle Road, Devonshire
P.O. Box HM325, Hamilton
FPO NY 09560-5300
Tel: (809) 295-1342
Fax: (809) 295-1592
Telex: HMBX AMCON

BOLIVIA
Banco Popular Del Peru Bldg
Corner of Calles Mercado & Colon
P.O. Box 425, La Paz
APO Miami 34032
Tel: 011 (591) 2 350251
Fax: 011 (591) 2 359875
Telex: AMEMB BV 3268

BOTSWANA
P.O. Box 90, Gaborone
Tel: 011 (267) 353-982
Fax: 011 (267) 356-947

BRAZIL
Avenida das Nacoes, Lote 3
70403 Brasilia, D.F.
APO Miami 34030
Tel: 011 (55) 61 321-7272
Fax: 011 (55) 61 225-3981
Telex: 061-1091

BRUNEI
Third Floor Teck Guan Plaza
Jalan Sultan, American Ambassy Box B
Bandar Seri Begawan
APO San Francisco 96528
Tel: 011 (673) 2 29670
Fax: 011 (673) 2 25293

BULGARIA
One A. Stamboliski Blvd
Sofia
APO NY 09213-5740
Tel: (359) 2 884801
Telex: 22690 BG

BURKINA FASO
01 B.P. 35
Ouagadougou
Tel: (226) 306723
Fax: (226) 312368
Telex: AEMB 5290 BF

BURMA/MYANMAR
581 Merchant Street
GPO Box 521, Rangoon
APO San Francisco 96346, AM, Box B
Tel: 011 (95) 1 82055/82181
Fax: 011 (95) 1 80409
Telex: 083-21230 AIDRGN BM

BURUNDI
Avenue des Etats-Unis
Rwagasore
B.P. 1720
Bujumbura
Tel: 011 (257) 222-454
Fax: 011 (257) 222-926

CAMBODIA
27 EO Street 240
or
Box P, APO AP 96546
Tel: 011 (855) 23-26436/26438
Fax: 011 (855) 23-26437

CAMEROON
Rue Nachtigal , B.P. 817
Yaounde
Tel: (237) 234-014
Telex: 8223 KN
Consulate
21 Avenue du General De Gaulle,
B.P. 4006, Douala
Tel: 011 (237) 42 0688
Fax: 011 (237) 42 7790
Telex: 5233KN

CANADA
(Ottawa, Ontario)
100 Wellington Street
K1P 5T1; P.O. Box 5000
Ogdensburg, NY 13669
Tel: (613) 238-5338
Fax: (613) 233-8511
Telex: 053-3582

CAPE VERDE, REPUBLIC OF
Rua Hoji Ya Henda 81
C.P. 201, Praia
Tel: 011 (238) 614-363
6068 AMEMB CV

CENTRAL AFRICAN REPUBLIC
Avenue President Dacko
B.P. 924
Bangui
Tel: 011 (190) 61-02-00
Fax: 011 (190) 236 61-44-94
Telex: 5287 RC

CHAD
Ave. Felix Eboue
B.P. 413
N'Djamena
Tel: 011 (235) 516 218
5203 KD

CHILE
Codina Building
1343 Agustinas
Santiago
APO Miami 34033
Tel: 011 (56) 2 671-0133
Fax: 011 (56) 2 699-1141
Telex: 240062-USA-CL

CHINA (PRC)
Xiu Shui Bei Jie 3
1006000 Beijing
PSC 461, Box 50
FPO AP 96521-0002
Tel: 011 (86) 1 532-3831
Fax: 011 (86) 1 532-3178
Telex: AMEMB CN 22701

COLOMBIA
Calle 38, No. 8-61
P.O. Box A.A. 3831 Bogota
APO Miami 34038
Tel: 011 (57) 1 285-1300
Fax: 011 (57) 1 285-7945
Telex: 44843

COMOROS
Boite Postale 1318
Moroni
Tel: 011- 732203/22
Telex: 257 AMEMB KO

THE CONGO
Avenue Amilcar Cabral
B.P. 1015; Box C
Brazzaville
APO NY 09662-0006

COSTA RICA
Pavas, San Jose
APO Miami 34020
Tel: 011 (506) 203939
Fax: 011 (506) 204703

COTE D'IVOIRE
5 Rue Jesse Owens
01 B.P. 1712
Abidjan
Tel: 011 (225) 210979
Fax: 011 (225) 22-32-59
Telex: 23660

CUBA
Swiss Embassy
Calzada entre L&M
Vedado Seccion
Havana
Tel: 320551
Telex: 512206

CYPRUS
Therissos and Dositheos Streets
Nicosia
FPO NY 09530
Tel: 011 (357) 2 4651511
Fax: 011 (357) 2 459571
Telex: 4160 AMEMY CY

CZECH REPUBLIC
Trziste 15-125 48 Praha
APO AMEM, Box 5630
APO NY 09213-5630
Tel: 011 (42) 2 53 6641/9
Telex: 21196 AMEMBC

DENMARK
Dag Hammarskjolds Alle 24
2100 Copenhagen O
APO NY 09170
Tel: 011 (45) 31 423144
Fax: 011 (45) 35 430223
Telex: 22216 AMEMB DK

DJIBOUTI, REPUBLIC OF
Plateau du Serpent
Blvd. Marechal Joffre
B.P. 185, Djibouti
Tel: 011 (253) 353940
Fax: 011 (253) 353940

DOMINICAN REPUBLIC
Corner of Calle Cesar Nicolas Penson
& Calle Leopoldo Navarro
Santo Domingo
APO Miami 34041-0008
Tel: 011 (809) 541-2171
Telex: 3460013

ECUADOR
120 Avenida Patria, Quito
Tel: 011 (593) 2 562890
Fax: (593) 2 502052

EGYPT
3 Lazougi Street
Garden City
Cairo
Unit 64900, Box 11
APO AE 09839-4900
Tel: 011 (20) 2 354-2320
Fax: 011 (20) 2 355-8368
Telex: 93773 AMEMB

EL SALVADOR
25 Avenida Norte No. 1230
San Salvador
APO Miami 34023
Tel: 011 (503) 267100
Fax: 011 (503) 234067

EQUATORIAL GUINEA
Calle de Los Ministros
P.O. Box 597
Malabo
Tel: 011 (240) 9 2185
Fax: 011 (240) 9 2164

ERITEA
34 Zera Yacob Street
P.O. Box 211
Tel: 011 (291) 1-12-00-04
Fax: 011 (291) 1-12-75-84

ESTONIA
Kentmanni 20
EE 0001
Tel: 011 (372) 6-312-021/2/3/4
Fax: 011 (372) 6-312-025

ETHIOPIA
Entoto Street, P.O. Box 1014
Addis Ababa
Tel: 011 (251) 1 550666
Fax: 011 (251) 1 551166
Telex: 21282

FIJI
31 Loftus Street
P.O. Box 218
Suva
Tel: 011 (679) 314466
Telex: 2255 AMEMBASY FJ

FINLAND
Itainen Puistotie 14A
SF-00140, Helsinki
APO NY 09664
Tel: 011 (358) 0 171931
Fax: 011 (358) 0 635322
Telex: 121644 USEMB SF
TELEX (Commercial Section): 125541

FRANCE
2 Avenue Gabriel
75382 Paris CEDEX 8
Paris
APO NY 09777
Tel: 011 (33) 1 42664827
Telex: 650221 AMEMB

FRENCH CARIBBEAN
Consulate General
14 Rue Blenac; B.P. 561
Martinique
Fort-de-France 97206
Tel: 011 (596) 631303
Fax: 011 (596) 602080
Telex: 912670

GABON
Boulevard de la Mer
B.P. 4000, Libreville
Tel: 011 (241) 762003
Fax: 011 (241) 745-507
Telex: 5250 GO

THE GAMBIA
Fajara, Kairaba Ave
P.M.B. No. l9, Banjul
Tel: 011 (220) 92856
Fax: 011 (220) 92475

GEORGIA
#25 Antonely Str.
380026 Tiblisi
Tel: 011 (7-8832) 98-99-68
Fax: 011 (7-8832) 93-37-59

GERMANY
Diechmanns Alle 29
5300 Bonn 2
Tel: 011 (49) 228-339-2895
Fax: 011 (49) 228-334-649

GHANA
Ring Road East,
P.O. Box 194
Accra
Tel: 011 (233) 21 775348
Fax: 011 (233) 21 706008
Telex: 2579 EMBUSA GH

GREECE
91 Vasilissis Sophias Rd.
GR - 101 60 Athens
Tel: 011 (301) 721-2951
Fax: 011 (301) 721-8660

GRENADA
Ross Point Inn; P.O. Box 54
St. George's, Grenada, W.I.
Tel: (809) 440-1731
Fax: (809) 444-4820

GUATEMALA
7-01 Avenida de la Reforma
Zone 10
01010 Guatemala City
APO Miami 34024
Tel: (502) 2 31-15-41

GUINEA
2nd Blvd and 9th Ave
B.P. 603, Conakry
Tel: 011 (244) 44-15-20
Fax: 011 (244) 44-15-22

GUINEA-BISSAU
Avenida Domingos Ramos
C.P.297, Bissau
Tel: 011 (245) 20-1139
Fax: 011 (245) 20-1159

GUYANA
99-100 Young and Duke Streets
Kingstown, Georgetown
Tel: 011 (592) 2 54900-9

HAITI
Harry Truman Boulevard
P.O. Box 1761
Port-Au-Prince
Tel: 011 (509) 1 20354
Fax: 011 (509) 1 39007

HONDURAS
Avenida La Paz
Apdo. Postal 3453
Tegucigalpa, D.C.
APO Miami 34022
Tel: 011 (504) 32-3120
Fax: 011 (504) 32-0027 (Emb)
Fax: 011 (504) 32-2888 (Comm Sect)

HONG KONG
Consulate General
PSC 464 , Hong Kong
FPO San Francisco 96552-0002
Tel: 011 (852) 5 239011
Fax: 011 (852) 5 845-1598

HUNGARY
V. Szabadsag Ter 12
1054 Budapest
Tel: 011 (36) 11 126450
Fax: 011 (36) 11 328934
Telex: 18048 224222

ICELAND
Laufasvegur 21, Box 40
FPO NY 09571-0001
Reykjavik
Tel: 011 (354) 1 629100
Fax: 011 (354) 1 629139
Telex: USEMB IS3044

INDIA
Shanti Path,
Chanakyapuri 110021,
New Delhi
Tel: 011 (91) 11 600651
Fax: 011 (91) 11 672476
Telex: 031-82065 USEMIN

INDONESIA
Medan Merdeka Selatan 5
Jakarta
APO AP 96520
Tel: 011 (62) 21 360360
Fax: 011 (62) 21 3851632
Telex: 44218 AMEMB JKT

IRELAND
42 Elgin Road
Ballsbridge, Dublin
Tel: 011 (353) 1 687122
Fax: 011 (353) 1 689946

ISRAEL
71 Hayarkon Street
Tel Aviv
APO NY 09672
Tel: 011 (972) 3 517-4338
Fax: 011 (972) 3 658-0330
Telex: 33376/371386 USFCSIL

ITALY
Via Veneto 119/A
00187-Rome
APO AE 09624
Tel: 011 (39) 6 46741
Fax: 011 (39) 6 46742
Telex: 622322 AMBRMA

JAMAICA
Jamaica Mutual Life Center
2 Oxford Road, 3rd Floor
Kingston
Tel: (809) 929-6743

JAPAN
10-1, Alasaka 1-chome
Minato-ku (107), Tokyo
APO San Francisco 96503
Tel: 011 (81) 3 224-5000
Fax: 011 (81) 3 505-1862
Telex: 2422118 AMEMBJ

U.S Export Development Office
7th Floor, World Import Mart
1-3 Higashi Ikebukuro 3-chome
Toshima-ku, Tokyo 170

JERUSALEM
Consulate General
18 Agron Road, P.O. Box 290
Jerusalem 94190
APO NY 09672
Tel: 011 (972) 2 253288
Consular & Commercial Offices
27 Nablus Road

JORDAN
Jabel Amman
P.O. Box 354
APO NY 09892
Tel: 011 (962) 6 644371 6
Fax: 011 (962) 6 659667
Telex: 21510 USEMB JO
Commercial Office
Telex: 24070 USCOMM JO

KAZAKHSTAN
99/97 Furmanova Str.
Almaty, Republic of Kazakhstan 480012
Tel: 011 (7-3272) 63-24-26
Fax: 011 (7-3272) 63-38-83

KENYA
Moi/Haile Selassie Avenue
Nairobi
P.O. Box 30137
Tel: 011 (254) 2 334141
Telex: 22964

KOREA, REPUBLIC OF
82 Sejong-Ro;
Chongro-ku
Seoul
APO San Francisco 96301
Tel: 011 (82) 2 397-4114
Telex: AMEMB 23108

KYRGYZSTAN
Erkindik Prospekt 66
Bishkek 720002
Tel: 011 (7-3312) 22-29-20, 22-27-77
Fax: 011 (7-3312) 22-35-51
Telex: 245133 AMEMB SU

KUWAIT
P.O. Box 77
13001 SAFAT
Tel: 011 (965) 242-4151
Fax: 011 (965) 240-7368

LATVIA
Raina Boulevard 7
Riga 226050
Tel: 011 (371) 2-213-962
Fax: 011 (371) 2-882-0047

LAOS
Rue Bartholonie; B.P. 114
Vientiane; Box V
APO San Francisco 96346
Tel: 011 (2220) 2384,3570

LEBANON
Antelias, P.O. Box 70-840
Beirut
FPO New York 09530
Tel: 011 (961) 417774

LESOTHO
P.O. Box 333, Maseru 100
Tel: 011 (266) 312666
Fax: 011 (266) 310116
Telex: 4506 USAID LO

LIBERIA
111 United Nations Drive
P.O. Box 98, Monrovia
APO New York 09155
Tel: (231) 22299
Fax: (231) 222450

LITHUANIA
Akmenu 6,
Vilnus 2600
APO AE 09723
Tel: (370) 2-223-031
Fax: (370) 2-222-779

LUXEMBOURG
22 Blvd. Emmanuel-Servais
L-2535 Luxembourg
APO AE 09132-5380
Tel: 011 (352) 460123
Fax: 011 (352) 461401

MACEDONIA
c/o USAID
26 Veljko Vlahovic
9100 Skopje
APO AE 009213-5740 (c/o US Embassy Sofia)
Tel: 011 (389) 91-117-2121
Fax: 011 (389) 91-118-105

MADAGASCAR
14 and 16 Rue Rainitovo
Antsahavola, B.P. 620
Antananarivo
Tel: 011 (261) 2 212-57
Telex: USA EMB MG 22202

MALAWI
P.O. Box 30016, Lilongwe
Tel: 011 (265) 783-166
Fax: 011 (265) 780-471
Telex: 44627

MALAYSIA
376 Jalan Tun Razak
P.O. Box No. 10035
50400 Kuala Lumpur
Tel: 011 (60) 3 248-9011
Fax: 011 (60) 3 243-2207

MALI
Rue Testard and Rue Mohamed V.
B.P. 34, Bamako
Tel: 011 (223) 225470
Fax: 011 (223) 228059
Telex: AMEMB MJ

MALTA
Development House, 2nd Flr
St. Anne Street, PO Box 535
Floriana , Valletta
Tel: 011 (356) 240424
Fax: 011 (356) 243229

MARSHALL ISLANDS
P.O. Box 680
Republic of the Marshall Islands
Majuro 96960-4380
Tel: 011 (692) 4011

MAURITANIA
B.P. 222
Nouakchott
Tel: 011 (222) 2 252660
Fax: 011 (222) 2 52589
Telex: AMEMB 5558 MTN

MAURITIUS
Rogers Building, 4th Floor
John Kennedy Street
Port Louis
Tel: (230) 208-9534

MEXICO
Paseo de la Reforma 305
Colonia Cuauhtemoc
06500 Mexico, D.F.
Laredo, TX 78044-3087
Tel: 011 (52) 5 211-0042
Fax: 011 (52) 5 511-9980
Telex: 017-73-091

MICRONESIA
P.O. Box 1286, Pohnpei
Kolonia, Federated States
 of Micronesia 96941
Tel: 011 (691) 320-2187

MOLDOVA
Strada Alexei Mateevici 103
Tel: 011 (373) 2-23-37-72/3004
Fax: (7-0422) 23-34-94

MONGOLIA
Ulaanbaatar
PSC 461, Box 300
FPO AP 96521-2000
Tel: 29095/27411
Telex: 080079253 AMEMB MH

MOROCCO
2 Ave. de Marrakech
P.O. Box 120, Rabat
APO NY 09284
Tel: 011 (212) 7 762265
Telex: 31005M

MOZAMBIQUE
Avenida Kaunda 193
P.O. Box 783, Maputo
Tel: 011 (258) 1 492797
Fax: 011 (258) 1 490114

NAMIBIA
Ausplan Building
14 Lossen St, Private Bag 12029
Windhoek
Tel: 011 (264) 61 221601/222675
Fax: 011 (264) 61 229792

NEPAL
Pani Pokhari
GPO Box 295
Kathmandu
Tel: 011 (977) 1 411179
Fax: 011 (977) 1 419963

NETHERLANDS
Lange Voorhout 102
The Hague
APO AE 09715
Tel: 011 (31) 70 310-9417
Fax: 011 (31) 70 263-2985

NETHERLANDS ANTILLES
Consulate General
St. Anna Blvd. 19
P.O. Box 158
Willemstad, Curacao
Tel: 011 (599) 9 613066
Fax: 011 (599) 9 616489
Telex: 1062 AMCON NA

NEW ZEALAND
29 Fitzherbert Terrace
Thorndon, Wellington
P.O. Box 1190
FPO San Francisco 96690-0002
Tel: 011 (64) 4 722068
Fax: 011 (64) 4 712380
Telex: NZ 3305

NICARAGUA
Km. 4-1/2 Carretera Sur.
Managua
APO Miami 34021
Tel: 011 (505) 2 662291

NIGER
Niamey, B.P. 11201
Tel: 011 (227) 722661
Fax: 011 (277) 733167
Telex: EMB NIA 5444NI

NIGERIA
12 Eleke Crescent
P.O. Box 554, Lagos
Tel: 011 (234) 1 610097
Fax: 011 (234) 1 610257
Telex: 23616 EMLA NG

NORWAY
Drammensveien 18
N-0244 Oslo
APO AE 09707
Tel: 011 (47) 2 448550
Fax: 011 (47) 2 558803
Telex: 78470

OMAN
P.O Box 50202
Madinat Qaboos, Muscat
Tel: 011 (968) 698989
Fax: 011 (968) 604316
Telex: 3785 AMEMBMUS ON

PAKISTAN
Diplomatic Enclave
Ramna 5, P.O. Box 1048
Islamabad
Unit 6220, Box 2000
APO AE 09812-2000
Tel: 011 (92) 51 826161
Fax: 011 (92) 51 822004
Telex: 825864 AEISL PK

REPUBLIC OF PALAU
P. 0. Box 6028
Republic of Palau 96940
Koror (USLO)
Tel: 160-680-920

PANAMA
Apartado 6959
Panama 5
Rep. de Panama, Box E
APO Miami 34002
Tel: 011 (507) 271777
Fax: 011 (507) 039470

PAPUA NEW GUINEA
Armit Street
P.O. Box 1492
Port Moresby
Tel: 011 (675) 211455
Fax: 011 (675) 213-423
Telex: 22189 USAEM

PARAGUAY
1776 Mariscal Lopez Avenue
Casilla Postal 402
Asuncion
APO Miami 34036
Tel: 011 (595) 21 213715
Fax: 011 (595) 21 213728

PERU
Corner Avenidas Inca Garcilaso
 de la Vega & Espana
P.O. Box 1995,
Lima 100
APO Miami 34031
Tel: 011 (51) 14 330555
Fax: 011 (51) 14 334687
Telex: 25212 PE(USEMBGSO)

PHILIPPINES
1201 Roxas Boulevard
Manila
APO San Francisco 96528
Tel: 011 (63) 2 521-7116
Telex: 722-23766 AME PH

Commercial Office
395 Buenida Avenue,
Extension Makati
Tel: 011 (63) 2 818-6674
Fax: 011 (63) 2 818-2684
Telex: 22708 COSEC PH

POLAND
Aleje Ujazdowskie 29/31
Am Warsaw, Box 5010
c/o AmConGen (WAW)
APO NY 09213
Tel: 011 (48) 2 628-3041
Fax: 011 (48) 2 628-8298
Telex: 813304 USA POL

PORTUGAL
Avenida das Forcas Armadas
1600 Lisbon
APO NY 09678-0002
Tel: 011 (351) 1 726-6600
Fax: 011 (351) 1 726-9109

QATAR
Fariq Bin Omran
P.O. Box 2399
Doha
Tel: 011 (974) 864701
Fax: 011 (974) 861669
Telex: 4847

ROMANIA
Strada Tudor Arghezi 7-9
Bucharest
APO NY 09213
Tel: 011 (40) 0 104040

RUSSIA
U.S. Ulitsa Chaykovskovo 1
9/21/23 Moscow
APO NY 09862
Tel: 011 (7095) 252-2450

RWANDA
Blvd. de la Revolution
B.P. 28, Kigali
Tel: 011 (205) 75601/3
Fax: (250) 72128

SAUDI ARABIA
Collector Road M
Riyadh Diplomatic Quarter
Unit 61307
APO AE 09803-1307
Tel: 011 (966) 1 488-3800
Fax: 011 (966) 1 488-3278
Telex: 406866 AMEMB SJ

SENEGAL
B.P. 49, Ave Jean XXIII
Tel: 011 (221) 214296
Fax: 011 (221) 111991
Telex: 21793 AMEMB SG

SERBIA-MONTENEGRO
American Embassy Box 5070
Unit 1310, APO AE 09213-1310
Tel: 011 (381) 11-645-221
Fax: 011 (381) 11-645-096

SEYCHELLES
Box 148, Victoria House
APO NY 09030
Tel: 011 (248) 25256

SIERRA LEONE
Corner of Walpole and
Siaka Stevens Streets
Freetown
Tel: 011 (232) 22 26481
Telex: 9893509 USEMBSL

SINGAPORE
30 Hill Street, Singapore 0617
APO AP 96534
Tel: 011 (65) 338-0251
Fax: 011 (65) 338-4550
Telex: 42289 AMEMB

SLOVAK REPUBLIC
Hviezdoslavovo Namestie 4
81102 Bratislava
Tel: 011 (42) 7-330861
Fax: 011 (42) 7-330096

SLOVENIA
Box 254, Prazakova 4
61000 Ljubljana
Tel: 011 (386) 61-301-427/472/485
Fax: 011 (386) 61-301-401

SOLOMON ISLANDS
Mud Alley, P.O. Box 561
Honiara
Tel: 011 (677) 23890
Fax: 011 (677) 23488
Telex: 66461 HQ USACON

SOUTH AFRICA
Thibault House, 225 Pretorius St
Pretoria
Tel: 011 (27) 12 284266
Fax: 011 (27) 12 284266 x259
Telex: 3751

SPAIN
Serrano 75, Madrid 28006
Tel: 011 (34) 1 577-4000
Fax: 011 (34) 1 577-8655
Telex: 27763

SRI LANKA
210 Galle Road, P.O. Box 106
Colombo 3
Tel: 011 (94) 1 448007
Fax: 011 (94) 1 549070
Telex: 21305 AMEMB CE

SUDAN
Sharia Ali Abdul Latif
P.O. Box 699
Khartoum
APO NY 09668
Tel: 74700
Telex: 22619 AMEM SD

SURINAME
Dr. Sophie Redmondstraat 129
P.O. Box 1821
Paramaribo
Tel: 597) 72900
Fax: 011 (597) 10025
Telex: 373 AMEMSU SN

SWEDEN
Strandvagen 101
S-115 89 Stockholm
Tel: (46) 8 783-5300
Fax: (46) 8 661-1964
Telex: 12060 AMEMB S

SWITZERLAND
Jubilaeumstrasse 93
3005 Bern
Tel: (41) 31 437011
Telex: 845 912603

SYRIA
Abu Rumaneh
Al Mansur Street, No.2
P.O. Box 29
Damascus
Tel: 011 (963) 11 332814/15
Fax: 011 (963) 11 718687
Telex: 411919 USDAMA SY

TAIWAN

(Note: Unofficial relations with Taiwan are conducted through the American Institute in Taiwan, which has offices in Taipei and Kaohsiung.)

American Institute in Taiwan
7 Lane 134, Hsin Yi Road
Section 3
Tel: 011 (866) 2 709-2000
Fax: 011 (886) 2 702-7675
Telex: 23890 USTRADE

American Institute in Taiwan
Kaohsuing
3rd Floor, No. 2
Chung Cheng, 3rd Road
Tel: 011 (886) 7 224-0154

TAKIJISTAN

Interim Chancery
39 Ainii Street
Oktyabraskaya Hotl
Tel: 011 (7-3772) 21-03-56

TANZANIA

36 Laibon Road
P.O. Box 9123
Dar Es Salaam
Tel: 011 (255) 51 375014
Telex: 41250 USA TZ
Fax: 011 (255) 513 37408

THAILAND

Diethlem Towers, A-302
93/1 Wireless Road
Bangkok 10330
APO AP 96546
Tel: 011 (66) 2 255-4365/7
Fax: 011 (66) 2 255-2915
Telex: 20966 FCSBKK

TOGO

Rue Pelletier Caventou
  & Rue Vauban, B.P. 852
Lome
Tel: 011 (228) 217717
Fax: 011 (228) 217952

TRINIDAD AND TOBAGO

15 Queen's Park West
P.O. Box 752
Port-of-Spain
Tel: (809) 622-6372
Fax: (809) 628-5462

TUNISIA

144 Ave. de la Liberte
1002 Tunis-Belvedere
Tel: 011 (216) 1 782566
Fax: 011 (011 216) 1 789719
Telex: 13379 AMTUN TN

TURKEY

110 Ataturk Boulevard
Ankara
APO NY 09257-0006
Tel: 011 (90) 4 467-0949
Fax: 011 (90) 4 467-1366
Telex: 43144 USIA TR

TURKMENISTAN

6 Teheran Street
Yubilenaya Hotel
Tel: 011 (7-36320) 24-49-25/49-22

UGANDA

Parliament Avenue
P.O. Box 7007
Kampala
Tel: 011 (256) 41 259792

UKRAINE

10 Yuria Kotsyubinskovo
252053 Kiev 53
Tel: 011 (7-044) 244-7349
Fax: 011 (7-044) 279-1485
Telex: 131142 CGKIV SU

UNITED ARAB EMIRATES

Al-Sudan Street
P.O. Box 4009
Abu Dhabi
Tel: (971) 2 336691
Commercial Section
Blue Tower Building, 8th Floor
Shaikh Kalifa Bin Zayed Street
Telex: 22229 AMEMBY EM

UNITED KINGDOM
24/31 Grosvenor Square
W. 1A 1AE, Box 40
London, England
FPO NY 09509
Tel: 011 (44) 01 499-9000
Fax: 011 (44) 71 409-1637
Telex: 266777

URUGUAY
Lauro Muller 1776
Montevideo
APO Miami 34035
Tel: 011 (598) 2 236061
Fax: 011 (598) 2 488611

VENEZUELA
Avenida Francisco de Miranda &
Avenida Principal de la Floresta
P.O. Box 62291
Caracas 1060-A
APO Miami 34037
Tel: 011 (58) 2 285-3111
25501 AMEMB VE
TELEX 25501 AMEMB VE

YEMEN ARAB REPUBLIC
Dhahr Himyar Zone
Sheraton Hotel District
P.O. Box 22347
Tel: 011 (967) 1 238-843 through 52
Fax: 011 (967) 1 251-563

ZAIRE
310 Avenue des Aviateurs
Kinshasha
APO NY 09662
Tel: 011 (243) 12 21532
Fax: 011 (243) 12 21232
Telex: 21405 US EMB ZR

ZAMBIA
Corner of Independence and
United Nations Avenues
P.O. Box 31617
Lusaka
Tel: 011 (2601) 228595
Telex: AMEMB ZA 41970

ZIMBABWE
172 Herbert Chitapo Avenue
P.O. Box 3340
Commercial Section
First Floor, Century House West
36 Baker Avenue
Harare
Tel: 011 (263) 14 794521
Fax: 011 (263) 4 796488
Telex: 4591 USFCS ZW

Appendix E:

Foreign Embassies in the United States

Afghanistan
2341 Wyoming Avenue, NW
Washington, DC 20008
Tel: (202) 234-3770

Albania
1150 18th Street., NW
Washington, DC 20006
Tel: (202) 223-4942

Algeria
2118 Kalorama Road, NW
Washington, DC 20008
Tel: (202) 265-2800

Angola
125 East 73rd Street.
New York, NY 10021
Tel: (212) 861-5656

Antigua & Barbuda
3007 Tilden Street, NW
Washington, DC 20007
Tel: (202) 362-5122

Argentina
1600 New Hampshire Avenue, NW
Washington, DC 20009
Tel: (202) 939-6400

Armenia
1600 L Street, Suite 210, NW
Washington, DC 20036
Tel: (202) 628-5766

Australia
1601 Massachusetts Avenue, NW
Washington, DC 20036
Tel: (202) 797-3000

Austria
3524 International Court, NW
Washington, DC 20008
Tel: (202) 895-6767

Azerbaijan
927 15th Street, Suite 700, NW
Washington, DC 20005
Tel: (202) 842-0001

Bahamas
2220 Massachusetts Avenue, NW
Washington, DC 20008
Tel: (202) 319-2660

Bahrain
3502 International Drive, NW
Washington, DC 20008
Tel: (202) 342-0741

Bangladesh
2201 Wisconsin Avenue, NW
Washington, DC 20007
Tel: (202) 342-8372

Barbados
2144 Wyoming Avenue, NW
Washington, DC 20008
Tel: (202) 939-9200

Belarus
1511 K Street, NW
Washington, DC 20001
Tel: (202) 986-1606

Belgium
3330 Garfield Street, NW
Washington, DC 20008
Tel: (202) 333-6900

Belize
2435 Massachusetts Avenue, NW
Washington, DC 20008
Tel: (202) 363-4505

Benin
Cathedral Avenue, NW
Washington, DC 20008
Tel: (202) 232-6656

Bhutan
2 U.N. Plaza,
27th Floor
New York, NY 10017
Tel: (212) 826-1919

Bolivia
3014 Massachusetts Avenue, NW
Washington, DC 20008
Tel: (202) 483-4410

Botswana
3007 Tilden Street, NW
Washington, DC 20007
Tel: (202) 244-4990

Brazil
3006 Massachusetts Avenue, NW
Washington, DC 20008
Tel: (202) 745-2700

Brunei
Watergate, Suite 300,
3rd Floor
2600 Virginia Avenue, NW
Washington, DC 20037
Tel: (202) 342-0159

Bulgaria
1621 22nd Street, NW
Washington, DC 20008
Tel: (202) 387-7969

Burkina Faso
2340 Massachusetts Avenue, NW
Washington, DC 20008
Tel: (202) 332-5577

Burundi
Wisconsin Avenue, NW, Suite 212
Washington, DC 20007
Tel: (202) 342-2574

Cameroon
2349 Massachusetts Avenue, NW
Washington, DC 20008
Tel: (202) 265-8790

Canada
501 Pennsylvania Avenue, NW
Washington, DC 20001
Tel: (202) 682-1740

Cape Verde
3415 Massachusetts Avenue, NW
Washington, DC 20007
Tel: (202) 965-6820

Central African Republic
1618 22nd Street, NW
Washington, DC 20008
Tel: (202) 483-7800

Chad
2002 R Street, NW
Washington, DC 20009
Tel: (202) 462-4009

Chile
1732 Massachusetts Avenue, NW
Washington, DC 20036
Tel: (202) 785-1746

China, People's Republic of
2300 Connecticut Avenue, NW
Washington, DC 20008
Tel: (202) 328-2500

Colombia
2118 LeRoy Place, NW
Washington, DC 20008
Tel: (202) 387-8338

Comoros
336 E. 45th St. Tel: (2nd Fl)
Washington, DC 20017
Tel: (202) 972-8010

Congo, People's Republic
4891 Colorado Avenue, NW
Washington, DC 20011
Tel: (202) 726-5500

Costa Rica
2114 S Street, NW
Washington, DC 20008
Tel: (202) 234-2945

Cote D'Ivoire
2412 Massachusetts Avenue, NW
Washington, DC 20008
Tel: (202) 797-0300

Croatia
236 Massachusetts Avenue, NE
Washington, DC 20002
Tel: (202) 543-5580

Cyprus
2211 R Street, NW
Washington, DC 20008
Tel: (202) 462-5772

Czech Republic
3900 Linnean Avenue, NW
Washington, DC 20008
Tel: (202) 363-6315

European Communities
2100 M Street, NW 7th floor
Washington, DC 20037
Tel: (202) 862-9500

Denmark
3200 Whitehaven Street, NW
Washington, DC 20008
Tel: (202) 234-4300

Djibouti
1156 15th Street, NW Suite 515
Washington, DC 20005
Tel: (202) 331-0270

Dominican Republic
1715 22nd Street, NW
Washington, DC 20008
Tel: (202) 332-6280

Ecuador
2535 15th Street, NW
Washington, DC 20009
Tel: (202) 234-7200

Egypt, Arab Rep. of
2310 Decatur Place, NW
Washington, DC 20008
Tel: (202) 232-5400

El Salvador
1010 16th Street, NW 3rd Floor
Washington, DC 20036
Tel: (202) 265-9671

Eritrea
910 17th Street, NW Suite 400
Washington, DC 20005
Tel: (202) 265-3070

Estonia
630 Fifth Avenue, Suite 2415
New York, NY 10111
Tel: (212) 247-1450

Ethiopia
2134 Kalorama Road, NW
Washington, DC 20008
Tel: (202) 234-2281

Fiji
2233 Wisconsin Avenue, NW, Suite 240
Washington, DC 20007
Tel: (202) 337-8320

Finland
3216 New Mexico Avenue, NW
Washington, DC 20016
Tel: (202) 363-2430

France
4101 Reservoir Road, NW
Washington, DC 20007
Tel: (202) 944-6000

Gabon
2034 20th Street, NW
Washington, DC 20009
Tel: (202) 797-1000

Gambia
1155 15th Street, NW Suite 1000
Washington, DC 20005
Tel: (202) 785-1399

Germany
4645 Reservoir Road, NW
Washington, DC 20007
Tel: (202) 298-4000

Ghana
3512 International Drive, NW
Washington, DC 20008
Tel: (202) 686-4520

Greece
2221 Massachusetts Avenue, NW
Washington, DC 20008
Tel: (202) 939-5800

Grenada
1701 New Hampshire Avenue, NW
Washington, DC 20009
Tel: (202) 265-2561

Guatemala
2220 R Street, NW
Washington, DC 20008
Tel: (202) 745-4952

Guinea
2112 Leroy Place, NW
Washington, DC 20008
Tel: (202) 483-9420

Guinea-Bissau, Rep.
918 16th Street, NW
Washington, DC 20006
Tel: (202) 872-4222

Guyana
2490 Tracy Place, NW
Washington, DC 20008
Tel: (202) 265-6900

Haiti
2311 Massachusetts Avenue, NW
Washington, DC 20008
Tel: (202) 332-4090

Honduras
3007 Tilden Street, NW
Washington, DC 20008
Tel: (202) 966-7702

Hungary
3910 Shoemaker Street, NW
Washington, DC 20008
Tel: (202) 362-6730

Iceland
2022 Connecticut Avenue, NW
Washington, DC 20008
Tel: (202) 265-6653

India
2107 Massachusetts Avenue, NW
Washington, DC 20008
Tel: (202) 939-7000

Indonesia
2020 Massachusetts Avenue, NW
Washington, DC 20036
Tel: (202) 775-5200

Iran
2209 Wisconsin Avenue, NW, 2nd Floor
Washington, DC 20007
Tel: (202) 965-4990

Ireland
2234 Massachusetts Avenue, NW
Washington, DC 20008
Tel: (202) 462-3939

Israel
3514 International Drive, NW
Washington, DC 20008
Tel: (202) 364-5527

Italy
1601 Fuller Street, NW
Washington, DC 20009
Tel: (202) 328-5500

Jamaica
1850 K Street, NW, Suite 355
Washington, DC 20006
Tel: (202) 452-0660

Japan
2520 Massachusetts Avenue, NW
Washington, DC 20008
Tel: (202) 939-6700

Jordan
3504 International Drive, NW
Washington, DC 20008
Tel: (202) 966-2664

Kazakhstan
3421 Massachusetts Avenue, NW
Washington, DC 20008
Tel: (202) 333-4507

Kenya
2249 R Street, NW
Washington, DC 20007
Tel: (202) 387-6101

Korea (South)
2320 Massachusetts Ave, NW
Washington, DC 20008
Tel: (202) 939-5600

Kuwait
2940 Tilden Street, NW
Washington, DC 20037
Tel: (202) 966-0702

Kyrgyz Republic
1511 K Street, NW
Washington, DC 20008
Tel: (202) 628- 0433

Lao People's Democratic Republic
2222 S Street, NW
Washington, DC 20008
Tel: (202) 332-6416

Latvia
4325 17th Street, NW
Washington, DC 20011
Tel: (202) 726-8213

Lebanon
2560 28th Street, NW
Washington, DC 20008
Tel: (202) 939-6300

Lesotho
2511 Massachusetts Avenue, NW
Washington, DC 20008
Tel: (202) 797-5533

Liberia
5303 Colorado Avenue, NW
Washington, DC 20011
Tel: (202) 723-0437

Lithuania
2622 16th Street, NW
Washington, DC 20009
Tel: (202) 234-5860

Luxembourg
2200 Massachusetts Avenue, NW
Washington, DC 20008
Tel: (202) 265-4171

Madagascar
2374 Massachusetts Avenue, NW
Washington, DC 20008
Tel: (202) 265-5525

Malawi
2408 Massachusetts Avenue, NW
Washington, DC 20008
Tel: (202) 797-1007

Malaysia
2401 Massachusetts Avenue, NW
Washington, DC 20008
Tel: (202) 328-2700

Mali
2130 R Street, NW
Washington, DC 20008
Tel: (202) 332-2249

Malta
2017 Connecticut Avenue, NW
Washington, DC 20008
Tel: (202) 462-3611

Marshall Islands
2433 Massachusetts Avenue, NW
Washington, DC 20008
Tel: (202) 234-5414

Mauritania
2129 Leroy Place, NW
Washington, DC 20008
Tel: (202) 232-5700

Mauritius
4301 Connecticut Avenue, NW , Suite 441
Washington, DC 20008
Tel: (202) 244-1491

Mexico
1911 Pennsylvania Avenue, NW
Washington, DC 20009
Tel: (202) 728-1600

Micronesia
1725 N Street, NW
Washington, DC 20036
Tel: (202) 223-4383

Mongolia
2833 M Street, NW
Washington, DC 20007
Tel: (202) 298-7137

Morocco
1601 21st Street, NW
Washington, DC 20009
Tel: (202) 462-7979

Mozambique
1990 M Street, Suite 570 NW
Washington, DC 20036
Tel: (202) 293-7146

Myanmar
2300 S Street, NW
Washington, DC 20008
Tel: (202) 332-9044

Namibia
1605 New Hampshire Avenue, NW
Washington, DC 20009
Tel: (202) 986-0540

Nepal
2131 Leroy Place, NW
Washington, DC 20008
Tel: (202) 667-4550

Netherlands
4200 Linnean Avenue, NW
Washington, DC 20008
Tel: (202) 244-5300

New Zealand
37 Observatory Circle, NW
Washington, DC 20008
Tel: (202) 328-4800

Nicaragua
1627 New Hampshire Avenue, NW
Washington, DC 20009
Tel: (202) 939-6570

Niger
2204 R Street, NW
Washington, DC 20008
Tel: (202) 483-4224

Nigeria
2201 M Street, NW
Washington, DC 20037
Tel: (202) 822-1500

Norway
2720 34th Street, NW
Washington, DC 20008
Tel: (202) 333-6000

Oman
2342 Massachusetts Avenue, NW
Washington, DC 20008
Tel: (202) 387-1980

Pakistan
2315 Massachusetts Avenue, NW
Washington, DC 20008
Tel: (202) 939-6200

Panama
2862 McGill Terrace, NW
Washington, DC 20008
Tel: (202) 483-1407

Papua New Guinea
1615 New Hampshire Avenue, NW
Washington, DC 20009
Tel: (202) 745-3680

Paraguay
2400 Massachusetts Avenue, NW
Washington, DC 20008
Tel: (202) 483-6960

Peru
1700 Massachusetts Avenue, NW
Washington, DC 20036
Tel: (202) 833-9860

Philippines
1600 Massachusetts Avenue, NW
Washington, DC 20036
Tel: (202) 467-9300

Poland
2224 Wyoming Avenue, NW
Washington, DC 20008
Tel: (202) 234-3800

Portugal
2125 Kalorama Road, NW
Washington, DC 20008
Tel: (202) 332-3007

Qatar
600 New Hampshire Avenue, NW, #1180
Washington, DC 20037
Tel: (202) 338-0111

Romania
1607 23rd Street, NW
Washington, DC 20008
Tel: (202) 232-4747

Russia
2650 Wisconsin Avenue, NW
Washington, DC 20007
Tel: (202) 298-5700

Rwanda
1714 New Hampshire Avenue, NW
Washington, DC 20009
Tel: (202) 232-2882

Saint Kitts & Nevis
2100 M Street, NW, Suite 608
Washington, DC 20037
Tel: (202) 833-3550

Saint Lucia
2100 M Street, NW, Suite 309
Washington, DC 20037
Tel: (202) 463-7378

Saint Vincent & Grenadines
1717 Massachusetts Avenue, NW, #102
Washington, DC 20036
Tel: (202) 462-7806

Sao Tome & Principe
122 East 42nd Street, Suite 1604
New York, NY 10168
Tel: (212) 697-4211

Saudi Arabia
601 New Hampshire Avenue, NW
Washington, DC 20037
Tel: (202) 342-3800

Senegal
2112 Wyoming Avenue, NW
Washington, DC 20008
Tel: (202) 234-0540

Seychelles
820 Second Avenue, Suite 900 F
New York, NY 10017
Tel: (212) 687-9766

Sierra Leone
1701 19th Street, NW
Washington, DC 20009
Tel: (202) 939-9261

Singapore
3501 International Place, NW
Washington, DC 20008
Tel: (202) 537-3100

Slovak Republic
3900 Linnean Avenue, NW
Washington, DC 20008
Tel: (202) 363-6315

Solomon Islands
820 Second Avenue, Suite 800
New York, NY 10017
Tel: (212) 599-6193

South Africa
3201 New Mexico Avenue, NW
Washington, DC 20016
Tel: (202) 232-4400

Spain
2700 15th Street, NW
Washington, DC 20009
Tel: (202) 265-0190

Sri Lanka, Rep. of
2148 Wyoming Avenue, NW
Washington, DC 20008
Tel: (202) 483-4025

Sudan
2210 Massachusetts Avenue, NW
Washington, DC 20008
Tel: (202) 338-8564

Suriname
4301 Connecticut Avenue, NW, Suite 108
Washington, DC 20008
Tel: (202) 244-7488

Swaziland
3400 International Drive, NW
Washington, DC 20008
Tel: (202) 362-6683

Sweden
600 New Hampshire Avenue, NW, #1200
Washington, DC 20037
Tel: (202) 944-5600

Switzerland
2900 Cathedral Avenue, NW
Washington, DC 20008
Tel: (202) 745-7900

Syrian Arab Republic
2215 Wyoming Avenue, NW
Washington, DC 20008
Tel: (202) 232-6313

Tanzania
2139 R Street, NW
Washington, DC 20008
Tel: (202) 939-6125

Thailand
2300 Kalorama Road, NW
Washington, DC 20008
Tel: (202) 483-7200

Togo
2208 Massachusetts Avenue, NW
Washington, DC 20008
Tel: (202) 234-4212

Trinidad & Tobago
1708 Massachusetts Avenue, NW
Washington, DC 20036
Tel: (202) 467-6490

Tunisia
1515 Massachusetts Avenue, NW
Washington, DC 20005
Tel: (202) 862-1850

Turkey
1714 Massachusetts Avenue, NW
Washington, DC 20036
Tel: (202) 659-8200

Uganda
5909 16th Street, NW
Washington, DC 20011
Tel: (202) 726-7100

Ukraine
3359 M Street, NW
Washington, DC 20007
Tel: (202) 333-0606

United Arab Emirates
3000 K Street, NW, Room 600
Washington, DC 20007
Tel: (202) 338-6500

United Kingdom
3100 Massachusetts Avenue, NW
Washington, DC 20008
Tel: (202) 462-1340

Uruguay
1918 F Street, NW
Washington, DC 20006
Tel: (202) 331-1313

Venezuela
1099 30th Street, NW
Washington, DC 20007
Tel: (202) 342-2214

Western Samoa
1155 15th Street, NW, Suite 510
Washington, DC 20005
Tel: (202) 833-2214

Yemen, Republic of
2600 Virginia Avenue, NW, 7th Floor
Washington, DC 20037
Tel: (202) 965-4760

Zaire
1800 New Hampshire Avenue, NW
Washington, DC 20009
Tel: (202) 234-7690

Zambia
2419 Massachusetts Avenue, NW
Washington, DC 20008
Tel: (202) 265-9717

Zimbabwe
1608 New Hampshire Avenue, NW
Washington, DC 20009
Tel: (202) 332-7100

African Development Bank

Harare Office
P.O. Box 8404
Harare, Zimbabwe
Tel: 011 (263) 79-43-91 /92

Nairobi Office
P.O. Box 52617
Nairobi, Kenya
Tel: 011 (2542) 72-31-85 /86
Fax: 011 (2542) 72-77-49

Rabat Office
9 Charii Tradbless
BP 1459,
R.P. Rabat, Morocco
Tel: 011 (2127) 73 05 18 /32
Fax: 011 (2127) 73 05 31

Yaounde Office
BP 264
Yaounde, Cameroon
Tel: 011 (237) 23 05 33

North America Office
2001 Pennsylvania Avenue, NW #350
Washington, DC 20006
Tel: (202) 429-5160
Fax: (202) 659-4704

Addis-Ababa Office
P.O. Box 5794
Addis-Ababa, Ethiopia
Tel: 011 (251) 51 90 78

European Office
58-60 Moortgate, 4th Flr.
London EC2 M65 B, U.K.
Tel: 011 (4471) 374-43 51
Fax: 011 (4471) 638 75 08

Conakry Office
BP, 1852,
Conakry, Guinea
Tel: 011 (224) 22 23 07

Lagos Office
12 B Oko Awo Close
P.O. Box 74657
Victoria Island, Nigeria
Tel: 011 (2341) 61-31-00
Fax: 011 (2341) 61-20-70

Asian Development Bank

Bangladesh
7th floor, BSEC Bhaban
102 Kazi Nazrul Islam Avenue
Karwan Bazar Commercial Area
Dhaka 1215, Bangladesh
Tel: 011 (880) 2-814380-5
Fax: 011 (880) 2-813242

Indonesia
Gedung Garuda Indonesia, 6th Floor
Jalan Medan Merdoka Selatan, 13
Jakarta Pusat 10110, Indonesia
Tel: 011 (62) 21-3808151/54
Fax: 011 (62) 21-3808155

Pakistan
20 A Shahrah-eJamhuriat
Ramna 5 (G 5/1)
Islamabad, Pakistan
Tel: 011 (92) 214320
Fax: 011 (92) 824335

India
37 Golf Links
P.O. Box 3019, Lodi Road HPO
New Delhi 110 003, India
Tel: 011 (9111) 469-2576, 469-2589
Fax: 011 (9111) 463-6175

Nepal
Srikunj Kamaiadi Ward No. 31
Block 2/597, Ka. Na. Pa.
P.O. Box 5017 K.D.P.O.
Kathmandu, Nepal
Tel: 011 (977) 1-227779, 227784
Fax: 011 (977) 1-225063

South Pacific
La Casa de Andrea, Kumul Highway
P.O. Box 127, Port Vila, Vanuatu
Tel: 011 (678) 2-3300
Fax: 011 (678) 2-3183

European Bank for Reconstuction and Development

Albania
Rruga Seshmoret 4
Shkurit No. 26
Tirana, Albania
Tel/Fax: 011 (355) 42-32-898

Baltic States
Latvian International Trade
Center Room 440
2 Elizabetes Street
LV 1010 Riga, Latvia
Tel: 011 (371) 2321-690
Fax: 011 (371) 8830-301

Belarus
17 Kirov Street
Minsk 220002
Belarus

Bulgaria
17 Moscovska Street
Sofia 1000, Bulgaria
Tel: 011 (359) 2 876 611
Fax: 011 (359) 2 803 036

Czech Republic
38 Rijna 9
Praha 1, Czech Republic
Tel: 011 (422) 2423 0247
Fax: 011 (422) 267 876

Hungary
Kecskemeti utca 7
H-1053 Budapest, Hungary
Tel: 011 (361) 266 6000
Fax: 011 (361) 266 6003

Poland
Room 15-14 LIM Centre-Marriott
Al-Jerozolimskie 65/79
00-697 Warsaw, Poland
Tel: 011 (482) 630 7275
Fax: 011 (482) 630 6551

Romania
Strada Sipotul Fintinilor 8
Sector 1
70718 Bucharest, Romania
Tel: 011 (401) 615 6999
Fax: 011 (401) 312 2233

Russian Federation
8/10 Gasheka Street
125047 Moscow
Russian Federation
Tel: 011 (7 503) 956 1111
Fax: 011 (7 503) 956 1122

Slovak Republic
Grosslingova 4
814 18 Bratislava
Slovak Republic
Tel: 011 (427) 367 835
Fax: 011 (427) 398-314

Ukraine
Room 407
The National Hotel
Corpus 1, 5 Lypska Street
252021 Kiev, Ukraine
Tel: 011 (7 044) 230 2626
Fax: 011 (7 044) 291 6246

Uzbekistan
Room 1328
Hotel Uzbekistan
Tashkent, Uzbekistan
Tel: 011 (7 3712) 336 343
Fax: 011 (7 3712) 891 121

Inter-American Development Bank

Argentina
Calle Esmeralda 130, 19 y 30 piso
Casilla de Correo No. 181, Sccursal 1
Buenos Aires, Argentina
Tel: 011 (54 1) 334-1756

Bahamas
IDB House, East Bay Street
P.O. Box N-3743
Nassau, Bahamas
Tel: (809) 393-7159

Barbados
Maple Manor, Hastings
P.O. Box 402
Christ Church, Barbados
Tel: (809) 427-3612

Belize
Social Security Building
Bliss Parade
Belmopan, Belize
Tel: 011 (501 8) 82-3914

Bolivia
Edificio BISA, 5 Piso
Avenida 16 de Julio, No. 1628
Casilla de Correo No. 5872
La Paz, Bolivia
Tel: 011 (591 2) 35-1221

Brazil
Setor Comercial Sul (SCS)
Quadra 3 - No. 40
Edificio Planalto - 2 andar, 70300
Brasilia, D.F., Brazil
Tel: 011 (55 61) 321-1848

Chile
Avenida Pedro de Valdivia 0193, 11 Piso
Casilla No. 16611, Correo 9
Providencia
Santiago, Chile
Tel: 011 (56 2) 231-7986

Colombia
Avenida 40 A No. 13-09, 8 Piso
Apartado Aereo 12037
Bogota, Colombia
Tel: 011 (57 1) 288-0366

Costa Rica
Edificio Centro Colon, 12 Piso
Paseo Colon, entre calles 38 y 40
San Jose, Costa Rica
Tel: 011 (506) 33-3244

Dominican Republic
Avenida Winston Churchill esquina
calle Luis F. Thomen, Torre BHD
Apartado Postal No. 1386
Santo Domingo
Dominican Republic
Tel: (809) 562-6400

Ecuador
Avenida Amazonas 477 y Roca
Edificio Banco de Los Andes, 9 Piso
Apartado Postal No. 17-07-9041
Quito, Ecuador
Tel: 011 (593-4) 56-2141

El Salvador
Condominio Torres Del Bosque
10 Piso, Colonia La Mascota
Apartado Postal No. (01) 199
San Salvador, El Salvador
Tel: 011 (503) 23-8300

Guatemala
Edificio Ceminis 10
12 calle 1-25, Zona 10, Nivel 19
Apartado Postal 935
Guatemala City, Guatemala
Tel: 011 (502-2) 35-2650

Guyana
47- High Street, Kingston
P.O. Box 10867
Georgetown, Guyana
Tel: 011 (592 29) 5-7951

Haiti
Bourdon 389
Boite postale 1321
Port-au-Prince, Haiti
Tel: 011 (509-1) 45-5711

Honduras
Edificio Los Castanos, 5 y 6 Pisos
Colonia Los Castanos
Apartado Postal No. 3180
Tegucigalpa, Honduras
Tel: 011 (504) 32-4238

Jamaica
40-46 Knutsford Blvd., 6th floor
P.O. Box 429
Kingston, 10, Jamaica
Tel: (809) 926-2342

Mexico
Avenida Horacio No. 1855
6 Piso (Esquina Periferico)
Los Morales- Polanco, 11510
Mexico D.F., Mexico
Tel: 011 (52-5) 580-2122

Nicaragua
Eddicio BID
Km 4-1/2 Carretera a Masaya
Apartado Postal 2512
Managua, Nicaragua
Tel: 011 (505-2) 67-0831

Panama
Avenida Samuel Lewis
Edifico Banco Union, 14 Piso
Apartado Postal 7297
Panama 5, Panama
Tel: 011 (507) 63-6944

Paraguay
Edificio Aurora I, 2 y 3 Pisos
Calle Cabellero esquina
Eligio Ayala, Casilla 1209
Asuncion, Paraguay
Tel: 011 (595 21) 49-2061

Peru
Paseo de la Republica 3245, 14 Piso
Apartado Postal No. 270154
San Isidro, Lima
Peru
Tel: 011 (51 14) 42-3400

Trinidad and Tobago
Tatil Building
11 Maraval Rd., P.O. Box 68
Port of Spain, Trinidad and Tobago
Tel: (809) 622-8367

Uruguay
Andes 1365, 13 Piso
Casilla de Correo 5029, Sucursal 1
Montevideo, Urauguay
Tel: 011 (598 2) 92-0444

Venezuela
Edificio Cremerca, 3 Piso
Avenida Venezuela, El Rosal
Caracas 1060
Venezuela
Tel: 011 (58 2) 951-5533

World Bank

Albania
Chief, Resident Mission
World Bank
Deshmoret e 4 Shkurtit, No. 34
Tirana, Albania
Tel: 011 (355-42) 28657
Fax: 011 (355-42) 32332

Angola
Chief, Resident Mission
Banco Mundiale
Rua Alfredo Troni (Edificio BPC)
14 Andars
CP 1331, Luanda, Angola
Tel: 011 (244-2) 394877
Fax: 011 (244-2) 394784

Argentina
Chief, Resident Mission
Banco Mundial
Avenida Leandro N. Alem 628-30
Piso 12
Buenos Aires, Argentina
Tel: 011 (54-1) 313-6816
Fax: 011 (54-1) 313-1233

Bangladesh
Chief, Resident Mission
World Bank
3A Paribagh
G.P.O. 97
Dhaka, Bangladesh
Tel: 011 (880-2) 86-105669
Fax: 011 (880-2) 86-3220

Benin
Chief, Resident Mission
World Bank
Zone Residentielle de la Radio
Boite Postale 03-2112
Cotonou, Benin
Tel: 011 (229) 312124
Fax: 011 (229) 312751

Bolivia
Chief, Resident Mission
Banco Mundial
Edificio BISA, Piso 9
16 de Julio 1628
Casilla 8692
La Paz, Bolivia
Tel: 011 (591-2) 356844
Fax: 011 (591-2) 391038

Brazil
Chief, Resident Mission
Banco Mundial
Sector Commercial Sul,
Quandra 1 Bloco H
Edificio Morro Vermelho - 8 Andar
Brasilia, DF 70399-900, Brazil
Tel: 011 (55-61) 322-7180
Fax: 011 (55-61) 322-8722

Bulgaria
Chief, Resident Mission
World Bank
World Trade Center
36 Dragan Tsankov Blvd.
Sofia, Bulgaria
Tel: 011 (359-2) 73-65-57
Fax: 011 (359-2) 80-15-95

Burkina Faso
Chief, Resident Mission
World Bank
Immeuble BICIA
3-eme Etage
Boite Postale 622
Ouagadougo, Burkina Faso
Tel: 011 (226) 30-62-37
Fax: 011 (226) 30-86-49

Burundi
Chief, Resident Mission
World Bank
Bujumbura, Burundi
B.P. 2637, Bujumbura
Tel: 011 (257-2) 22443
Fax: 011 (257-2) 26005

Cameroon
Chief, Resident Mission
World Bank
Immeuble Kennedy, Avenue Kennedy
Boite Postale 1128
Yaounde, Cameroon
Tel: 011 (237) 20 38 15
Fax: 011 (237) 21 07 22

Central African Republic
Chief, Resident Mission
Rue des Missions
P.O. Box 819
Bangui, Central African Republic
Tel: 011 (236) 616 138
Fax: 011 (236) 616 087

Chad
Chief, Resident Mission
World Bank, P.O. Box 146
N'djamena, Chad
Tel: 011 (235-51) 3247
Fax: 011 (235-51) 4484

China
Chief, Resident Mission
World Bank, P.O. Box 802
Beijing 100830, China
Tel: 011 (86-1) 851-2227
Fax: 011 (86-1) 852-4140

Colombia
Chief, Resident Mission
Banco Mundial
Diagonal 35 No. 5-98
Apartado Aereo 10229
Bogota, DE Colombia
Tel: 011 (57-1) 320-3577
Fax: 011 (57-1) 245-5744

Cote d'Ivoire
Chief, Resident Mission
World Bank
Corner of Booker Washington &
 Jacques AKA Street
B.P. 1850
Abidjan 01, Cote d'Ivoire
Tel: 011 (225) 44 22 27
Fax: 011 (225) 44 16 87

Egypt
Chief, Resident Mission
World Bank
World Trade Center
1191 Corniche El-Nil
15th Floor
Cairo, Egypt
Tel: 011 (20-2) 574-1662
Fax: 011 (20-2) 574-1676

Ethiopia
Chief, Resident Mission
World Bank
Africa Avenue, Bole
Addis Ababa, Ethiopia
Tel: 011 (251-1) 51 42 00
Fax: 011 (251-1) 51 14 41

Ghana
Chief, Resident Mission
World Bank
69 Eighth Avenue Extension
Northridge Residential Area
P.O. Box M27
Accra, Ghana
Tel: 011 (233-21) 22 96 81
Fax: 011 (233-21) 22 78 87

Guinea
Chief, Resident Mission
Banque Mondiale
Immeuble de l'Archevesche
Face Baie des Anges
B.P. 1420
Conakry, Guinea
Tel: 011 (224-4) 4-50-61
Fax: 011 (224-4) 4-26-74

Guinea-Bissau
Chief, Resident Mission
World Bank, Apartado 700
1041 Guinea-Bissau
Tel: 011 (245) 21-24-32
Fax: 011 (245) 20-12-84

Hungary
Chief, Resident Mission
World Bank
Suba Trade Center, 4th Floor
Nagymezo Utca 44
Budapest 1065, Hungary
Tel: 011 (36-1) 269-0389
Fax: 011 (36-1) 269-0396

India
Chief, Resident Mission
World Bank, 70 Lodi Estate
New Delhi 110003, India
Tel: 011 (91-11) 4617241-4
Fax: 011 (91-11) 4619393

Indonesia
Director, Resident Staff, World Bank
P.O. Box 324/JCT
Jakarta, Indonesia
Tel: 011 (62-21) 52 07 316
Fax: 011 (62-21) 52 00 438

Japan
Director, Tokyo Office, World Bank
Kokusai Building, Room 916
1-1, Marunouchi 3-chome
Chiyoda-ku, Tokyo 100, Japan
Tel: 011 (81-3) 3214-5001 or 3214-1001
Fax: 011 (81-3) 3214-3657

Kazakhstan
Chief, Resident Mission
World Bank
Almaty liaison Office
c/o Ministry of Economy
115 Zheltokson Street
Almaty, Kazakhstan 480091
Tel: 011 (7-3272) 627-378
Fax: 011 (7-3272) 627-378

Kenya
Chief, Resident Mission
View Park Towers
Monrovia Street
P.O. Box 30577
Nairobi, Kenya
Tel: 011 (254-2) 228477
Fax: 011 (254-2) 213925

Latvia
Chief, Resident Mission
World Bank
Regional Office, Baltic Countries
Kalku Street 15
Riga, Latvia 1050
Tel: 011 (371-2) 364-432
Fax: 011 (371-8) 828-058

Madagascar
Chief, Resident Mission
World Bank
1 Rue Patrice Lumumba
Boite Postale 4140
Antananarivo 101, Madagascar
Tel: 011 (261-2) 289 17
Fax: 011 (261-2) 329 02

Malawi
Chief, Resident Mission
World Bank Field Office
Development House
Capital City
P.O. Box 30557
Lilongwe 3, Malawi
Tel: 011 (265) 780-611
Fax: 011 (265) 781-158

Mali
Chief, Resident Mission
Banque Mondiale
Immeuble SOGEFIH
Avenue Moussa Travele
Quartier du Fleuve
Boite Postale 1864
Bamako, Mali
Tel: 011 (223) 22 22 83
Fax: 011 (223) 22 66 82

Mauritania
Chief, Resident Mission
World Bank, Villa No. 30, llot A
Quarter Socofim
Boite Postale 667
Nouakchott, Mauritania
Tel: 011 (222-2) 251017
Fax: 011 (222-2) 251334

Mexico
Chief, Resident Mission
Banco Mundial, Plaza Nafin
Nivel Paseo, Locales 71 y 72
Col. Guadelupe Inn
01020 Mexico D.F.
Tel: 011 (52-5) 661-8054
Fax: 011 (52-5) 661-0917

Mozambique
Chief, Resident Mission
World Bank Field Office
Caixa Postal 4053
Maputo, Mozambique
Tel: 011 (258-1) 492-841
Fax: 011 (258-1) 492-893

Nepal
Resident Representative
World Bank
P.O. Box 798, Kathmandu, Nepal
Tel: 011 (977-1) 226792, 226793
Fax: 011 (977-1) 225112

Nicaragua
Chief, Resident Mission
World Bank Field Office
Edificio malaga, Modula A-1
Managua, Nicaragua C.A.
Tel: 011 (505-2) 66 19 70
Fax: 011 (505-2) 66 10 00

Niger
Chief, Resident Mission
World Bank Field Office
B.P. 12402, Niajey, Niger
Tel: 011 (227) 73 51 21
Fax: 011 (227) 73 55 06

Nigeria
Chief, Resident Mission
World Bank
P.O. Box 127
Lagos, Nigeria
Tel: 011 (234-1) 26 16 016
Fax: 011 (234-1) 23 16 205

The Philippines
Resident Representative
World Bank
Central Bank of the Philippines
Multi-Storey Building
Room 200, Roxas Boulevard
Manila, Philippines
Tel: 011 (63-2) 521-2726,
Fax: 011 (63-2) 521-1317

Poland
Chief, Resident Mission
World Bank
Intraco I Building
17th Floor, 2 Stawki Str.
00-193 Warsaw, Poland
Tel: 011 (48-2) 635-0553
Fax: 011 (48-2) 635-9857

Romania
Chief, Resident Mission
World Bank
Boulevard Dacia 83
Sector 2
Bucharest, Romania
Tel: 011 (40-1) 210 1804
Fax: 011 (40-1) 210-2021

Russia
Chief, Resident Mission
World Bank Regional Office
Sadovo-Kudrinskaya No.3
Moscow 123242
Russian Federation
Tel: 011 (7-095) 254-0388
Fax: 011 (7-095) 254-8765

Rwanda
Chief, Resident Mission
World Bank
Blvd. de la Revolution
P.O. Box 609
Kigali, Rwanda
Tel: 011 (250) 72204
Fax: 011 (250) 76385

Saudi Arabia
Chief, Resident Mission
World Bank
P.O. Box 5900
Riyadh, Saudi Arabia 11432
Tel: 011 (966-1) 465-9582
Fax: 011 (966-1) 465-5842

Senegal
Chief, Resident Mission
World Bank
B.P. 3296
Dakar, Senegal
Tel: 011 (221) 23 36 30
Fax: 011 (221) 23 62 77

Sri Lanka
Resident Representative
World Bank
P.O. Box 1761
Colombo, Sri Lanka
Tel: 011 (94-1) 421840, 448070-1
Fax: 011 (94-1) 440357

Sudan
Chief, Resident Mission
World Bank/UNDP
7 Block 5, R.F.E. Gamma'a Avenue
Khartoum, Sudan
Tel: 011 (873) 150 1602
Fax: 011 (873) 150 1650

Tanzania
Chief, Resident Mission
World Bank, P.O. Box 2054
Dar-es-Salaam, Tanzania
Tel: 011 (255-51) 46447
Fax: 011 (255-51) 46450

Thailand
Chief, Resident Mission
World Bank
14th Floor, Tower A
Diethelm Towers
93/1 Wireless Road
Bangkok 10330, Thailand
Tel: 011 (66-2) 252-2305/07
Fax: 011 (66-2) 256-7795

Togo
Chief, Resident Mission
World Bank
169 Boulevard du 13 Janvier
Immeuble BTCI
8eme Etage
Lome, Togo
Tel: 011 (228) 21 55 69
Fax: 011 (228) 21 78 56

Turkey
Chief, Resident Mission
World Bank
Ataturk Bulvari No. 211
Gama-Guris Building Kat 6
06683 Kavaklidere
Ankara, Turkey
Tel: 011 (90-312) 468-4527
Fax: 011 (90-312) 468-4526

Uganda
Chief, Resident Mission
World Bank
P.O. Box 4463
Kampala, Uganda
Tel: 011 (256-41) 24 21 39
Fax: 011 (256-41) 23 00 92

Ukraine
Chief, Resident Mission
World Bank
26 Shovkovychna St.
Suites Two and Three
Kiev 252024
Ukraine
Tel: 011 (7-044) 226-3533
Fax: 011 (7-044) 226-3525

Venezuela
Chief, Resident Mission
Banco Mundial
Edificio Parque Cristal
Torre Oeste, Piso 15 Oficina 15-05
Avenida Francisco de Miranda
Los Palos Grandes
Caracas, Venezuela
Tel: 011 (58-2) 284-3437
Fax: 011 (58-2) 285-0181

Zaire
Chief, Resident Mission
World Bank
P.O. Box 14816
Kinshasa, Zaire
Tel: 011 (243-12) 20177
Fax: 011 (243-12) 20176

Zambia
Chief, Resident Mission
World Bank, P.O. Box 35410
Lusaka, Zambia
Tel: 011 (260-1) 226774
Fax: 011 (260-1) 225749

Zimbabwe
Chief, Resident Mission
World Bank
P.O. Box 2960
Harare, Zimbabwe
Tel: 011 (263-4) 729611
Fax: 011 (263-4) 708659

International Finance Corporation

Argentina
IFC Regional Representative
International Finance Corporation
Edificio Pirelli
Maipu 1300, Piso 12
Buenos Aires, Argentina
Tel: 011 (54-1) 313-6816
Fax: 011 (54-1) 312-9435

Barbados
IFC Eastern Caribbean Regional Office
Musson Building, 2nd Floor
Hichs Street
P.O. Box 259
Bridgetown, Barbados
7473 CAIC WB
Tel: (809) 429-6298
Fax: (809) 429-5809

Brazil
IFC Regional Representative
International Finance Corporation
Rua Guararapes 2064
10th Floor, Room 104
Sao Paolo, Brazil CEP 04561-004
Tel: 011 (55-11) 531-1629
Fax: 011 (55-11) 241-3073

Cameroon
IFC Liaison
International Finance Corporation
Rue Flatters
P.O. Box 4616
Douala, Cameroon
Tel: 011 (237) 428-033
Fax: 011 (237) 428-014

Cote d'Ivoire
IFC Regional Representative
International Finance Corporation
B.P. 1850
Abidjan-01, Cote d'Ivoire
Tel: 011 (225) 44 32 44
Fax: 011 (225) 44 44 83

China
Resident Representative
International Finance Corporation
Unit 3711, 37 / F Jing Guang Centre
Hu Jia Lou Chaoyang District
Beijing 100020, China
Tel: 011 (86-1) 501-5171/72/73
Fax: 011 (86-1) 501-5176

Czech Republic
IFC Regional Representative
International Finance Corporation
Siroka 5
Praha 1, Czech Republic
Tel: 011 (42-2) 2481-2245
Fax: 011 (42-2) 2481-2267

Egypt
IFC Regional Representative
International Finance Corporation
5 el Falah Street
Mohandessin
Giza, Egypt
Tel: 011 (20-2) 302-6533
Fax: 011 (20-2) 347-3738

Ghana
IFC Liaison
International Finance Corporation
Patrice Lumamba Road
Roman Ridge
Private Mail Bag (OMB) CCC21
Tel: 011 (233-21) 22 96 81
Fax: 011 (223-21) 77 49 61

Hungary
IFC Regional Representative
International Finance Corporation
Suba Trade Center, Suite 72, 7th Floor
Nagymezo Utca 44
Budapest 1065
Hungary
Tel: 011 (36-1) 269-0384
Fax: 011 (36-1) 269-0388

India
New Delhi
Chief, South Asia
International Finance Corporation
No. 1 Panchsheel Marg
Chanakyapuri
New Delhi, 110021, India
Tel: 011 (91-11) 301-1306

Bombay
Chief, South Asia
International Finance Corporation
No. 25 Maker Chambers VI
Nariman Point
Bombay, India
Tel: 011 (91-22) 285-5262, 285-5263
Fax: 011 (91-22) 285-5272

Indonesia
IFC Regional Representative
International Finance Corporation
P.O. Box 324/JCT
Jakarta, Indonesia
Tel: 011 (62-21) 5207316
Fax: 011 (62-21) 5200438

Kenya
IFC Regional Representative
International Finance Corporation
P.O. Box 30577, Nairobi, Kenya
Tel: 011 (254-2) 22 47 26
Fax: 011 (254-2) 21 99 80

Mexico
International Finance Corporation
45 Andres Bello
Colonia Palanco
11560 Mexico, DF
Tel: 011 (52-5) 281-1299
Fax: 011 (52-5) 281-2061

Nigeria
IFC Regional Representative
International Finance Corporation
P.O. Box 127, Lagos, Nigeria
Tel: 011 (234-1) 611-400
Fax: 011 (234-1) 261-7164

Philippines
IFC Regional Representative
International Finance Corporation
3rd Floor, Corinthian Plaza
121 Paseo de Roxas, Makati
Metro Manila, Philippines
Tel: 011 (63-2) 813-0082 or 813-0083
Fax: 011 (63-2) 5211317

Poland
IFC Regional Representative
International Finance Corporation
ul. Emilii Plater 28
00-688 Warsaw, Poland
Tel: 011 (48-2) 630-3444
Fax: 011 (48-2) 630-6445

Russia
IFC Regional Representative
International Finance Corporation
Pushechnaya Street 2
Moscow 103012
Russian Federation
Tel: 011 (7-501) 882-1045
Fax: 011 (7-501) 882-1044

Thailand
IFC Regional Representative
International Finance Corporation
Udom Vidhya Building (5th Floor)
956 Rama IV Road
Bangkok 10500, Thailand
Tel: 011 (66-2) 235-5300/6
Fax: 011 (66-2) 2366467

Trinidad and Tobago
IFC Regional Representative
International Finance Corporation
The Mutual Centre
16 Queens Park West
NW Penthouse
Port of Spain, Trinidad
Tel: (809) 628-5074
Fax: (809) 622-1003

Turkey
IFC Regional Representative
International Finance corporation
Mete Caddessi No. 24/3
Taksim, Istanbul, Turkey
Tel: 011 (90-212) 243-2593
Fax: 011 (90-212) 249-2476

Zimbabwe
IFC Regional Representative
International Finance Corporation
P.O. Box 2960
Harare, Zimbabwe
Tel: 011 (263-4) 79 48 60
Fax: 011 (263-4) 70 86 59

Appendix G:

State International Trade Offices

Alabama

International Trade Specialist
Alabama Development Office
401 Adams Avenue
Montgomery, AL 36130
Tel: (205) 242-0400
Fax: (205) 242-0486

Alaska

Governor's Office of Int'l. Trade
3601 C Street, Suite 798
Anchorage, AK 99503
Tel: (907) 561-5585
Fax: (907) 561-4577

Arizona

International Trade and Investment
Arizona Department of Commerce
3800 N. Central, Suite 1500
Phoenix, AZ 85012
Tel: (602) 280-1371
Fax: (602) 280-1305

Arkansas

Arkansas Industrial
  Development Commission
One State Capitol Mall, Room 4C 300
Little Rock, AR 72201
Tel: (501) 682-7688
Fax: (501) 682-7691

Arkansas Development Finance Auth.
100 Main Street, Suite 200
Little Rock, AR 72201
Tel: (501) 682-7688
Fax: (501) 682-7691

California

California State World Trade Comm.
801 K Street, Suite 1700
Sacramento, CA 95814-3520
Tel: (916) 324-5511
Fax: (916) 324-5791

Director, Export Finance Office
California State World Trade Comm.
6 Centerpointe, Suite 760
La Palma, CA 90623
Tel: (714) 562-5519
Fax: (714) 562-5530

Colorado

Colorado International Trade Office
1625 Broadway, Suite 680
Denver, CO 80202
Tel: (303) 892-3850
Fax: (303) 892-3820

Connecticut

International Division, Connecticut
  Department of Economic Dev't.
865 Brook Street
Rocky Hill, CT 06067
Tel: (203) 258-4243
Fax: (203) 721-7650

Delaware

International Trade Section
Delaware Development Office
99 Kings Highway, Box 1401
Dover, DE 19903
Tel: (302) 739-4271
Fax: (302) 739-5749

International Trade Specialist
Delaware Development Office
International Trade Section
820 French Street
Wilmington, DE 19801
Tel: (302) 577-6262
Fax: (302) 577-3862

Florida

Director
Division of International Trade
  and Development
Florida Department of Commerce
107 West Gaines Street
366 Collins Building
Tallahassee, FL 32399-2000
Tel: (904) 488-9050
Fax: (904) 487-1407

Georgia

Deputy Commissioner
or
Director, Trade Division
Georgia Department of Industry,
  Trade and Tourism
P.O. Box 1776
Atlanta, GA 30301
Tel: (404) 656-3571
Fax: (404) 651-6505

Hawaii

Division Head
Industry Promotion Division
Hawaii Department of Business,
  Economic Development & Tourism
P.O. Box 2359
Honolulu, HI 96804
Tel: (808) 586-2610
Fax: (808) 586-2549

Director
Int'l. Business Center of Hawaii
Tel: (808) 587-2797
Fax: (808) 587-2790

Idaho

International Trade Specialist
Division of International Business
  Development
Idaho Department of Commerce
700 W. State Street
Boise, ID 83720
Tel: (208) 334-2470
Fax: (208) 334-2783

Illinois

International Business Development
Illinois Department of Commerce
  and Community Affairs
100 West Randolph, Suite C-400
Chicago, IL 60601
Tel: (312) 814-7164
Fax: (312) 814-6581
or
International Trade Centers and
  Domestic Trade Shows
Tel: (312) 814-7170
Fax: (312) 814-2807

Indiana

Director,
International Trade Division
Business Development Division
Indiana Department of Commerce
One North Capitol, Suite 700
Indianapolis, IN 46204-2248
Tel: (317) 232-3527
Fax: (317) 232-4146

Iowa

Division of International Trade
Iowa Department of Economic
  Development
200 East Grand Avenue
Des Moines, IA 50309
Tel: (515) 242-4729
Fax: (515) 242-4749

Kansas

International Trade Representative
Trade Development Division
Kansas Department of Commerce
700 Harrison Street, 13th Floor
Topeka, KS 66603-3957
Tel: (913) 296-4027
Fax: (913) 296-5263

Kentucky

Office of International Trade
Kentucky Cabinet for Economic
  Development
Capitol Plaza Tower, 24th Floor
Frankfort, KY 40601
Tel: (502) 564-7140
Fax: (502) 564-7697

Louisiana

Director, International Trade
Louisiana Department of
  Economic Development
P.O. Box 94185
Baton Rouge, LA 70804-9185
Tel: (504) 342-4320
Fax: (504) 342-5389

Maine

Maine Department of Economic
  and Community Development
State House Station 59
Augusta, ME 04333
Tel: (207) 287-3153
Fax: (207) 287-5701

Maryland

Maryland International Division
401 East Pratt Street, Suite 752
Baltimore, MD 21202
Tel: (410) 333-8180
Fax: (410) 333-8200
or
Export Finance Program
Tel: (410) 333-8189

Massachusetts

Office of International Trade
100 Cambridge Street, Room 902
Boston, MA 02202
Tel: (617) 367-1830
Fax: (617) 227-3488

Michigan

International Office
Michigan Department of Commerce
P.O. Box 30105
Lansing, MI 48909
Tel: (517) 373-6390
Fax: (517) 335-2521

Director, Grants Office
Michigan Department of Comm.
P.O. Box 30225
Lansing, MI 48908
Tel: (517) 373-6390
Fax: (517) 335-2521

Minnesota

Minnesota Trade Office
1000 MN World Trade Center
30 East 7th Street
St. Paul, MN 55101-4902
Tel: (612) 297-4227
Fax: (612) 296-3555
or
Director of Export Finance
Tel: (612) 297-4222

Mississippi

Deputy Director
International Trade and Investment
Mississippi Dep't.
of Economic Development
P.O. Box 849
Jackson, MS 39205
Tel: (601) 359-3449
Fax: (601) 359-2832

Missouri

Senior Trade Specialist
International Trade and Development
Missouri Economic Dev't. Programs
P.O. Box 118
Jefferson City, MO 65102
Tel: (314) 751-4999
Fax: (314) 751-7384

Montana

International Affairs Coordinator
International Trade Office
Montana Department of Commerce
1424 9th Avenue
Helena, MT 59620
Tel: (406) 444-3923
Fax: (406) 444-2903

Nebraska

International Trade Promotion
Department of Economic
 Development
301 Centennial Mail South
P.O. Box 94666
Lincoln, NE 68509
Tel: (402) 471-3111
Fax: (402) 471-3778
or
Development Consultant
Office of International Trade and
 Foreign Investment
Tel: (402) 471-3111

Nevada

Director
International Program
Nevada Commission on Economic
 Development
3770 Howard Hughes Parkway
Suite 295
Las Vegas, NV 89158
Tel: (702) 486-7282
Fax: (702) 486-7284

New Hampshire

Office of International Commerce
New Hampshire Int'l. Trade
Resource Center
601 Spaulding Turnpike, Suite 29
Portsmouth, NH 03801-2833
Tel: (603) 334-6074
Fax: (603) 334-6110

New Jersey

Governor's Special Trade Representative
 and Director
Division of International Trade
New Jersey Department of Commerce
 and Economic Development
P.O. Box 47024
Newark, NJ 07102
Tel: (201) 648-3518
Fax: (201) 623-1287

New Mexico

Economic Development Division
New Mexico Economic Development
 and Tourism Department
1100 St. Francis Drive
Santa Fe, NM 87503
Tel: (505) 827-0272
Fax: (505) 827-0263
or
Office of International Trade
Tel: (505) 827-0309

New York

Director, International Division
New York Dept. of
 Economic Development
1515 Broadway, 51st Floor
New York, NY 10036
Tel: (212) 827-6210
Fax: (212) 827-6263

North Carolina

Director of International Trade
International Division
North Carolina Dept. of Commerce
430 North Salisbury Street
Raleigh, NC 27611
Tel: (919) 733-7193
Fax: (919) 733-0110

Director, Business and Industrial
 Development
Tel: (919) 733-4979

North Dakota

International Trade Specialist
North Dakota Economic Dev't.
 and Finance
1833 E. Bismarck Expressway
Bismarck, ND 58504
Tel: (701) 221-5300
Fax: (701) 221-5320

Ohio

Deputy Director
International Trade Division
Ohio Department of Development
77 S. High Street, 29th Floor
P.O. Box 1001
Columbus, OH 43266-0101
Tel: (614) 466-2317
Fax: (614) 463-1540

Oklahoma

Director, International Trade
 and Investment
Oklahoma Department of Commerce
P.O. Box 26980
Oklahoma City, OK 73126-0980
Tel: (405) 841-5217
Fax: (405) 841-5245
or
Program Manager, Export Finance
Tel: (405) 841-5129
Fax: (405) 841-5142

Oregon

Director, International Trade Division
Oregon Economic Development Dept.
One World Trade Center
121 Southwest Salmon, Suite 300
Portland, OR 97204
Tel: (503) 229-5625
Fax: (503) 222-5050

Pennsylvania

Director
Office of International Trade
Pennsylvania Department of Commerce
463 Forum Building
Harrisburg, PA 17112
Tel: (717) 783-1356
Fax: (717) 234-4560

Puerto Rico

Assistant Secretary for External Trade
Puerto Rico Department of Commerce
G.P.O. 4275
San Juan, Puerto Rico 00905
Tel: (809) 725-7254
Fax: (809) 722-8477

Rhode Island

Business and Industry Representative
International Trade Division
Rhode Island Department of
Economic Development
7 Jackson Walkway
Providence, RI 02903
Tel: (401) 277-2601
Fax: (401) 277-2102

South Carolina

South Carolina State Development Board
P.O. Box 927
Columbia, SC 29202
Tel: (803) 737-0400
Fax: (803) 737-0818

South Dakota

Export, Trade and Marketing Div.
Governor's Office of Economic
 Development
711 Wells Avenue, Capitol Lake Plaza
Pierre, SD 57501
Tel: (605) 773-5735
Fax: (605) 773-5698

Tennessee

Tennessee Export Office
Tennessee Department of Economic
 and Community Development
320 6th Avenue North, 7th Floor
Nashville, TN 37243-0405
Tel: (615) 741-5870
Fax: (615) 741-5829

Texas

Director of International Marketing
 and Development
Texas Department of Commerce
P.O. Box 12728
Austin, TX 78711
Tel: (512) 320-9621
Fax: (512) 320-9424
or
Program Manager,
International Trade Relations
Tel: (512) 320-9672
Fax: (512) 320-9674

Utah

Director,
International Business and Economic
 Development
Economic and Industrial
Development Division
324 South State Street, Suite 200
Salt Lake City, UT 84111
Tel: (801) 538-8737
Fax: (801) 538-8889

Vermont

Director
International Trade and
 Investment
Vermont Agency of Development
and Community Affairs
Pavilion Office Building
Montpelier, VT 05609
Tel: (802) 828-3221
Fax: (802) 828-3258

Virgin Islands

Director
Virgin Islands Department of
Economic Development
 and Agriculture
Bureau of Economic Research
P.O. Box 6400
St. Thomas, Virgin Islands 00904
Tel: (809) 774-8784
Fax: (809) 774-8477

Virginia

Director
Division of International Trade, Travel
and Investment
Virginia Department of Economic
 Development
P.O. Box 798
Richmond, VA 23206-0798
Tel: (804) 371-8107
Fax: (804) 371-8112

or

Export Development Manager
Trade Development Group
Tel: (804) 371-8242
Fax: (804) 371-8860

Washington

Director, Domestic and International
 Trade Division
or
Business Expansion Program
Washington Department of Trade
 and Development
2001 6th Avenue, Suite 2700
Seattle, WA 98121-2522
Tel: (206) 464-7143
Fax: (206) 464-7222

West Virginia

International Trade and Investment
Governor's Office of Community and
 Industrial Development
State Capitol, Room M-146
Charleston, WV 25306
Tel: (304) 558-2234
Fax: (304) 558-0449

Wisconsin

Director, Bureau of International
 Development
Wisconsin Department of Development
P.O. Box 7970
Madison, WI 53707
Tel: (608) 266-1767

Wyoming

Management Assistant
International Trade Office
Wyoming Division of Economic and
 Community Development
4th Floor North, Barrett Building
Cheyenne, WY 82002
Tel: (302) 777-6412
Fax: (302) 777-5804

Small Business
Development Centers (SBDCs)

Alabama

State Director
Small Business Development Center
University of Alabama
1717 11th Avenue South, Suite 419
Birmingham, AL 35294-4410
Tel: (205) 934-7260
Fax: (205) 934-7645

Alabama International Trade Center
University of Alabama
400 North Martha Parham
Tuscaloosa, AL 35487-0396
Tel: (205) 348-7621
Fax: (205) 348-6974

Alaska

State Director
Small Business Development Center
University of Alaska/Anchorage
430 West 7th Avenue, Suite 110
Anchorage, AK 99501
Tel: (907) 274-7232
Fax: (907) 274-9524

Arizona

State Director
Small Business Development Center
Maricopa Country Community College
2411 West 14th Street
Tempe, AZ 85281-6941
Tel: (602) 731-8720
Fax: (602) 731-8729

Arkansas

Small Business Development Center
University of Arkansas
Little Rock Technology Center Building
100 South Main, Suite 401
Little Rock, AR 72201
Tel: (501) 324-9043
Fax: (501) 324-9049

California

State Director
Small Business Development Center
California Trade and Commerce Agency
801 K Street, Suite 1700
Sacramento, CA 95814
Tel: (916) 324-5068
Fax: (916) 322-5084

Export Small Business
Development Center of Southern
 California
110 East Ninth Street, Suite A-761
Los Angeles, CA 90079
Tel: (213) 892-1111
Fax: (213) 892-8232

Colorado

Small Business Development Center
Office of Business Development
1625 Broadway, Suite 1719
Denver, CO 80202
Tel: (303) 892-3809
Fax: (303) 892-3848

Connecticut

Small Business Development Center
University of Connecticut
Box U-41, Room 422
368 Fairfield Road
Storrs, CT 06269-2041
Tel: (203) 486-4135
Fax: (203) 486-1576

Delaware

Small Business Development Center
University of Delaware
Suite 005 - Purnell Hall
Newark, DE 19711
Tel: (302) 831-2747
Fax: (302) 831-1423

District of Columbia

Howard University
2600 6th Street, NW, Room 128
Washington, DC 20059
Tel: (202) 806-1550
Fax: (202) 806-1777

Florida

University of West Florida
19 West Garden Street, Third Floor
Pensacola, FL 32501
Tel: (904) 444-2060
(904) 444-2070

Florida Atlantic University
P.O. Box 3091
Boca Raton, FL 33431
Tel: (407) 367-2273, 367-2271
Fax: (407) 367-2272

Georgia

University of Georgia
Chicopee Complex
1180 East Broad Street
Athens, GA 30602
Tel: (706) 542-6762
Fax: (706) 542-6776

Hawaii

State Director
Small Business Development Center
University of Hawaii at Hilo
523 West Lanikaula Street
Hilo, HI 96720
Tel: (808) 933-3515
Fax: (808) 933-3683

Idaho

Small Business Development Center
Boise State University
College of Business
1910 University Drive
Boise, ID 83725
Tel: (208) 385-1640
Fax: (208) 385-3877

International Trade Coordinator
Lewis Clark State College
500 Eighth Avenue
Lewiston, ID 83501
Tel: (208) 799-2465
Fax: (208) 799-2831

Illinois

Small Business Development Center
Department of Commerce and
  Community Affairs
620 East Adams Street
Springfield, IL 62701
Tel: (217) 524-5856
Fax: (217) 785-6328

College of Dupate
22nd & Lambert Road
Glen Ellyn, IL 60137
Tel: (708) 858-2800, Ext. 3052
(708) 790-1179

Bradley University
141 North Jobst Hall, First Floor
Peoria, IL 61625
Tel: (309) 677-3075
Fax: (309) 677-3386

Small Business Development Center

Southern Illinois University, Edwardsville
Campus Box 1107
Edwardsville, IL 62026
Tel: (618) 692-2929
Fax: (618) 692-2647

Indiana

Small Business Development Center
Economic Development Council
One North Capital, Suite 420
Indianapolis, IN 46204-2248
Tel: (317) 264-6871
Fax: (371) 264-3102

Iowa

Small Business Development Center
Iowa State University
137 Lynn Avenue
Ames, IA 50010
Tel: (515) 292-6351
Fax: (515) 292-0020

Northeast Iowa Small Business
  Development Center
Dubuque Area Chamber of Commerce
770 Town Clock Plaza
Dubuque, IA 52001
Tel: (319) 588-3350
Fax: (319) 557-1591

Eastern Iowa Small Business
  Development Center
304 West Second Avenue
Davenport, IA 52801
Tel: (319) 322-4499
Fax: (319) 322-3956

Kansas

Small Business Development Center
Wichita State University
1845 Fairmount
Wichita, KS 67260-0148
Tel: (316) 689-3193
Fax: (316) 689-3647

Kentucky

State Director
Small Business Development Center
University of Kentucky
College of Business and Economics
  Building
Lexington, KY 40506-0034
Tel: (606) 257-7668
Fax: (606) 258-1907

Louisiana

State Director
Small Business Development Center
Northeast Louisiana University
College of Business Administration
700 University Avenue
Monroe, LA 71209
Tel: (318) 342-5506
Fax: (318) 342-5510

Director of Development
University of New Orleans
368 Business Administration Building
New Orleans, LA 70148
Tel: (504) 286-6978
Fax: (504) 286-7197

Maine

Small Business Development Center
University of Southern Maine
96 Falmouth Street
Portland, ME 04103
Tel: (207) 780-4420
Fax: (207) 780-4810

Maryland

Small Business Development Center
Department of Economic and
  Employment Development
217 East Redwood Street,
Ninth Floor
Baltimore, MD 21202
Tel: (410) 333-6995
Fax: (410) 333-4460

Massachusetts

Small Business Development Center
University of Massachusetts
School of Management, Room 205
Amherst, MA 01003-4935
Tel: (413) 545-6301
Fax: (413) 545-1273

Michigan

Wayne State University
2727 Second Avenue
Detroit, MI 48201
Tel: (313) 964-1798
Fax: (313) 964-3648

Center for International Business
 Development
Michigan State University
6 Kellogg Center
East Lansing, MI 48824-1022
Tel: (517) 353-4336 or (800) 852-5727
Fax: (517) 336-1009

Minnesota

Department of Trade and Economic
 Development
500 Metro Square, 121 Seventh Place East
St. Paul, MN 55101-2146
Tel: (612) 297-5770
Fax: (612) 296-1290

Mississippi

University of Mississippi
Old Chemistry Building, Suite 216
University, MS 38677
Tel: (601) 232-5001
Fax: (601) 232-5650

International Trade Center
Hinds Community College
P.O. Box 1179
Raymond, MS 39154
Tel: (601) 857-3536
Fax: (601) 857-3535

Missouri

Small Business Development Center
University of Missouri, Columbia
Suite 300, University Place
Columbia, MO 65211
Tel: (314) 882-0344
Fax: (314) 884-4297

Central Missouri State University
Small Business Development Center
Grinstead 75
Warrensburg, MO 64093-5087
Tel: (816) 543-4402
Fax: (816) 543-8159

Missouri Southern State College
Small Business Development Center
107 Matthews Hall
3950 Newman Road
Joplin, MO 64801
Tel: (417) 625-9313
Fax: (417) 625-9782

Southwest Missouri State University
Small Business Development Center
901 South National, Box 88
Springfield, MO 65804
Tel: (417) 836-5685
Fax: (417) 836-6337

Montana

Small Business Development Center
Montana Department of Commerce
1424 Ninth Avenue
Helena, MT 59620
Tel: (406) 444-4780
Fax: (406) 444-2808

Nebraska

Small Business Development Center
University of Nebraska, Omaha
60th & Dodge Streets, CBA Room 407
Omaha, NE 68182
Tel: (402) 554-2521
Fax: (402) 554-3747

University of Nebraska, Omaha
1313 Farnam, Room 132
Omaha, NE 68182
Tel: (402) 595-2381
Fax: (402) 595-2388

Nevada

Small Business Development Center
University of Nevada in Reno
College of Business Administration,
 Room 411
Reno, NV 89557-0100
Tel: (702) 784-1717
Fax: (702) 784-4337

New Hampshire

Small Business Development Center
University of New Hampshire
108 McConnell Hall
Durham, NH 03824
Tel: (603) 862-2200
Fax: (603) 862-4468

International Resource Center
601 Spaulding Turnpike, Suite 29
Portsmouth, NH 03801-2833
Tel: (603) 334-6074
Fax: (603) 334-6110

New Jersey

Small Business Development Center
Rutgers University
Ackerson Hall, Third Floor
180 University Street
Newark, NJ 07102
Tel: (201) 648-5950
Fax: (201) 648-1110

New Mexico

Small Business Development Center
Santa Fe Community College
P.O. Box 4187
Santa Fe, NM 87502-4187
Tel: (505) 438-1362
Fax: (505 438-1237

New York

Small Business Development Center
State University of New York
SUNY UPSTATE
SUNY Plaza, S-523
Albany, NY 12246
Tel: (518) 443-5398
Fax: (518) 465-4992

State University College, Buffalo
1300 Elmwood Avenue
Buffalo, NY 14222
Tel: (716) 878-4030
Fax: (716) 878-4067

Rockland Community College at Suffern
145 College Road
Suffern, NY 10901
Tel: (914) 356-0370
Fax: (914) 356-0381

North Carolina

Small Business Development Center
University of North Carolina
4509 Creedmoor Road, Suite 201
Raleigh, NC 27612
Tel: (919) 571-4154
Fax: (919) 571-4161

North Dakota

Small Business Development Center
University of North Dakota
Gramble Hall, University Station
Grand Forks, ND 58202-7308
Tel: (701) 777-3700
Fax: (701) 777-3225

Ohio

Small Business Development Center
Department of Development
77 South High Street
Columbus, OH 43266-1001
Tel: (614) 466-2711
Fax: (614) 466-0829

Southeast Ohio
Small Business Development Center
Ohio University at Athens
Innovation Center
One President Street, Suite 014
Athens, OH 45701
Tel: (614) 593-1797
Fax: (614) 593-1795

Small Business Development Center
218 North Huron Street
Toledo, OH 43604
Tel: (419) 243-8191
Fax: (419) 241-8302

Small Business Development Center
Lake County
 Economic Development Center
Lakeland Community College
Mentor, OH 44080
Tel: (216) 951-1290
Fax: (216) 953-4413

Marietta College SBDC
Marietta, OH 45750
Tel: (614) 374-4649
Fax: (614) 374-7585

Oklahoma

Small Business Development Center
Southeast Oklahoma State University
517 West University
Station A, Box 2584
Durant, OK 74701
Tel: (405) 920-0277
Fax: (405) 920-7471

Oregon

State Director
Small Business Development Center
Lane Community College
99 West 10th Avenue, Suite 216
Eugene, OR 97401
Tel: (503) 726-2250
Fax: (503) 345-6006

Portland Community College
Small Business Development Center
121 SW Salmon Street, Suite 210
Portland, OR 97204
Tel: (503) 274-7482
Fax: (503) 228-6350

Pennsylvania

Small Business Development Center
University of Pennsylvania
The Wharton School
444 Vance Hall
Philadelphia, PA 19104
Tel: (215) 898-1219
Fax: (215) 573-2135

Wharton Export Network
3733 Spruce Street, Suite 413
Philadelphia, PA 19104
Tel: (215) 898-4861
Fax: (215) 898-1299

Lehigh Small Business Development
 Center
The Rauzh Business Center, No. 37
Bethlehem, PA 18015
Tel: (215) 758-3980
Fax: (215) 758-5205

Kutztown University Small Business
 Development Center
2986 North Second Street
Harrisburg, PA 17110
Tel: (717) 233-3120
Fax: (717) 233-3181

Puerto Rico

Director
Small Business Development Center
University of Puerto Rico
Box 5253 - College Station
Building B
Mayaguez, PR 00681
Tel: (809) 834-3590
Fax: (809) 834-3790

Rhode Island

Small Business Development Center
Bryant College
1150 Douglas Pike
Smithfield, RI 02917
Tel: (401) 232-6111
Fax: (401) 232-6416

South Carolina

Small Business Development Center
University of South Carolina
College of Business Administration
1710 College Street
Columbia, SC 29208
Tel: (803) 777-4907
Fax: (803) 777-4403

South Dakota

Small Business Development Center
University of South Dakota
School of Business
414 East Clark
Vermillion, SD 57069
Tel: (605) 677-5498
Fax: (605) 677-5427

Tennessee

Small Business Development Center
Memphis State University
South Campus
Getwell Road, Building #1
Memphis, TN 38152
Tel: (901) 678-2500
Fax: (901) 678-4072

Texas

Region Director, North Texas
North Texas Small Business
  Development Center
Dallas County Community College
1402 Corinth Street
Dallas, TX 75215
(214) 565-5833
Fax: Tel: (214) 565-5815

Small Business Development Center
P.O. Box 58299
2050 Stemmons Freeway
World Trade Center,
Suite 150
Dallas, TX 75258
Tel: (214) 747-1300, Code 68
Fax: (214) 748-5774

Region Director
Small Business Development Center
University of Houston
1100 Louisiana, Suite 500
Houston, TX 77002
Tel: (713) 752-8444
Fax: (713) 756-1500

Region Director
South Texas Border
Small Business Development Center
University of Texas at San Antonio
Cypress Tower, Suite 410
1222 North Main Street
San Antonio, TX 78212
Tel: (210) 558-2450
Fax: (210) 558-2464

Region Director
Northwest Texas
Small Business Development Center
Texas Tech University
2579 South Loop 289, Suite 114
Lubbock, TX 79423-1637
Tel: (806) 745-3973
Fax: (806) 745-6207

Utah

Small Business Development Center
University of Utah
102 West 500 South
Salt Lake City, UT 84101
Tel: (801) 581-7905
Fax: (801) 581-7814

Vermont

Small Business Development Center
Vermont Technical College
P.O. Box 422
Randolph Center, VT 05060
Tel: (802) 728-9101
Fax: (802) 728-3026

Virginia

State Director
Small Business Development Center
Department of Economic Development
1021 East Cary Street
Richmond, VA 23206-0798
Tel: (804) 371-8258
Fax: (804) 371-8185

Northern Virginia
Small Business Development Center
4260 Chainbridge Road, Suite B-1
Fair, VA 22030
Tel: (703) 993-2131
Fax: (703) 993-2126

Longwood Small Business Development
Center
Longwood College
515 Main Street
Farmville, VA 23901
Tel: (804) 395-2086
Fax: (804) 395-2359

James Madison University
Small Business Development Center
College of Business
Zane Showker Hall, Room 523
Harrisonburg, VA 22807
Tel: (703) 568-3227
Fax: (703) 568-3299

SBDC of Hampton Roads
420 Bank Street, P.O. Box 327
Norfolk, VA 23501
Tel: (804) 622-6414, 825-2957
Fax: (804) 622-5563, 825-2960

Virgin Islands

Small Business Development Center
University of the Virgin Islands
8000 Nisky Center, Suite 202
Charlotte Amalie
St. Thomas, Virgin Islands 00802-5804
Tel: (809) 776-3206
Fax: (809) 775-3756

Washington

Small Business Development Center
Washington State University
College of Business and Economics
245 Todd Hall
Pullman, WA 99164-4727
Tel: (509) 335-1576
Fax: (509) 335-0949

International Trade Institute
Small Business Development Center
North Seattle Community College
9600 College Way North
Seattle, WA 98103
Tel: (206) 527-3732
Fax: (206) 527-3734

West Virginia

Small Business Development Center
Governor's Office of Community and
 Industrial Development
1115 Virginia Street, East
Charleston, WV 25301
Tel: (304) 558-2960
Fax: (304) 558-0127

Wisconsin

Small Business Development Center
University of Wisconsin
432 North Lake Street, Room 423
Madison, WI 53706
Tel: (608) 263-7794
Fax: (608) 262-3878

Argentina

Argentina Export Financing Program

Contact
General Manager
Banco Central de la Republica Argentina
Edificio Reconquista 266
Buenos Aires, Argentina
Tel: 011 (54-1) 394-1811, 393-1042

Australia

**Australian Trade
Commission--Export Finance and
Insurance Corporation
(Austrade-EFIC)**

Contact
AUSTRADE-EFIC
Level 24, AIDC Tower
Maritime Centre
201 Kent Street
Sydney, NSW 2000
Tel: (61) 2-3902111

Austria

Austrian National Bank

Contact
The Export Fund
Oesterreichischer Exportsfonds Ges.
m.b.H.
Gottfried Keller-G 1
A-1030 Vienna, Austria
Tel: 011 (43) 1-72-61-51-0

Additional Addresses:
Oesterreichische Kredit-
Versicherungs AG
Stubenring 24, A1011
Vienna, Austria
Tel: 011 (43) 1-51-5-54-0

Oesterreichische Kontrollbank (OKB)

Contact
Oesterreichische Kontrollbank AG
Abteilung Exportgarantien
Postfach 70
A-1011 Vienna, Austria
Tel: 011 (43-1) 53127-0
Fax: 011 (43-1) 53127/69

Belgium/Luxembourg

Creditexport

Contact
Creditexport
Rue du Commerce 78
B-1040 Brussels, Belgium
Tel: 011 (32) 2 511-73-30
Fax: 011 (32) 2 514-34-50

**Societe Nationale de Credit et
d'Investissement**

Contact
Societe Nationale de Credit et
d'Investissement (SNCI)
7 rue du St. Esprit
L-1475 Luxembourg
Tel: 011 (352) 461971-1
Fax: 011 (352) 461979

Office du Ducroire

Contact
Office du Ducroire
L-2981 Luxembourg
Tel; (352) 435853
Fax: 011 (352) 438326

Delcredere

Contact
Office National du Ducroire
Square de Meeus 40
1040 Brussels, Belgium
Tel: 011 (32) 2 509-42-11
Fax: 011 (32) 2 513-50-59

General Administration for Development and Cooperation (AGCD)

Contact
General Administration for Development Cooperation (AGCD)
Place du Champ de Mars 5
bte. 57
Brussels, Belgium
Tel: 011 (32) 2-519-02-11
Tlx: 21-376

Bolivia

Bolivia Export Financing Line

Contact
Interested exporters should contact Bolivian-based commercial banks.

Brazil

Brazil Export Financing Program

Contact
General Manager
Banco Central do Brasil
730 Ave. Presidente Vargas
Rio de Janeiro, Brazil
Tel: 011 (55-21) 216-2244

Canada

Export Development Corporation (EDC)

Contact
Export Development Corporation
151 O'Connor Street
Ottawa, Canada K1A 1K3
Tel: 011 (613) 598-2500
Fax: 011 (613) 237-2690

Colombia

Colombian National Export Bank (BANCOLDEX)

Contact
National Export Bank
Calle 28, No. 13A-15, Piso 42
Bogota, Colombia
Tel: 011 (57) 1-341-0677
Fax: 011 (57) 1-284-5087

Denmark

Eksportkreditradet (EKR)

Contact
Eksportkreditradet (EKR)
Codanhus
Gl. Kongevej 60
1850 Frederiksberg C
Copenhagen, Denmark
Tel: 011 (45) 313835
Fax: 011 (45) 312425

Finland

Finnish Export Credit (FEC)

Contact
Finnish Export Credit Ltd.
Eteläesplanadi 8 Helsinki
P.O. Box 123
SF-00131 Helsinki, Finland
Tel:(358) 0-131171
Fax:(358) 0-174819
Tlx:121893 FEC SF
Cable: EXPORTCREDIT HELSINKI

Takuukeskus (Finnish Guarantee Board FEG)

Contact
Takuukeskus
Finnish Guarantee Board (FGB)
Eteläranta 6, Helsinki
P.O. Box 1010
SF-00101 Helsinki
Finland
Tel:(358) 0-134111
Fax:(358) 0-651181
Tlx:121778 VTL SF

France

Banque Francaise du Commerce Exterieur (BFCE)

Contact
Banque Francaise du Commerce Exterieur
(BFCE)
21, Boulevard Haussman
75427 Paris Cedex 09
France
Tel: 011 (33) 1-48004800

Caisse Centrale de Cooperation Economique

Contact
Caisse Centrale de Cooperation
Economique (CCCE)
Cite du Retiro, 35-37,
r. Boissy-d'Anglas
75379 Paris CEDEX 08
Tel: 011 (33) 40 06 31 31
Fax: 011 (33) 42 66 03 31
Tlx: 212632

French Chamber of Industry and Commerce in Japan (CODEX)

Contact
Secrétariat Général CODEX / DREE
139, rue de Bercy
Télédoc 216, France
Tel: 011 (33) 40-24-82-01/02

COFACE (Compagnie Francaise d'Assurance pour le Commerce Exterieur)

Contact
COFACE
12, cours Michelet
La Defense 10
92800 PUTEAUX
France
Tel: 011 (33) 1 49022000

Postal Address:
Cedex 51
92065 Paris-La Defense
France

Germany

Hermes Kreditversicherungs-AG

Contact
Hermes Kreditversicherungs-AG
22746 Hamburg
Friedensallee 254,
22763 Hamburg
Germany
Tel: 011 (49) 40-887-0
Fax: 011 (49) 40-887-7744

Greece

Export Credit Insurance Organization (ECIO)

Contact
Export Credit Insurance Organization
(ECIO)
57, Panepistimiou Street
Athens, P.O.C. 10564
Greece
Tel: 011 (301) 324-42-47, 16-47
Fax: 011 (301) 324-40-74
Tlx: 215206 BNGR-ECIO

Guatemala

Guatemala Revolving Credit for Nontraditional Exports

Contact
Applicants should contact a
Guatemalan-based commercial bank or
private finance company.

Ireland

Coras Trachtala (CTT)

Contact
Coras Trachtala
Irish Export Board
Merrion Hall, Strand Road
Dublin, Rep. of Ireland
Tel: 011 (353-1) 695011
Fax: 011 (353-1) 695820

Insurance Corporation of Ireland (ICI)

Contact
Insurance Corporation of Ireland plc (ICI)
Burlington House
Burlington Road
Dublin 4, Ireland
Tel: 011 (353) 1 601377
Fax: 011 (353) 1 609220

Israel

Israel Foreign Trade and Risks Insurance Corporation

Contact
Israel Foreign Trade and Risks Insurance
Corporation
65 Derech Petach Tikua
Tel Aviv, Israel
Tel: 011 (972) 3-563-1777
Fax: 011 (972) 3-561-0313

Italy

Mediocredito Centrale

Contact
Mediocredito Centrale
Via Piemonte, 51
00187 Roma
Tel: 011 (39) 6-47911
Tlx: 621699 MEDIOC

Special Section for Export Credit Insurance (SACE)

Contact
Sezione Speciale per l'Assicurazione del
Credito all'Esportazione
Casella Postale 253 Roma Centro
00100 Roma
Tel: 011 (396) 67361
Fax: 011 (396) 6736225

Jamaica

National Export-Import Bank of Jamaica (J-Ex-Im)

Contact
Managing Director
The National Export-Import Bank of
Jamaica
48 Duke Street
Kingston, Jamaica
Tel: 011 (809) 92-29690-4

Japan

Export-Import Bank of Japan (JEXIM)

Contact
Public Information Office
Policy Coordination and Planning
Department at the Head Office
Export-Import Bank of Japan
4-1, Ohtemachi 1-chome, Chiyoda-ku,
Tokyo 100, Japan
Tel: 011 (81) 3-3287-9108
Fax: 011 (81) 3-3287-9539

Additional Addresses:
Representative Office in Washington. DC
2000 Pennsylvania Ave, NW, Suite 3350
Washington, DC 20006
Tel: 011 (202) 331-8547
Fax: 011 (202) 775-1990
Tlx: 23-248547 (AAB) 248547 YUGIN
UR

Representative Office in New York
375 Park Avenue, Suite 3601
New York, NY 10152
Tel: 011 (212) 888-9500
Fax: 011 (212) 888-9503
Tlx: 23-7607841 (AAB) 7607841
YUGIN UC

Ministry of International Trade and Industry (MITI)

Export-Import Insurance Division

Contact
EID/MITI
1221 Ave. of the Americas
New York, NY 10020
Tel: 011 (212) 819-7770
Fax: 011 (212) 819-7796

Korea

Export-Import Bank of Korea (Ko-Exim)

Contact
Export-Import Bank of Korea
16-1, Yoido-dong, Youngdungpo-gu
Seoul 150-010, Korea
Tel: (82) 2-784-1021, 7071
Fax: (82) 2-784-1030
Tlx: K26595 EXIMBK
Cable: EXIMKOREA SEOUL

Additional Addresses:
Postal Address
Yoido P.O. Box 641
Seoul 150-606, Korea

Overseas Representative Offices
460 Park Ave., 20th Floor
New York, NY 10022-1906
Tel: (212) 355-7280/3
Fax: (212) 308-6106
Tlx: 428144 EXIMBK
Cable: EXIMKOREA NEW YORK

Latin America

Latin American Export Bank (BLADEX)

Contact
Latin American Export Bank
Apartado 6-1497, El Dorado
Panama City, Republic of Panama
Tel: 011 (507) 63-6766
Fax: 011 (507) 69-6333
Tlx: INTEL 2356

Additional Addresses:
750 Lexington Avenue, 26th Floor
New York, NY 10022
Tel: (212) 754-2600
Fax: (212) 754-2606

Malaysia

Malaysia Export Credit Insurance Bhd. (MECIB)

Contact
Malaysia Export Credit Insurance Bhd.
(MECIB)
Level 12 & 13
Bangunan Bank Industri
Jalan Sultan Ismail
P.O. Box 11048
50734 Kuala Lumpur
Tel: 011 (60) 3-291-0677
Fax: 011 (60) 3-291-0353
Tlx: MA 31190

Netherlands

Netherlands Credit Insurance Company (NMC)

Contact
Netherlands Credit Insurance Company
P.O. Box 473
1000 Amsterdam
The Netherlands
Tel: 011 (31) 20-553-9111
Fax: 011 (31) 20-553-2811

Norway

Exportfinans

Contact
Exportfinans
P.O. Box 1601 Vika
N-0119 Oslo 1, Norway
Tel: 011 (47) 283-0100
Fax: 011 (47) 283-2237

Guarantee-Institute for Export Credits (GIEK)

Contact
The Guarantee-Institute for Export
Credits
(GIEK)
P.O. Box 1763 Vika
N-0122 Oslo, Norway
Tel: 011 (47) 283-2835
Fax: 011 (47) 283-2445
Tlx: 8121153

Portugal

Fundo de Garantia de Riscos Cambiais (FGRC)

Contact
Instituto do Comercio Externo de Portugal
Av. 5 de Outubro, 101
1016 LISBOA CODEX
Tel: 011 (35) 1-1-793 01 03
Fax: 011 (35) 1-1-793 50 28

Additional Addresses:
Banco de Portugal (Bank of Portugal)
Sede: Rua Comercio, 148
1100 Lisbon
Tel: 011 (351) 346-2931
Fax: 011 (351) 346-4843

Comissao Nacional das Garantias de Creditos (CNGC)

Contact
Comissao Nacional das Garantias de
Creditos
Avenida da Republica, 58-13
P-1000 Lisbon
Tel: 011 (351-1) 775140
Fax: 011 (351-1) 734614

Companhia de Seguro de Creditos EP (COSEC)

Contact
Companhia de Seguro de Creditos EP
Avenida de Republica 58
1094 Lisbon Codex
Tel: 011 (351-1) 760131, 6051
Fax: 011 (351-1) 7934614

South Africa

Industrial Development Corporation of South Africa (IDC)

Contact
Industrial Development Corporation of
South Africa, Ltd.
Head Office
19 Fredman Drive, Sandown, RSA
P.O. Box 784055
Sandton 2146, RSA
Tel: (27-11) 883-1600
Fax: (27-11) 883-1655
Tlx: 4-27174 SA, 4-27201 SA
Cable: IDECE

Credit Guarantee Insurance Corporation (CGIC)

Contact
Credit Guarantee Insurance Corporation
of Africa, Ltd.
31 Dover Street, Randburg
P.O. Box 9244
Johannesburg 2000 RSA
Tel: (27-11) 889-7000
Fax: (27-11) 886-5715, 886-1027
Tlx: 4-20508
Cable: CREDINSUR JOHANNESBURG

Spain

Banco Exterior de Espana (BEX)

Contact
Banco Exterior de Espana
Carrera de San Jeronimo, 36
28014 Madrid, Spain
Tel: 011 (34) 1 429-4477
Fax: 011 (34) 1 429-8342

Cia Española de Seguros de Crédito a la Exportación (CESCE)

Export-Credit Guarantee System

Contact
CESCE
Velazquez, 74
28001 Madrid, Spain
Tel: 011 (34) 1-577-6066
Fax: 011 (34) 1-576-5140

Sweden

Swedish Export Credit Corporation (SEK)

Contact
AB Svensk Exportkredit (SEK)
Box 16368
S-103 27 Stockholm
Tel: 011 (46-8) 613 8000
Fax: 011 (46-8) 203894

Swedish Export Credits Guarantee Board (EKN)

Contact
The Swedish Export Credits Guarantee
Board
Box 7334
S-103 90 Stockholm
Tel: 011 (46-8) 7010000
Fax: 011 (46-8) 118149

Switzerland

Export Risk Guarantee Fund (ERG)

Contact
Geschaftsstelle fur die
Exprtsrisikogarantie-ERG
(Office for the Export Risk Guarantee)
Kirchenweg 4
8032 Zurich
Tel: 011 (41-1) 3844777
Fax: 011 (41-1) 3844848

Taiwan

Export-Import Bank of the Republic of China (Taiwan) (T-Eximbank)

Contact
Finance Department
Export-Import Bank of the Republic of
China (Taiwan)
8th Fl., 3 Nan Hai Road
Taipei 10728, Taiwan
Tel: (886) 397-1505, 321-0511
Fax: (886) 886-02-394-0630
Tlx: 26044
Cable: EXIMBANK Taipei

Trinidad & Tobago

Trinidad and Tobago Export Credit Insurance Company (EXICO)

Contact
Manager
Trinidad and Tobago Export Credit
Insurance Company, Ltd.
92 Queen Street
Port-of-Spain, Trinidad
Tel: 011 (809) 624-0028
Fax: 011 (809) 624-0028

Turkey

Export Credit Bank of Turkey (Turk Eximbank)

Contact
Export Credit Bank of Turkey, Inc.
Müdafa Cad. No: 20
06100 Ankara, Turkey
Tel: (90) 312-417-1300
Fax: (90) 312-418-0015

United Kingdom

Export Credit Guarantee Department (ECGD)

Contact
Export Credit Guarantee Department
(ECGD)
P.O. Box 272, Export House
50 Ludgate Hill
London EC4M 7AY, England
Tel: 011 (44) 71-382-7000
Fax: 011 (44) 71-382-7649
Tlx: 883601 ECGD HQ G

USDA Agricultural Trade Offices Abroad

China

Beijing
8th Floor, China World Tower
No. 1 Jian guo men wai Avenue
Beijing, China 10004
Tel: 011 (86-1) 505-4575-4576
Fax: 011 (86-1) 505-4574

(U.S. mailing address)
ATO/U.S. Embassy
PSC 461, Box 50
FPO AP 96521-0002

Guangzhou
China Hotel Office Tower
Rm 1259, Liu Hua Road
Guangzhou, China

(U.S. mailing address)
ATO/U.S. Consulate (Guangzhou)
PSC 461, Box 100
FPO AP 96521-0002

Germany

Hamburg
Grosse Theaterstrasse 42
D-20354 Hamburg, Germany
Tel: (49) 40-34-12-07
Fax: (49) 40-34-12-00

(U.S. mailing address)
Agricultural Trade Office
American Consulate General, Hamburg
Department of State
Washington, DC 20251-5180

Hong Kong

18th Floor, St. John's Building
Hong Kong
Tel: (852) 841-2350
Fax: (852) 845-0943

(U.S. mailing address)
ATO/U.S. Consulate Hong Kong
PSC 464, Box 30
FPO AP 96522-0002

Japan

Osaka
ATO/Shima Office Bldg., 3F
1-18, Kitahama 3-chome
Chuo-ku, Osaka 541, Japan
Tel: (81) 6-208-0303
Fax: (81) 6-208-0306

(U.S. mailing address)
ATO/American Consulate General
Unit 45004, Box 239
APO AP 96337-0002

Tokyo
7th Floor, Tameike Tokyu Bldg.
1-14, Akasaka 1-chome
Minato-ku, Tokyo 107, Japan
Tel: (81) 3-3224-5115/3505-6050
Fax: (81) 3-3582-6429

(U.S. mailing address)
ATO American Embassy
Unit 45004, Box 241
APO AP 96337-5004

Korea

Seoul
Rm. 303, Leema Bldg.
146-1 Susong-dong, Chongro-ku
Seoul, South Korea (110-140)
Tel: (82-2) 397-4188
Fax: (82-2) 720-7921

(U.S. mailing address)
ATO American Embassy
Unit 15550-001
APO AP 96205-0001

Mexico

Mexico City
Monte Pelvoux, No. 220-PH2
Lomas de Chaupultepec
011000 Mexico D.F.
Tel: (52) 5-202-0168/0434/0212
Fax: (52) 5-202-0528

(U.S. mailing address)
ATO American Embassy
P.O. Box 3087
Laredo, TX 78044-3087

Saudi Arabia

Riyadh
American Embassy
P.O. Box 94309
Riyadh 11693, Saudi Arabia
Tel: (966) 1-488-3800. ext 560
Fax: (966) 1-482-4364

(U.S. mailing address)
ATO American Embassy
Unit 61307
APO AE 09803-1307

Jeddah
U.S. Consulate
Palestine Road
P.O. Box 149
Jeddah 21411, Saudi Arabia
Tel: (966) 2-661-2408/667-0080, ext 299
Fax: (966) 2-667-6196

(U.S. mailing address)
Agricultural Trade Office
Unit 62112
APO AE 09811-2112

Singapore

(including Brunei, Papua New Guinea, Indonesia, Malaysia, and the Philippines)
Agricultural Trade Office
541 Orchard Rd., #08-03
Liat Towers
Singapore 0923
Tel: (65) 737-1233/1729
Fax: (65) 732-8307

(U.S. mailing address)
Agricultural Trade Office
American Embassy
FPO AP 96534-0001

Taiwan

Taipei
American Institute in Taiwan
54 Nan Hai Road
Taipei, Taiwan
Tel: (886) 2-305-4883
Fax: (886) 2-305-7073

(U.S. mailing address)
Agricultural Trade Office
AIT, Taipei
P.O. Box 1612
Washington, DC 20013

United Arab Emirates

(including Dubai, Bahrain, Kuwait, and Oman)
U.S. Consulate General
Dubai World Trade Center
P.O. Box 9343
Dubai, UAE
Tel: (971) 4-313-612/314-063
Fax: (971) 4-314-998

(U.S. mailing address)
Agricultural Trade Office/American Consulate General
U.S. Department of Agriculture, FAS
Washington, DC 20250-6000

United Kingdom

(including Ireland)
Regent Arcade House
19-25 Argyll Street
London, W1V 1AA U.K.
Tel: (44) 171-287-2624
Fax: (44) 171-287-2629

(U.S. mailing address)
Agricultural Trade Office/American Embassy
PSC 801, Box 48
FPO AE 09498-4048

ALPHABETICAL INDEX

I

J-L

M

S

T

U

V-W

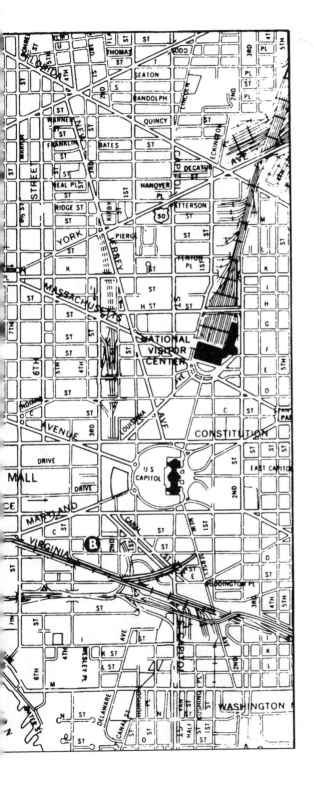

A Overseas Private
   Investment Corporation
   1100 New York Avenue, NW
   Washington, DC 20527
   (202) 336-8799

B Small Business Administration
   409 Third Street, SW
   Washington, DC 20416
   (202) 205-6600

C Export-Import Bank of the
   United States
   811 Vermont Avenue, NW
   Washington, DC 20571
   (202) 565-3946

D Office of the
   U.S. Trade Representative
   600 17th Street, NW
   Washington, DC 20506
   (202) 395-3230

E U.S. Trade and
   Development Agency
   1621 North Kent Street
   Rosslyn, VA 22209
   (703) 875-4357

F U.S. Agency for
   International Development
   Department of State Building
   320 Twenty-First Street, NW
   Washington, DC 20523
   (202) 647-1850

G U.S. Department of Commerce
   14th Street and Constitution
   Avenue, NW
   Washington, DC 20230
   (202) 482-2000

H U.S. Department of Agriculture
   14th Street and Independence
   Avenue, SW
   Washington, DC 20250
   (202) 720-8732

I International Bank for
   Reconstruction and Development
   1818 H Street, NW
   Washington, DC 20433
   (202) 473-1234

J International Finance Corporation
   1850 Eye Street, NW
   Washington, DC 20433
   (202) 473-7711